THE BLUE RIDER
IN THE LENBACHHAUS, MUNICH

Helmut Friedel
Annegret Hoberg

THE BLUE RIDER
IN THE LENBACHHAUS, MUNICH

Prestel

Munich · London · New York

© 2000, Prestel Verlag, Munich · London · New York,
and the Städtische Galerie im Lenbachhaus, Munich

© of works illustrated by the artists, their heirs and assigns, except in
the following cases: Heinrich Campendonk, Alexei Jawlensky, Wassily
Kandinsky, Paul Klee, Alfred Kubin, Gabriele Münter by VG Bild-Kunst,
Bonn 2000; Robert Delaunay by L & M Services, B. V. Amsterdam;
Marianne von Werefkin by Fondazione Marianne Werefkin, Ascona

Cover:
(Hardcover edition) Franz Marc, *The Tiger*, 1912 (plate 48)
(Paperback edition) Franz Marc, *Blue Horse I*, 1911 (plate 45)

Frontispiece: Wassily Kandinsky, Design for the cover
of The Blue Rider almanac, 1911

Translated from the German by: John Ormrod (plate texts), Almuth
Seebohm (plate texts and preface), Ishbel Flett (essay by Helmut
Friedel)

Copyedited by Curt Holtz
Editorial direction: Christopher Wynne

Die Deutsche Bibliothek CIP data is available

Prestel Verlag
Mandlstrasse 26, 80802 Munich
Tel.: +49 (89) 38 17 09-0
Fax: +49 (89) 38 17 09-35;

4 Bloomsbury Place, London WC1A 2QA
Tel.: +44 (020) 7323-5004
Fax: +44 (020) 7636-8004;

175 Fifth Avenue, Suite 402, New York, NY 10010,
Tel.: +1 (212) 995-2720
Fax: +1 (212) 995-2733

www.prestel.com

Design and Layout: WIGEL, Munich
Lithography: Repro Karl Dörfel GmbH, Munich/ReproLine, Munich
Printing and Binding: Passavia Druckservice GmbH, Passau
ISBN 3-7913-2216-8

Preface

The Blue Rider (*Der Blaue Reiter*) was formed by the artists Wassily Kandinsky, Franz Marc, Gabriele Münter, August Macke, Alexei Jawlensky, and Paul Klee. Beyond all doubt, it is the one group of artists that made the most important and influential contribution to the art of the 20th century in Munich, itself a center of the arts. Their particular, expressive kind of painting made use of bright colors and a concentrated formal idiom that was moving towards abstraction. Through a unique spiritual approach it opened the way to a new potential for conveying meaning, ranging in style from "grand realism" to "abstraction." The story of the Blue Rider begins with its long prehistory of how the artists came together to work in Munich and Murnau. The subsequent period of extremely intense activity and revolutionary innovations in the years just before the outbreak of World War I culminated in two Blue Rider exhibitions in 1911 and 1912 and the publication of the The Blue Rider almanac in May 1912.

The Blue Rider united different artistic personalities working together on the basis of diversity. What they had in common was a striving after new forms in art to express an inner vision in a direct and original way. Art was to be independent of any traditionally binding formal canon and of any "external, modernistic program of the day," as Kandinsky and Marc tended to refer to the various 'isms' of the avant-garde. In this openness towards expressive means, which extended to the choice of both technique and style, the Blue Rider differed considerably from other artists' groups of the period. It represented a modernity that has maintained this art's acceptability to this day. Moreover, at the first Blue Rider exhibition in the winter of 1911–12, "no particular and special form" was to be presented, as Kandinsky wrote on the title page of the catalogue. Rather, "in the diversity of the forms represented, we aim to show the various ways the artists' inner desire is manifested." The search for the forms of "inner necessity" indicates one of the Blue Rider's basic concerns. It was, at least for Kandinsky, to lead the way towards abstraction.

The works of the Blue Rider, especially the collection held by the Lenbachhaus, are now world famous. For today's viewer they have lost nothing of their splendid color, of innovation or of the artistic brilliance of those pioneering years. In fact, their popularity is growing steadily. On the walls of the museum and in the selection of over 120 major works in this book, their undiminished aura reveals something of the astounding self-confidence of the Blue Rider at being the avant-garde – above and beyond all the other modern endeavors at the time, such as Cubism, Futurism, and the Expressionism of *Die Brücke* (The Bridge) group. This self-confidence, challengingly justified by the overwhelming reception their works have continually received over many decades right up to the present day, is evidently a crucial part of the essence and influence of this group of artists.

Munich is still a center for the art of the Blue Rider today thanks to its world famous collection in the Städtische Galerie im Lenbachhaus. Many of the works form part of an extraordinarily generous donation made by Gabriele Münter who was a founding member of the group and Wassily Kandinsky's companion until 1914. On the occasion of her 80th birthday in 1957, Münter gave Munich the biggest and most important gift in recent museum history, namely the large collection of works by Blue Rider artists in her possession. These included "over 90 oil paintings by Kandinsky, over 300 watercolors, tempera paintings, and drawings, 29 sketchbooks with over 250 studies and designs, 24 paintings on glass, a selection of applied art, and a large number of prints in varying states. The collection also included 25 of her own paintings, together with a variety of works by her friends form the period preceding World War I. In addition, Münter generously supported the efforts of the Städtische Galerie to purchase further works in order to augment this extraordinary donation, which determined the future direction of the museum's collection policy. Since the original statutes of the Städtische Galerie, which had not been opened to the public until 1929, stipulated that it should limit its collecting activities to the work of local artists, the wisdom and circumspection of Gabriele Münter was instrumental in the building of its international reputation."

This short description of the magnitude of the donation cites the words of Armin Zweite, Director of the Städtische Galerie im Lenbachhaus from 1972 to 1990, under whose supervision two inventory catalogues of the collection were published, including the forerunner of this volume. I would like to join Armin Zweite in commending our predecessor Hans Konrad Roethel, who, right at the beginning of his term of office as Director of the gallery in February 1957, accepted Gabriele Münter's donation. For many years he had been in contact with the artist and her second companion, Johannes Eichner, striving to obtain her work and gradually discovering what an astounding treasure of works by the Blue Rider artists was preserved in her house in Murnau.

With regard to the adventurous history of this collection, I would like to quote Armin Zweite from the first edition of *The Blue Rider in the Lenbachhaus, Munich*, at some length:

"As a Russian citizen, Kandinsky was forced to leave Germany when war broke out in the late summer of 1914, taking with him only a few of his large-format paintings for exhibition purposes and leaving behind an extensive collection of medium-sized and smaller pictures, sketches, books, and furniture, which was entrusted to the care of Münter. Like so many of his contemporaries, Kandinsky believed that the war would soon be over and that he would then be able to return to Munich and resume his life and work, despite the fact that his relationship with Münter had recently begun to show signs of deterioration. The couple met once more in Stockholm in 1916, but then decided to go their separate ways; shortly afterward, Kandinsky married Nina von Andreyevskaya, a much younger woman, in Moscow. Münter, who was bitterly disappointed, lived for several years in Scandinavia, but eventually returned to the house in Murnau which she had bought in 1909 and which she had shared for a time with Kandinsky. The Russian painter, on the other hand, remained in Moscow until 1921, moving to Weimar the following year to take up a teaching post at the Bauhaus. Immediately after he arrived back in Germany, Münter claimed an entitlement to maintenance, [whereby she was less concerned with material than with moral reparation], but it was not until 1926 that the couple finally signed a legal agreement dividing up their property. Kandinsky recovered his books and furniture, together with a number of drawings, watercolors, and major paintings; the remainder of the works which he had abandoned in Munich was left to Münter. Until the 1950s few people were aware that she was in possession of such a rich hoard of pictures.

Shortly after the appointment in 1956 of Hans Konrad Roethel as director of the Städtische Galerie, the museum and the city of Munich received one of the biggest donations of its kind ever made, on the occasion of [Münter's] 80th birthday. . . .

Roethel had not only been inordinately lucky in securing the donation for the city of Munich; he had also worked hard to convince the elderly painter in Murnau that he was the right person to look after this exciting collection of modern art. Münter, who had managed to preserve intact the works left to her by Kandinsky through the duration of the Nazi dictatorship, deliberately chose to donate her precious hoard to a museum which at that time was still relatively small and in which the paintings in her possession would stand out as major examples of early Modernism. She trusted Roethel implicitly as a committed advocate of modern art. . . ."

In 1965 Gabriele Münter's donation was complemented by that of Bernhard Koehler, completing the Blue Rider collection beautifully with paintings mainly by Franz Marc, August Macke, and Jean Bloé Niestlé. Bernhard Koehler Senior, a wealthy Berlin industrialist, was the uncle of August Macke's wife Elisabeth. During trips together to Paris, for instance, the young painter had advised Koehler on his outstanding collection, which included many works by avant-garde artists living in France, including Van Gogh, Cézanne, Gauguin, Matisse, Bonnard, Degas, Delaunay, Picasso, and Chagall. Koehler became not only August Macke's most important patron but also, from 1910 on, that of his friend Franz Marc and soon of the Blue Rider as a whole. In the process he purchased major works from all artists in the group and subsidized the publication of the almanac by taking over a considerable guarantee. A large part of the Koehler collection disappeared towards the end of World War II in Berlin or went missing as war booty. Following the magnanimous example of Gabriele Münter, the remaining works, largely comprising masterpieces by Macke and Marc, were given by Elly Koehler, the widow of Bernhard Koehler Junior, to the Lenbachhaus in 1965.

A year later, in 1966, the Gabriele Münter and Johannes Eichner Foundation entered into effect. Housed in the Lenbachhaus, it contains Münter's entire personal estate, which besides many of her own pictures, includes writings by herself and Kandinsky, letters, diaries, documents, photos, and their joint collection of folk art, such as paintings on glass and religious carvings. An important part of this legacy is the house in Murnau which the artist shared with Kandinsky during the decisive years of the Blue Rider up to 1914, and where she died in 1962. Partly accessible to the public since the seventies, it was reopened to the public in 1999 after renovations making it true to the original. It is an especially attractive and authentic artistic and memorial site.

A further addition to the above-mentioned gifts to the Lenbachhaus is the Kubin Archive, purchased in 1971. The archive had been assembled by the Hamburg pharmacist Kurt Otto over many decades, in close collaboration with the artist. This largest existing single archive on an artist, which includes numerous documents concerning Kubin's artist friends in Schwabing, suitably complements the existing collection and has become a center for research on Kubin.

Ever since Hans Konrad Roethel's term of office, when he presented Münter's donation to an amazed public in 1957, the Lenbachhaus has contributed considerably to the knowledge, scholarly research and artistic awareness of the Blue Rider by holding a series of major exhibitions on both the group and the individual artists. I would like to point out that the art of the Blue Rider at that time, after years of being defamed by the National Socialist regime, was only gradually re-entering public consciousness. The first decisive impetus behind the revival of its reception after World War II was the major exhibition "Der Blaue Reiter: München und die Kunst des 20. Jahrhunderts" (The Blue Rider: Munich and 20th-Century Art) curated by Ludwig Grote, partly in collaboration with living members of the group or their survivors, and shown in Munich's Haus der Kunst in 1949. Grote had discussed plans for a similar Blue Rider exhibition with Kandinsky early in the thirties in Dessau. Among other things this project, which failed because of the political situation at the time, was to rectify Kandinsky's role in the group. He was the undisputed intellectual and artistic mind behind the Blue Rider besides Franz Marc. The group's name, among other things, was due to him alone. After World War I, a turning point in the lives of all the artists involved, the works of the pre-war avant-garde and interrelated developments were soon forgotten. Because of Marc's death on the front and a certain hero-worship of him as a person, his achievement received more attention. It was a similar situation with Paul Klee, who rose to a "master of contemporary art" in the twenties, exaggerating the role he had in the Blue Rider group around 1911–12. On the other hand, the membership of Alexei Jawlensky and Marianne von Werefkin had long been unclear. Since the fifties, both artists had been considered members without a second thought. Jawlensky and Werefkin had belonged to the *Neue Künstler-vereinigung München* (NKVM, New Artists Association of Munich), along with Kandinsky, Münter, Marc, and Kubin. Adolf Erbslöh, Alexander Kanoldt, Erma Bossi, Vladimir Bekhteyev, and a series of other artists, were also members of the NKVM which had been founded in 1909, and which with some reservations, can be called the precursor of the Blue Rider. However, Jawlensky and Werefkin did not join the other artists in the decisive step of quitting the NKVM after a dispute about the almost entirely abstract *Composition V* by Kandinsky, nor were they involved in founding the Blue Rider in late 1911. Only a few months later, however, their works were included with others in the traveling Blue Rider exhibition. After its first venue at the Thannhauser Gallery in Munich, it went to several cities and toured until 1914.

In the previous edition of this book, Jawlensky was represented with over 15 works found in the Lenbachhaus collection. His paintings created before World War I, while staying in Murnau in 1908 with his painter companion Werefkin, and Kandinsky and Münter, developed out of a mutual inspiration and close interchange with the other artists. This reciprocality belongs to the immediate prehistory of the Blue Rider. We have also included the best works by Marianne von Werefkin from our collection in this new volume. Artistically close to Symbolism while nevertheless belonging to the inner circle of the developing group, she enhanced it with theoretical discussions. Furthermore, we have included a few works representing Alfred Kubin as a Blue Rider artist. Kubin was one of the group's first members after quitting the NKVM. While he was not in the first Blue Rider exhibition, being a draughtsman he and Paul Klee participated in the second one, devoted exclusively to graphic art, in the spring of 1912. Besides works from the riches of the Kubin Archive, we have selected two drawings that joined the collection as part of Münter's donation. They were among Kandinsky's and Münter's literary and artistic papers and thus document the personal relationships between the artists. We have also included Heinrich Campendonk as a Blue Rider artist in this new volume. Campendonk appeared on the scene in the decisive period just before the first Blue Rider exhibition in the winter of 1911–12. He moved to the group's immediate neighborhood to be near his revered artist friend Franz Marc in Sindelsdorf. Long after Marc's death on the front he still remained under his influence. Finally, we have also included a piece by the French artist Robert Delaunay. Prominent in the first Blue Rider exhibition with four of his major works, his first showing in Germany, he had a great influence on the German artists, especially Macke, Marc, and Klee.

The introductory essay, "The History of the Blue Rider" has also been rewritten, attempting to provide a lively and detailed account of the development of the movement and characteristics of its members' art. We were able to add hitherto unknown information from the apparently inexhaustible resources in the Lenbachhaus and the Münter and Eichner Foundation. New findings had already been discovered by Annegret Hoberg in connection with her research for the exhibition "Der Blaue Reiter und das Neue Bild" (The Blue Rider and the New Painting) held at the Lenbachhaus in 1999 on the occasion of the 90th anniversary of the foundation of the NKVM. As the Lenbachhaus also has the largest museum collection of works by NKVM artists who are less well known than Kandinsky, Münter, Marc, Jawlensky and Werefkin, we decided to illustrate a number of these major works in color with the essay, in order to present them to the reader in the best possible way.

Nowhere else in the world can the history and art of the Blue Rider be studied with such a wealth of works in a chronological sequence as in the Lenbachhaus in Munich. The finest paintings in the collection have been assembled in this volume of plates providing a comprehensive survey of the art of the Blue Rider. Finally, I would like to thank my colleague Annegret Hoberg, Curator of the Blue Rider department, very sincerely for her knowledgeable and articulate catalogue entries on the selected plates. Last, but not least, my thanks are due to Prestel Publishing for producing a book that shows off the works of art to their best advantage.

Helmut Friedel
Director of the Städtische Galerie im Lenbachhaus

Helmut Friedel, Annegret Hoberg

The History of the Blue Rider

The Blue Rider group of artists, formed in Munich in 1911, was the single most important movement of artistic renewal to emerge in twentieth century Germany. Only the *Brücke* group, founded in Dresden in 1905, had a comparable impact. Whereas the members of the *Brücke* lived and worked together until they moved to Berlin in 1911, and developed a unified style of figurative expressionism, the Blue Rider was a loose-knit group of artists whose creative aims differed widely. Under the auspices of its two key figures, Wassily Kandinsky and Franz Marc, the Blue Rider mounted joint exhibitions in 1911 and 1912 and published the legendary Blue Rider almanac in 1912. This publication, created with almost visionary fervor, has remained an eloquent chronicle of the group and its aims right up to the present day. The Blue Rider almanac, like many other writings by Kandinsky and his fellow artists, propounds the notion of the 'inner necessity' of true art which can be expressed in very different forms and styles. This central tenet goes a long way towards explaining the pluralism of the Blue Rider as a group embracing an exacting range of formal approaches, from the naive realism of Henri Rousseau to the vividly colored stylized landscapes and portraits by Gabriele Münter and Alexei Jawlensky, the Orphism of Robert Delaunay, the fantastic drawings of Alfred Kubin, the spiritual animal portrayals by Franz Marc, and Wassily Kandinsky's own abstract compositions. What is more, the Blue Rider group was receptive to other arts, especially music, and recognized the value of creative expression beyond the conventional confines of 'high art' – such as art by children, amateurs, the mentally ill, folk art and the art of non-European 'primitives' which had begun to attract the appreciation of the avant-garde since the turn of the century. The much vaunted claim of lending form to 'the spiritual' in art points towards an intellectual aspect of the Blue Rider group as the second major movement of German Expressionism that clearly sets it apart from other avant-garde movements such as Cubism and Futurism, and finally culminates in Kandinsky's revolutionary breakthrough to abstraction.

That such a development was possible at all was due to a number of artistic and theoretical givens that coincided in the fertile climate of the fin de siècle, and also owed much to the presence in Munich of certain artists who, together, paved the way for the enormous renewal embodied in the Blue Rider. Munich's reputation as a city of art had attracted them all, providing a catalyst for the emergence of the Blue Rider as a movement that was to roll back the boundaries of artistic expression. Renowned as a fountainhead of art with excellent training possibilities for painters, turn-of-the-century Munich was a magnet for students from Eastern and Central Europe, Belgium, England, Scotland and the USA. In 1896, for example, Wassily Kandinsky, Alexei Jawlensky, Marianne von Werefkin, Igor Grabar and Dmitry Kardovsky had all come to Munich from Russia, followed in 1898 by the Swiss artist Paul Klee, the Austrian Alfred Kubin and the ethnic German Russian Alexander von Salzmann. In 1901, Gabriele Münter from the Rhineland and Eugen von Kahler from Prague, Vladimir Bekhteyev and Moisey Kogan, as well as their Russian compatriot, the dancer Aleksandr Sakharov, all came to Munich, followed in 1904 and 1908 respectively, by Adolf Erbslöh and Alexander Kanoldt, who came to the Bavarian capital from the Karlsruhe Academy. In 1909, Albert Bloch, an American of German Bohemian extraction, came to Munich from St. Louis, and at the beginning of 1910, August Macke from the Rhineland first met Franz Marc, the only one of the circle who had actually been born in Munich.

Many of these artists who met in Munich around the turn of the century became members of the *Neue Künstlervereinigung München* (NKVM), founded in 1909, which may be regarded in some ways as a forerunner of the Blue Rider. The history and development of the NKVM and the later splinter group that was to become the Blue Rider, is discussed later. First of all, however, the focus of attention is on the prevailing climate that Kandinsky and his fellow artists found in Munich's art world as the nineteenth century drew to a close.

Artists flocked to Munich, drawn by its reputation as a center of art. This image that had been consolidated by the generous patronage and architectural commissions of Ludwig I, who, from 1815 onwards, had single-mindedly pursued his ambition of transforming the residence of the dynastic House of Wittelsbach from a quiet backwater into a regal capital and culturally sophisticated metropolis. His father, Max I Joseph, had been promoted by Napoleon from the rank of elector to that of king, and even when he was still crown prince, Ludwig I had eagerly collected works of art and had commissioned major buildings from the architect Leo von Klenze, whose late Neoclassical edifices are still dominant features of present-day Munich. It is no coincidence that several museums were built during the reign of Ludwig I to house the extensive Wittelsbach collections, among them the *Glyptothek*, the *Alte Pinakothek* and the *Neue Pinakothek*. In the mid-nineteenth century, the *Kunstakademie*, founded in 1808 – at a time when its fame rested on the presence of such illustrious teachers as Wilhelm von Kaulbach and Karl Piloty and had already earned the city the epithet 'Athens on the Isar' – was given a pompous new building on the border between Klenze's museum quarter and the district of Schwabing which was rapidly becoming the home of the art scene and the bohème. Almost all the artists in the Blue Rider group and its circle were later to live and work in Schwabing.

Under Ludwig's successor Maximillian II, the first glass and iron building on the European continent was built. From 1869 onwards, this so-called *Glaspalast* housed the major international art exhibitions organized by the Münchner Künstlergenossenschaft that were to put Munich firmly on the map of the art world. Officially recognized from 1868 onwards as a formally registered association, the Münchner Künstlergenossenschaft was solely responsible for the representation of the artists and supervision of the exhibitions until the

Secession was founded almost thirty years later. Franz von Lenbach – president for only four years – was, for a long time, one of its most influential members. Granted a peerage in 1882, von Lenbach's meteoric rise to become the most sought-after and highly paid portraitist of Munich society, whose sitters included heads of state, European nobility and leading figures of public life and industry, was inextricably linked with the specific conditions that prevailed in the economic boom years of the so-called *Gründerjahre* – with all the affluence, pomp and circumstance that entailed.

At the height of his fame, Franz von Lenbach, whose rank as 'painter prince' was paralleled only by Hans Makart in Vienna – and somewhat later by the younger Franz von Stuck – had a house built between 1887 and 1891 to plans by the architect Gabriel von Seidl. This magnificent Italianate villa and exhibition hall right next to the Propylaeum on Munich's prestigious Königsplatz (fig. 1) and close to the city's major museums, underlined Lenbach's position as an artist of influence. Vintage photographs of his studio indicate that it was furnished and decorated in the flamboyantly elaborate style of the period (fig. 2). At the same time, however, one can also discern a certain aspect of Lenbach's approach to art based on a combination of different styles and techniques that later won the admiration of such artists as Paul Klee. In 1924, Franz von Lenbach's widow donated the villa to the city of Munich and since 1929 it has housed the *Städtische Galerie im Lenbachhaus*. There is a certain irony in the fact that just two generations later, the house belonging to Lenbach, that prototypical conservative artist of history painting, should be used to house the collection of the Blue Rider group. Gabriele Münter's bequest in 1957 and subsequent gifts and acquisitions have made the Lenbachhaus a museum of international rank, home to a major collection of works by the most important exponents of the avant-garde in Munich, whose art was so highly controversial in their own day and defamed in the Nazi exhibition of *Entartete Kunst* ("degenerate art") in 1937.

Yet even before the Blue Rider group was formed in Munich, the conservative art scene and traditional teaching at the Academy had already come under fire. Shortly after 1870, Wilhelm Leibl had adopted what was then the provocative

3　Franz von Stuck, exhibition poster, "VII. Internationale Kunst-ausstellung," 1897, Münchner Stadtmuseum

simplicity of recent French painting, especially that of Manet, imbuing German painting with a nascent realism of precise observation that would develop into the atmospheric naturalism of his followers, such as Karl Schuch, Johann Sperl, and Wilhelm Trübner. Yet Leibl and his circle, misunderstood by a Munich public eager for the sumptuous interiors and anecdotal painting of the *Gründerzeit*, withdrew to the rural setting of Bad Aibling in Upper Bavaria and remained on the margins of Munich's art scene.

In 1888, the fourth International Exhibition at the *Glaspalast* featured more than 3,000 works, among them many genre paintings and history paintings of mediocre quality. It triggered the crucial protest that was to culminate in the foundation of the Munich Secession in 1892, splitting away from the Münchner Künstlergenossenschaft and breaking its monopoly on the city's art scene. The founding members included Hugo von Habermann, Bruno Piglhein, Heinrich von Zügel, Gustav Kuehl, Franz von Stuck, Fritz von Uhde and Leibl's student Wilhelm Trübner. It should be noted that the Munich Secession was founded earlier than the two other Secession movements of the late nineteenth century – the Vienna Secession around Gustav Klimt and the Berlin Secession around Max Liebermann. In other words, Munich was at the vanguard of a movement that blazed a trail for new forces such as Naturalism, Symbolism, and even Jugendstil.

Initially, the Munich Secession had its own exhibition space at the Königs-platz. Yet by the end of the 1890s, opposition had weakened and by 1897 they were holding joint exhibitions with the Künstlergenossenschaft in the famous 7th International Exhibition at the *Glaspalast* (fig. 3). In 1898, the Secession also included the new international decorative arts of high standard, including Henry van der Velde and René Lalique in their annual exhibition. One year earlier, in 1897, the famous Vereinigte Werkstätten für Kunst im Handwerk had been founded in Munich. This workshop, like the Secession was to become a pioneering movement in the field of applied arts. Peter Behrens, who later founded the Deutscher Werkbund, Richard Riemerschmid, Heinrich Obrist and Otto Eckmann were all among the founding members. Their names, in turn, are closely linked with the emergence of German Jugendstil, which, in its early days, was in fact a Munich Jugendstil. The German term for Art Nouveau – Jugendstil – was coined in Munich with the founding of the magazine *Jugend* by publisher Georg Hirth in 1896. His colleague and rival Albert Langen, who came from Paris, founded a similarly important periodical in 1896 called *Simplicissimus* along the lines of the French satirical magazine *Gil Blas*. The *Jugend* that gave its name to the entire Jugendstil movement and *Simplicissimus* were the leading periodicals in Germany until World War I, shaping opinions with their articles and influencing style with their illustrations. Whereas *Jugend* tended to concentrate on the aesthetic aspects of layout and virtuoso ornament, the magazine *Simplicissimus* commissioned some of the same artists – Thomas Theodor Heine, Rudolf and Erich Wilke, Ferdinand von Reznicek, Olaf Gulbransson, Bruno Paul, Eduard Thöny, Karl Arnold and others – to produce political and socially critical caricatures.

Given all this activity, Schwabing had become the center of artistic life and home to a new artistic and literary bohème. Its heyday, from 1896 until the outbreak of World War I in 1914, prompted Kandinsky, like so many of his contemporaries, to muse in 1930 that Schwabing, in retrospect, had been not so much a place as a state of mind. "The rather odd, somewhat eccentric and self-confident Schwabing, in whose streets a man or a woman – without a palette, a canvas, or at least a portfolio – seemed out of place. Like a cuckoo in the nest. Everyone was painting … or writing, or making music, or dancing." Apart from writers such as Frank Wedekind, Thomas and Heinrich Mann, the circle around Stefan George with Karl Wolfskehl, Ludwig Klages, Friedrich Gundolf and Countess Franziska zu Reventlow, Rainer Maria Rilke and Eduard Graf von Keyserling, the streets and cafés of Schwabing were full of artists. One of their favorite meeting places was the Café am Siegestor, frequented among others, by the founding members of the Jugendstil magazine *Die Insel* that had moved from Berlin to Munich in 1901 – Otto Julius Bierbaum and Alfred Walter Heymel – whereas Café Stefanie was the haunt of Alfred Kubin, Hans von Weber, Max Dauthendey and artists of the later Café du Dôme in Paris, including Rudolf Levy and Albert Weisgerber. In a back room of the Simpl, run by Kathi Kobus on Türkenstrasse, the famous *Elf Scharfrichter* cabaret performed every evening in the early years of the century, and commissioned its posters and stage sets from such artists Ernst Stern and Alexander von Salzmann.

Wassily Kandinsky was born in Moscow in 1866. He had studied law and economics in his native city and stood on the threshold of a promising university career with a call to the University of Dorpart, when he decided in 1896 to move to Munich and study painting instead. The very fact that, in the last year before he left Moscow, he had worked as an artistic head of a printer's shop, indicates that he pursued other interests besides his academic career. In his

memoirs, published in 1913, he mentions two key experiences that strengthened his resolve to become a painter. One was hearing a performance of Richard Wagner's *Lohengrin* in Moscow and the other was seeing a painting by Claude Monet from his *Haystacks* series, in which he had at first been unable to discern the haystack, dissolved by the artist's impressionist handling of light. Almost a decade later, when he was involved in *Phalanx*, Kandinsky would organize the first exhibition in Munich to feature works by Claude Monet.

When Kandinsky came to Munich at the end of 1896, he studied for more than two years at the then highly regarded and popular private art school run by the Slovenian Anton Ažbe, which attracted a great number of students from Central and Eastern Europe. In the same year, Alexei Jawlensky and Marianne von Werefkin had arrived in Munich from Russia, together with their fellow artists Dmitry Kardovsky and Igor Grabar, to study painting. Marianne von Werefkin had been a master student of the famous Russian Realist Ilja Repin in St. Petersburg since 1887 and it was there that she had met the young officer cadet and painting student Jawlensky, who became a student of Repin's in 1890. When Werefkin's father, Commander of the Fortress of St. Peter and St. Paul, died in 1896, leaving her a generous allowance for the rest of her life, she and her partner Jawlensky took the opportunity of moving to Munich, where they rented a magnificent double apartment on Giselastrasse in Schwabing. Once settled in Munich, Werefkin interrupted her own painting for almost ten years, and dedicated herself entirely to nurturing and promoting Jawlensky's talent, while holding a salon in her apartment which became a meeting place of progressive thinkers, artists, painters, stage designers and Russian émigrés around the turn of the century. Jawlensky, Kardovsky and Grabar studied until 1899 at the art school of Anton Ažbe, where they eventually became teaching assistants. In a letter to his brother, recently published in Russian, Igor Grabar describes Kandinsky's arrival at the Ažbe school in February 1897: "Along comes a gentleman with a box of paints, takes a seat and starts working. His appearance is typically Russian, even with a touch of the Moscow university scene and a hint of the graduate ... that's exactly how we summed him up: a Moscow don. Well, you can imagine my astonishment when I actually heard his Russian accent ... that was Kandinsky" (figs 4, 5). In those early years in the Ažbe school, there was little contact between Kandinsky, who could, incidentally, speak fluent German and French, and the circle around Alexei Jawlensky. It was not until 10 years later, from around 1908 in Murnau, that this early acquaintance with Jawlensky and Werefkin was to bear fruit, blossoming into the artistically important friendship from which Blue Rider would emerge.

The Phalanx Group 1901–1904

From 1900 onwards, Kandinsky studied for a year at the Munich Academy under Franz Stuck, having been turned down the previous year. Stuck (fig. 6), who was given a peerage in 1906, was not only Munich's most famous Jugendstil painter and second 'painter prince' but also a influential academy professor whose many students, at the time, included Hans Purrman, Albert Weisgerber, Eugen von Kahler, Hermann Haller and, somewhat later, Paul Klee. Yet, like many other artists of the new generation around the turn of the century, Kandinsky was dissatisfied with the academic teaching and life studies, and soon preferred to concentrate on what he called his "small oil studies" painted from nature, in which he was predominantly self-taught. According to Kandinsky, his intention was to make the colors "sing strongly" by applying them energetically to the carrier. A typical feature of all Kandinsky's oil studies is the way he uses the spatula to apply the paint thickly "in colored specks and stripes," leaving visible traces of the working process. Using this technique, he created a number of small

6   Franz von Stuck, *Double Portrait with his Wife Mary*, 1900
Oil on wood, Städtische Galerie im Lenbachhaus, Munich

7   Wassily Kandinsky, *Nikolaiplatz in Munich-Schwabing*, 1901/02
Oil on cardboard, Städtische Galerie im Lenbachhaus, Munich

views of Schwabing (fig. 7) and other parts of Munich, which differ from his Post-Impressionist style only in their impasto paintwork and intensity of color.

Modest as these beginnings may have been, Wassily Kandinsky, still unknown and working more or less alone, joined forces with the sculptors Wilhelm Hüsgen and Waldemar Hecker, draftsmen and stage designers such as Ernst Stern and Alexander von Salzmann – who all worked for the *Elf Scharfrichter* cabaret – and other members of the progressive Schwabing art scene to found a private exhibition association and art school known as *Phalanx*. Kandinsky had already tried to found a similar association the previous year, as a letter to Kardovsky in St. Petersburg dated 14 November 1900 indicates: "This summer I found acceptable conditions and decided to discuss my long-harbored plan with a number of people, to found a new association in Munich with a permanent exhibition of works from all fields of art. I shall not describe all the details, plans and stations of this idea, but just want to say that I have succeeded in interesting some of my artist friends (the idea of the artist is to get good commissions), so I hope that the association might be able to open its doors to the public in the spring."

This fundamental interest in creating opportunities for exhibitions and commissions by founding the *Phalanx* association is echoed eight years later in the founding of the *Neue Künstlervereinigung München* (NKVM). It shows that, right from the beginning, Kandinsky was a skilled, conscious and strategic "art politician" who sought to exploit the mechanisms of the emergent modern art market to his advantage and to further his own aims.

Until 1904, the *Phalanx,* of which Kandinsky became chairman soon after it was founded, organized no fewer than twelve major exhibitions of the international avant-garde in painting and decorative arts. The Munich public took little note. For the first *Phalanx* exhibition in August 1901, predominantly

8 Wassily Kandinsky, poster for the first Phalanx exhibition, 1901 Color lithograph, Städtische Galerie im Lenbachhaus, Munich

featuring works by the members themselves, Kandinsky created a poster whose stylized spear-wielding warrior, with his Jugendstil contours and Hellenistic helmet, is reminiscent of the Amazons in some of Franz Stuck's Secession posters (figs 8, 9). What is particularly interesting, however, is the fairy-tale aspect of these figures and the doubling, combined with a movement to the left against the direction of reading, which creates an overall effect of dissonance, energy and dynamism. The subsequent *Phalanx* exhibitions included such artists as Lovis Corinth, Wilhelm Trübner, the Finnish Symbolist Akseli Gallen-Kallela and the Munich Jugendstil artist Carl Strathmann, drawings by Alfred Kubin and John Jack Vrieslaender as well as works by Felix Vallotton, Paul Signac and Henri Toulouse-Lautrec. For the seventh *Phalanx* exhibition, which presented 16 works by Claude Monet, shown in Munich for the first time, Kandinsky also designed a poster (fig. 10). Even the lettering reflects the influence of Munich Jugendstil, which Kandinsky had explored in some of his decorative art designs. The unusual pictorial motif, however, with its boats reminiscent of Viking longships floating along a meandering river like heralds from some distant era lost in the mists of time, also betrays his involvement with the fantastic realms of Old Russian imagery and medieval scenes – inspired by Russian Symbolism and Jugendstil – which he had addressed between 1903 and 1907 in a number of woodcuts and tempera paintings, alongside his thematically less demanding and stylistically completely different 'small oil studies'.

In the *Phalanx* school, Kandinsky taught painting and a life study evening class. In early 1902, Gabriele Münter, who had arrived in Munich from the Rhineland in the Spring of 1901, enrolled as a student. Münter had dropped out of a private drawing class in Düsseldorf in 1898, following the death of her parents, to join her sister Emmy on a two-year trip to visit relatives in America. On her return in 1900, she decided to continue her studies in Munich. As the art academies did not accept female students in those days, she initially enrolled in the beginners' class given by Maximilian Dasio at the school of the *Künstlerinnen-Verein* (Association of Women Artists) and in the winter semester she joined the life-study class of Angelo Jank. A fellow student told her about the exhibitions and opportunities offered by the *Phalanx*. Münter would later describe these beginnings and her impression of Kandinsky's teaching in an interesting note: "Then a student at the 'Bellevue' pension at Theresienstrasse 30 suggested I should visit the interesting Phalanx exhibition at Finkenstrasse. There was a collection by the Finnish artist Axel Gallén — I remember the sunny, clear painting by Kandinsky of 'the old town' and 2 sculptors Hecker and Hüsgen. I liked Hüsgen's masks for the *Elf Scharfrichter*. It made me want to become a sculptor. I then went to the *Phalanx* school and enrolled in Hüsgen's sculptor class for the afternoon. That also included the evening life-study course with K.[andinsky] — I dropped the life-study classes I had visited before, and took the opportunity That was a new artistic experience, like K., quite different, from the other teachers — thorough and detailed explanation, looked at me as though I was a conscious and striving individual to whom one could entrust tasks and set goals. That was new to me and made quite an impression. It was also very nice on the third floor of the Hohenzollernstrasse *Phalanx* school." (fig. 11).

In the summer of 1902, Münter accepted Kandinsky's invitation to join his painting class on an excursion to Kochel. Painting from nature out of doors was,

11   Members of the Phalanx school, Munich, 1902
(from left to right: Olga Meerson, Emmy Dresler, Wilhelm Hüsgen, Gabriele Münter, Richard Kothe, Maria Giesler, Wassily Kandinsky)
Photograph: Gabriele Münter and Johannes Eichner Foundation, Munich

12 Kandinsky with his Phalanx
painting class in Kochel, summer
1902
Photograph: Gabriele Münter and
Johannes Eichner Foundation, Munich

for Kandinsky as it was for many avant-garde artists since the plein air painting
of the Impressionists, a principle of anti-academic teaching and working, which
he continued to pursue well into his Murnau period around 1912/13. In this,
he followed the example of other German movements such as the Dachau
school of painting, the Munich *Scholle* group and even the Worpswede artists'
colony in northern Germany, who had withdrawn to work in rural surroundings. In Kochel, Kandinsky and his student Gabriele Münter got to know each
other more intimately, aided no doubt by their shared love of cycling – at that
time still a most unusual sport for women (fig. 12). In 1903 they both traveled
with the *Phalanx* painting class on an excursion to Kallmünz in the Palatinate.
On this excursion, Münter, who had previously concentrated primarily on
drawing, painted a number of small landscape studies in oil, using the sketchy,
impasto technique that Kandinsky taught his students. Moreover, they both
experimented intensely with color woodcuts, and the woodcut continued to
play an important role in their work until 1908. The visit to Kallmünz inspired
Kandinsky to go beyond his Old Russian and Biedermeier imagery and explore
an increasing number of motifs from Old German and medieval street scenes
and costumes in what he called his "colored drawings" (fig. 13) – tempera
painting on a dark, clayey ground, culminating in his famous paintings from
the Paris period (see plates 3, 4).

In Kallmünz, Kandinsky and Münter became engaged – a move that created
an untenable situation in Munich for Kandinsky, married since 1892 to his

Russian cousin Anya Shemyakina, who had traveled with him to Germany. The nomadic life on which Kandinsky and Münter embarked for several years from 1904 onwards was due first and foremost to their personal circumstances. At the same time, however, some progressive artists were beginning to leave Munich for Berlin, and this factor, combined with the enormous effort involved in running the financially unviable *Phalanx* with its ambitious yet little appreciated program of exhibitions, may well have been further reasons. In the spring of 1904, Kandinsky resigned his chairmanship and was replaced by his fellow artist and cycling enthusiast Georg Treumann. He still had plans for the *Phalanx*, though, for he envisaged having Alexei Jawlensky elected as a member at the next meeting. Yet, soon after Kandinsky and Münter met up in Bonn

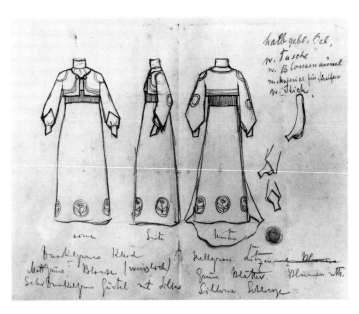

and Düsseldorf in May 1904, to continue on their first journey together to Holland, the *Phalanx* ceased its activities.

In the winter of 1904 to 1905, Münter and Kandinsky continued their travels and spent some months in Tunisia. There, Kandinsky studied decorative art techniques such as beading fabrics and clothing design, and he designed and made a loose-fitting dress for Münter of the kind known in Germany at the time as *Reformkleid* (figs 14, 15). For the summer of 1905 they took an apartment in Dresden where Kandinsky painted his portrait of Gabriele Münter (fig. 16). In the winter of 1905 to 1906, they spent several months in Rapallo on the Italian Riviera. Finally, from June 1906 to June 1907 they spent a year in Sèvres near Paris, with Münter staying occasionally in her own room in Paris and attending

16   Wassily Kandinsky,
Gabriele Münter, 1905,
Oil on canvas,
Städtische Galerie im Lenbachhaus,
Munich

17   Gabriele Münter,
Kandinsky, 1906,
Color linocut,
Städtische Galerie im Lenbachhaus,
Munich

courses given by Théophile Steinlen. In Paris, Münter and Kandinsky experienced at first hand the new French woodcut developed by such artists as Vallotton, Bonnard and Vuillard, who, in the closing years of the nineteenth century, had been inspired by the arrival of Japanese woodcuts to revive this ancient technique as a vehicle for their own modern interest in planarity and simplicity of form. In their own oeuvre, Münter and Kandinsky soon developed a consummate mastery of the art of the woodcut (fig. 17). After Paris, they stayed in Berlin until the spring of 1908, and then, having traveled to South Tyrol together in April 1908, they decided to settle again in Munich. Throughout these years of travel, Kandinsky and Münter retained their impasto, Post-Impressionist style of oil painting whose relief-like, compact and detailed rendering of the motif indicates little in the way of artistic development.

1908–1909: The Turning Point in Murnau

When Kandinsky and Münter decided in the spring of 1908 to move back to Munich for good, this not only consolidated their private situation, but paved the way for hitherto unknown opportunities in their creative development. It was on a trip to the surrounding countryside in search of a suitable place for plein air painting that they discovered the little market town of Murnau in the Alpine foothills of Upper Bavaria, not far from Kochel on the old trading route between Munich and Garmisch. They were enthralled by the picturesque setting on a hill overlooking the broad expanses of the Murnau moor against the sheer blue backdrop of the Alpine peaks, and they loved the brightly painted local houses. When they told their fellow artists Alexei Jawlensky and Marianne von Werefkin about it, they also visited Murnau, staying at the Griesbräu Inn on Obere Hauptstrasse. Jawlensky and Werefkin now urged their friends to join them on painting excursions there.

During August and September of 1908, Kandinsky, Jawlensky, Münter and Werefkin spent a few weeks together in Murnau – weeks that were to prove a turning point in the oeuvre of all four. 'Murnau 1908' stands for the break-through to a new, expressive painting that heralded the emergence of the Blue Rider group. Intense and luminous swathes of pure colors were juxtaposed in a way that no longer slavishly reiterated nature, and combined with a compositional planarity and simplification of forms that condensed what they saw to the verge of abstraction. They worked prolifically there, and the spontaneous, exuberant explosions of color in their Murnau paintings signal their emancipation from the constraints of conventional realism to which even Impressionism was still dedicated, by taking on a dynamically expressive life of their own. Gabriele Münter would later sum up this development in her retrospective journals of 1911: "After a brief period of torment, I made a great leap – from reproducing nature – more or less impressionistically – to feeling the content

18 Alexei Jawlensky, Marianne von Werefkin, Andreas Jawlensky and Gabriele Münter (from left to right) in Murnau, 1908
Photograph: Gabriele Münter and Johannes Eichner Foundation, Munich

19   Wassily Kandinsky, *Village*, 1908
Oil on cardboard, Städtische Galerie
im Lenbachhaus, Munich

20   Gabriele Münter,
View from the Griesbräu, 1908
Oil on cardboard, Städtische Galerie
im Lenbachhaus, Munich

– abstracting – giving an extract." She went on: "It was a beautiful, interesting, joyful time with many discussions about art with the enthusiastic 'Giselists'. I particularly enjoyed showing my work to Jawlenksy – on the one hand he liked to give lavish praise, and on the other hand he would explain things to me – sharing his experience and skills – he spoke of 'synthesis.' He is a nice colleague. All four of us worked very hard and each of us developed."(Fig. 18)

Van Gogh, Cézanne, and Gauguin were the fathers of this far-reaching process in modern painting, and it is by no coincidence that it was Jawlensky who was able to give the little group such important inspiration on the basis of his visits to France in 1903 and 1905. In 1905, in particular, during an extended voyage with Marianne von Werefkin to Brittany, Paris and Provence, he had seen the work produced by the School of Pont-Aven following Paul Gauguin, as well as the works of van Gogh and the 'wild' painting of the Fauves around Henri Matisse. He had even exhibited at the Salon d'automne. This second visit to France also inspired Marianne von Werefkin to return to painting after an interruption of almost 10 years. In 1906, on her return from Paris and Provence, she began to produce the first paintings in her new style, channelling the achievements of the French avant-garde and even the soul-searching paintings of Eduard Munch into the highly distinctive and specific form of symbolism that was to characterize the rest of her oeuvre. Jawlensky, for his part, met the Dutch painter and Benedictine monk Willibrord Verkade at the *Münchner Kunstverein* in the winter of 1906/07 and let him work in his studio for half a year. Verkade prompted Jawlensky to study the school of the Nabis around Maurice Denis more closely and also introduced him personally to Paul Sérusier. According to the memoirs of both Münter and Kandinsky, Jawlensky willingly shared his findings with others in the early Murnau period, encouraging his friends to adopt a free and 'wild' handling of color and the expressive planarity of the 'Nabis', while propagating a synthesis of the image into a independent formal unit (figs 19/20). Münter, in particular, adopted the technique of *cloisonnisme* developed by Gauguin – reducing the visual elements to a few colored planes enclosed (*cloisonné*) by black outlines – especially in her landscapes and still lifes after 1909, and also followed Jawlensky in reducing the individual object to an almost geometrical structure.

In February 1909, Kandinsky and Münter visited their friends, the Russian composers and musicians Thomas and Olga von Hartmann, in Kochel, where they painted a series of views of the town and its cemetery in the snow (fig. 21, and plates 6, 64). Here, Kandinsky and Thomas von Hartmann first drew up their plans for theater performances in which color and light, music and language, action, movement and dance were to merge into a single unit. Gabriele Münter goes into considerable detail in her retrospective journal of May 1911 on Kandinsky's early and little-known experiments in the use of stage design and theater as the vehicle for a new *gesamtkunstwerk*, noting that, in the winter of 1908, Kandinsky had dictated his first *Stage Composition – Black-White-Colored* to her. She adds, "Spent 14 days with Hartmann in Kochel. Hartmann designed (very interesting – very talented) with K. the music for *Die Riesen* (The Giants). . . . Nothing came of this work – although K. put a lot into it and had a structure made for a small stage (*c*. 60 cm) and all decorations (also for a fairy tale)." *Die Riesen* was to be the first preliminary work for Kandinsky's famous

21   Gabriele Münter in Kochel, 1909
Photograph: Gabriele Münter and
Johannes Eichner Foundation, Munich

22   The Münter House in Murnau,
1909
Photograph: Gabriele Münter and
Johannes Eichner Foundation, Munich

stage composition *Der Gelbe Klang* (The Yellow Sound), which he drew up in the fall of 1911 as a manuscript for the Blue Rider almanac, with music fragments by Thomas von Hartmann. The young dancer Aleksandr Sakharov was also closely involved in this work. He was a close friend of Jawlensky and Marianne von Werefkin, and visited their salon from 1908 almost daily until war broke out (see plate 79).

In the spring of 1909, Kandinsky, Münter, Jawlensky and Werefkin all met in Murnau, where they stayed until June, taking private accommodation at the home of the Echter family on Pfarrgasse, whose grandmother had her portrait painted in peasant costume by both Marianne von Werefkin and Gabriele Münter. From there, Kandinsky and Münter moved to a little house set on a slope at the western edge of the village. It had been built recently by a local carpenter named Streidel who intended to rent it out as a holiday home. Kandinsky,

23   Gabriele Münter, *Interior of the "Russian House,"* 1909
Oil on cardboard, Gabriele Münter and Johannes Eichner Foundation, Munich

24   Kandinsky in the garden of the Münter House, *c.* 1909
Photograph: Gabriele Münter and Johannes Eichner Foundation, Munich

as she recalled, immediately fell in love with the house directly opposite the hill on which the castle and the church stood. At his insistence, Münter bought the house in August 1909 using part of her inheritance (fig. 22). This purchase was to bind the couple to Murnau. Soon they began to paint the simple wooden furniture for their rooms on the upper floor in the style of Bavarian folk art. In 1911, Kandinsky used stencils to paint the curving wing of the wooden stairway that leads to the upper floor with brightly colored leaping riders, flowers, and suns. A painting by Gabriele Münter created in 1909 shows her own room in the Murnau house with a view through to Kandinsky's bedroom where he is lying on his narrow bed, and a rucksack and rough sandals can be seen on the floor (fig. 23). On the shelf to the left, a folk art Madonna can be seen, indicating another important influence during the Murnau period. It was here that Kandinsky and Münter began to collect regional crafts and religious folk art, especially paintings on glass and carved figures of Madonnas or Saints, which they bought in Murnau, or at the traditional Munich flea market known as Auer Dult, and later in Moscow. In this way, they built up a unique collection of paintings on glass as well as carvings in their Murnau house and in their Munich apartment on Ainmillerstrasse, bringing a specific touch of folk art to the broader context of the discovery of 'primitive' art by the contemporary avant-garde – such as the inclusion of African and Oceanic art by the Cubists in France and the Expressionists of the *Brücke* in Germany.

In Murnau, especially in the religious motifs of the paintings on glass, they found crucial inspiration and new forms of stylistic simplicity which they could transpose to their own art. Alexei Jawlensky had been the first to draw his friends' attention (by the spring of 1909 at the latest) to more than a thousand glass paintings of predominantly Bavarian and Bohemian origin in the collection

25 Paintings on glass in the
Münter House, Murnau, c. 1913
Photograph: Gabriele Münter and
Johannes Eichner Foundation,
Munich

of a Murnau brewer by the name of Krötz. These are now housed in the local history museum of Oberammergau. At first, Gabriele Münter began to copy works of this kind from old originals, and she learned the technique of glass painting from Heinrich Rambold, one of the last glass painters then still operating in Murnau. Soon, she was creating glass paintings to her own designs, and encouraged Kandinsky to try out the technique as well. It was the simplicity of form in these uncluttered and often schematic images with their black outlines and unblended juxtaposition of bright and luminous colors, quite apart from their primitive naturalness and emotive expression, that inspired the artists and confirmed the essence of their own artistic aims. It was around this time that they began painting the frames of their works as well, taking folk art's naive love of ornament one step further and at the same time heralding their endeavors to eliminate the boundaries of the image – a quest that Kandinsky was to continue, most notably in his Bauhaus years (figs 25–27). The estate of Münter and Kandinsky includes almost a hundred paintings on glass, religious carvings, figures of the Virgin, the saints and crib figures as well as other arts and crafts items, many of which can still be seen today in their original setting at the Münter House in Murnau, which is now a memorial museum. Jawlensky, too, had a considerable collection of local paintings on glass. His interest in these objects was largely forgotten, since he, unlike Münter, Kandinsky and somewhat later Franz Marc, August Macke and Heinrich Campendonk, did not actually work in this technique himself. Yet the memoirs of Elisabeth Macke-Erdmann and of Lily Klee, who looked after the apartment of Jawlensky and Werefkin on Giselastrasse in the Schwabing district of Munich during World War I, state that the walls there were covered in glass paintings. What is more, like Gabriele Münter, Jawlensky included glass paintings and religious folk art in some of his still life paintings (see plates 69, 70).

For Kandinsky, there was another aspect of painting on glass and folk art that had a crucial influence. From 1911 onwards, religious motifs, sometimes

26 Gabriele Münter, votive image,
c. 1908/09
Painting on glass. Städtische Galerie
im Lenbachhaus, Munich

blended with Russian elements, and often in coded symbolism, can be found increasingly in his large and semi-abstract paintings. In his own paintings on glass, based on the primitive figures of the older originals, this religious symbolism is much more evident and barely concealed in its figurative approach. It is quite possible that the anti-naturalistic portrayals of folk art appealed to Kandinsky, for they tended, in their own way, towards abstraction, as Wilhelm Worringer sought to point out in his treatise *Abstraktion und Einfühlung* (Abstraction and Empathy) at the time (see plates 41, 42). Even while he was still in Russia, Kandinsky had been deeply impressed by folk art and peasant painting during a study trip to Vologda in 1889, where, according to his memoirs (*Rückblicke*) he sometimes felt he was walking around inside a painting when he entered a peasant's home. "I have sketched a lot – these tables and various ornaments. They were never sparing, and so heavily painted that the object itself disappeared." All in all, in his first years in Murnau, Kandinsky succeeded in blending the hitherto distinctly separate areas of his work – the symbolic and figural aspects of his tempera paintings and prints, and the landscape elements of his oil paintings. Autonomous color, increasingly veiled and enigmatic symbols, and the use of graphic codes, merged to create a new unity in his paintings, paving the way towards abstraction and a breach with conventional pictorial contents. As Peg Weiss has noted, "Suddenly a way appeared to solve the dichotomy between his Impressionist landscapes and the lyrical works that had held him in thrall for so long. In various later statements, Kandinsky explained that his transition to abstraction had occurred primarily in three steps: by overcoming perspective through two-dimensionality, by applying graphic elements to oil painting, and finally, by emancipating color from line, so that the image becomes an entity hovering in the air."

27   Paintings on glass, Ainmillerstrasse 36 in Schwabing, *c.* 1911 Photograph: Gabriele Münter and Johannes Eichner Foundation, Munich

1909–1912: The Neue Künstlervereinigung München

Following the artistic turning point in Murnau in the late summer of 1908, which had a liberating effect on all those involved, generating a phase of prolific productivity and a new sense of community, they began to think of exhibiting together as well. Activities in Munich indicating the foundation of an artists' association are documented as early as December 1908, including a letter from Adolf Erbslöh to his friend and relation Oscar Wittenstein, both of whom were soon to become members of the group. The document of foundation of the *Neue Künstlervereinigung München* – the NKVM – was hand-written by Gabriele Münter on 22 January 1909. The founding members included Kandinsky, Jawlensky, Münter, Werefkin, Erbslöh and Wittenstein, Alexander Kanoldt (Erbslöh's close friend), Paul Baum, Vladimir Bekhteyev, Moisey Kogan, Alfred Kubin, Karl Hofer, Thomas von Hartmann and the painters Hugo Schimmel and Charles Palmié, who both left the group soon afterwards. Other founding members included Johanna Kanoldt, Alexander Kanoldt's sister, his wife, as well as the art lovers Heinrich Schnabel and Gustav Freytag, son of the writer and Munich eye specialist, who had been the secretary of the *Phalanx* group. In the course of the year, the dancer Aleksandr Sakharov also joined them, as is documented in the brief chronicle of the NKVM by art historian Otto Fischer in his 1912 publication *Das Neue Bild* (figs 28, 29).

28 Marianne von Werefkin and Alexei Jawlensky (above) with Alexandr Sakharov, his sister and a friend, Helene Nesnakomoff in front, Munich, 1909. Photograph: Fondazione Marianne Werefkin, Ascona, and Fäthke Archive

29 Wassily Kandinsky, poster for the first exhibition of the NKVM, 1909 Color lithograph, Städtische Galerie im Lenbachhaus, Munich

30   Wassily Kandinsky, membership card for the NKVM, 1909
Woodcut, Städtische Galerie im Lenbachhaus, Munich

31   Adolf Erbslöh (right) and Oscar Wittenstein in Munich, 1906
Private collection

Adolf Erbslöh (fig. 31), from Wuppertal-Barmen, had come in 1904 from the art academy of Karlsruhe to the Munich academy to study under Ludwig Herterich. By 1908, at the latest, he was a student in Jawlensky's small studio, which he continued to run on the same premises after the death of the much respected teacher Anton Ažbe in 1905. Alexander Kanoldt, son of the landscape painter Edmund Kanoldt, and a fellow student of Erbslöh in Karlsruhe, often visited him in Munich and also took private lessons from Jawlensky before moving to Munich permanently in early 1909. Vladimir Bekhteyev, who had been acquainted with Jawlensky and Werefkin since 1902 in Munich and had even known them in their St. Petersburg days, was also attracted to the group, having spent more than two years studying in Paris from 1906 onwards. Kandinsky also persuaded the composer Thomas von Hartmann, Gustav Freytag, and the young Austrian draughtsman Alfred Kubin to join the group. Kubin, who had presented a number of his drawings in the *Phalanx* in 1904, and whose work Kandinsky thought highly of in the Munich years – including the fantastic novel *Die Andere Seite* published in early 1909 – had known Jawlensky and Bekhteyev since at least 1905. Kubin's wife Hedwig, who had moved with him in 1906 to Zwickledt in Upper Austria, had her portrait painted by Jawlensky shortly before leaving Munich. The painter Erma Bossi, who also joined the group in the course of 1909, had clearly been a frequent visitor to the salon of Jawlensky and Werefkin. Because of his many and diverse connections, Jawlensky was initially envisaged as the first chairman of the new group, but after some debate it was decided that Kandinsky should be elected, "Because," as Münter noted, "nobody else could do it." On 25 January 1909, just a few days after the founding document had been drawn up, Erbslöh wrote to Kandinsky on the matter, saying, "I am delighted to hear that you are now prepared to chair our group, which means that this issue has been resolved in the best possible way. Yesterday, I spoke to Miss Kanoldt [Alexander Kanoldt's sister, Johanna] and she will be happy to take the post of treasurer." Jawlensky was elected the second chairman, and Erbslöh himself acted as secretary to the group for the next two years.

The well-organized and business-like structure of the NKVM suited the initially pragmatic objective that was formulated somewhat laconically in the founding document: "The aim of this association is to mount art exhibitions in Germany and abroad." The wish to present new works to the public within the scope of an official association equipped with an organizational structure and financial means was thus a central motive for the foundation of the NVKM, and in March 1909 a detailed eight-page brochure of statutes was duly printed. Shortly afterwards, Kandinsky created a membership card for the NKVM featuring his woodcut *Felsen* (Cliffs) (fig. 30). Soon, however, a programmatic declaration was added to the pragmatic formulation of aims drawn up by Kandinsky in the spring of 1909 and expounded in the founding circular of the NKVM: "Esteemed reader! Allow us to draw your attention to an alliance of artists founded in January 1909 which hopes, by exhibiting serious works of art, to contribute to the best of their ability to the promotion of artistic culture. We take as our starting point the notion that an artist is constantly collecting experiences in an inner world, apart from the impressions that he receives from the outside world of nature; and that the search for artistic forms by which to lend expression to all these interacting and mutually permeating experiences – forms that have to be free from all that is irrelevant so that they can strongly express the essential – in short, the quest for artistic synthesis, appears to us to be a solution that currently unites an increasing number of artists intellectually and spiritually. By founding this association, we hope to lend material form to this meeting of minds, and to create the opportunity of addressing the public with united energy. Respectfully, Neue Künstlervereinigung München."

Apart from the concept of "synthesis" it is this new blend of impressions from the "outer world" and the "inner world" that Kandinsky adopts as the watchword by which to describe the unique aspect of their painting. It specifies the prerequisite for separating the artistic image from the appearance of nature and, with that, its translation into a subjective portrayal. The "artistic synthesis" of form and content can now also express new dimensions of emotional, intellectual, spiritual and imaginative states by stylistic means that go far beyond anything achieved by previous movements, including Symbolism.

"With synthesis as the focus of artistic endeavor, the program adopted the concepts that Jawlensky was constantly talking about. It was a crystallization of the art theoretical debates in the circle around Jawlensky and Werefkin. The meaning of the term, so widely used at the time, is ambiguous and often contradictory. It was frequently used simply as a synonym for artistic unity, harmonious composition, unity of concept, coherence of color and form etc. It gained currency with the exhibition of the 'Groupe impressioniste et synthétiste' in Paris in 1890 and became such a point of discussion that in one of his commercial works, Gauguin even wrote the motto 'vive la sintaïze!'. The term introduced into the debate by Jawlensky took on such enormous importance because it was based on something that a number of different French artists also focused on: the mutual permeation of external expressions and inner experience and the pursuit of forms liberated from nature and free of irrelevant trivia, 'to strongly express the essential,' as formulated in the founding circular." (Armin Zweite)

Even the works by artists who were not direct members of the 'Murnau colony' – as Kandinsky light-heartedly wrote to his former *Phalanx* student and colleague Emmy Dresler, who had also visited Murnau in June 1909 – indicate a similar tendency towards a simplifying 'synthesis' of the subject matter. For example, Adolf Erbslöh, whose handling of color was still subdued and delicate in 1909, and whose painting *Märzsonne* (March Sun) has a structure of foreground and background that still betrays his previous involvement with Neo-Impressionism, was soon to turn his attention to strongly colored female nudes heavily contoured in black, using intensive colors and simple forms (fig. 33). Erma Bossi's *Zirkus* (Circus) with its expansive planes, ornamental and almost decorative figurations, and suggestively hermetic color effect display a 'synthetic' heightening of expressiveness in the diction of the artist (fig. 34). Marianne von Werefkin too, works specifically with the expressive force of her darkly

32 Marianne von Werefkin,
At the Ball, c. 1908
Tempera and oil crayon on cardboard,
Städtische Galerie im Lenbachhaus,
Munich
On permanent loan from the
Gabriele Münter and Johannes
Eichner Foundation, Munich

33   Adolf Erbslöh, *March Sun*, 1909
Oil on canvas, Städtische Galerie im
Lenbachhaus, Munich
On permanent loan from a private
collection

34   Erma Bossi, *Circus*, 1909
Oil on cardboard, Städtische Galerie
im Lenbachhaus, Munich
On permanent loan from a private
collection

smoldering colors; in her painting *Ballszene* (At the Ball) the enigmatic relationships between the main figures and the alignment and multiplication of similar figures in the background all point towards further typical stylistic instruments of her own personal form of symbolism in which she develops the inspiration of the Nabis and Eduard Munch, in particular, culminating in her large tempera paintings of the period (fig. 32).

In 1909, Alexander Kanoldt began to create a series of laconic portraits and figures in which simple planes of color are linked by clear, dark contours, signifying a radical departure from his previous Neo-Pointillist experiments. In a note written in 1910, Kandinsky seeks to describe the typical characteristics of various NKVM members: "Some paint directly from nature and change it, according to their emotional needs (Jawlensky, Münter, Kanoldt, Erbslöh). Others also address nature, but do not have it before their eyes at the moment of work (Werefkin, Bossi). Still others make things that, for the most part, they have never seen in real form (Kubin, Dresler, Kandinsky)."

By the spring of 1909, the recently founded NKVM was already trying to organize a public exhibition of its members' work, but the enterprise was fraught with difficulty. Kandinsky turned to Hugo von Tschudi, the recently appointed director-general of the Bavarian museums in Munich, who had been dismissed from his post at the Nationalgalerie in Berlin on grounds of his progressive acquisition policy. Tschudi was indeed open-minded in his approach to this unknown young group of artists. "Since he knew hardly any of us," wrote Kandinsky in retrospect, "he asked us to mount a little private exhibition of our works for him and this was immediately done at the studio of A. v. Jawlensky. H. v. Tschudi appeared punctually and spent at least an hour in the little exhibition. His remarks were most apt." Tschudi arranged for them to meet the art dealer and gallery owner Josef Brakl who had created a platform for moderate modernism by presenting the Munich group of artists known as *Scholle*. During the preparations for an exhibition, however, there was some disagreement, and the NKVM quickly changed to Heinrich Thannhauser, who had recently separated from his partner Brakl and had opened a gallery of his own at a prime city center location in the Arcopalais on Theatinerstrasse.

There, in the "beautiful skylit room" of the Galerie Thannhauser, the first exhibition of the NKVM was held from 1–15 December 1909. It showed no fewer than 128 works by members and guests: Paul Baum, Vladimir Bekhteyev, Erma Bossi, Emmy Dresler, Robert Eckert, Adolf Erbslöh, Pierre Girieud, Karl Hofer, Alexei Jawlensky, Wassily Kandinsky, Alexander Kanoldt, Moisey Kogan, Alfred Kubin, Gabriele Münter, Carla Pohle and Marianne von Werefkin. This first exhibition received scathing reviews in the Munich press, which reserved particular vitriol for the "orgies of color" by Kandinsky and Jawlensky, and cruelly mocked the unaccustomed simplicity of the works by Münter and Kanoldt. The public too, according to Kandinsky's memoirs, was appalled, and "raged and spat" at the paintings until Heinrich Thannhauser almost closed his gallery. "I willingly admit that our pictures, unlike the official *Secession*, the quiet *Scholle*, must have seemed like a bomb and that the excitement was only natural,"

wrote Kandinsky in his memoirs more than twenty years later. "For us as exhibitors, their fury was incomprehensible. We were already standing with both feet in the realms of awakened art, and were living in that spirit with body and soul. We were rather surprised that in Munich, the 'city of art', no one but Tschudi, had a good word to say about us." After the Munich show, the first NKVM exhibition went on tour until October of the following year to Brünn, Elberfeld, Barmen, Hamburg, Schwerin and Frankfurt am Main, and it was in the art world of the Rhineland, in particular, that the revolutionary innovation of their images at last met with some understanding. Irrespective of the extremely negative reception in Munich, the NKVM continued their work in the following year, 1910, when the French artists Pierre Girieud and Henri Le

Fauconnier joined the group. Girieud had already shown two works in the first exhibition, one of them a portrait (fig. 35) that the critics had described as very bold in its handling of color. Both Girieud, whom Adolf Erbslöh had visited in the early summer of 1910 in Paris to prepare for the second exhibition, and Le Fauconnier were to become active agents for the NKVM in Paris. Girieud apparently set up contacts with Picasso, while Le Fauconnier, who was vice-president of the *Indépendants,* did much to publicize the NKVM among the avant-garde of Paris, while his connections with the Russian artist colony in Paris meant that the word quickly spread to Moscow. The second NKVM exhibition from 1–14 September 1910, again at the Galerie Thannhauser, differed from the first in that it included a considerable number of foreign guest artists, among them members of the French avant-garde – Braque, Derain, van Dongen, Picasso, Rouault, and Vlaminck. With the works of Braque and Picasso, in particular, early Cubism was shown in Germany for the first time, shortly after the *Sonderbund* exhibition in Düsseldorf in the summer of 1910.

Kandinsky had also managed at the last minute, to invite the stars of the Russian avant-garde – the brothers David and Vladimir Burlyuk, Wassily Denisov and the Prague artist Eugen von Kahler – some of them ex catalogue. This time no fewer than five prefaces were included in the catalogue. "As chairman, Kandinsky undoubtedly had the necessary contacts and had ensured that texts by Le Fauconnier, the Burlyuk brothers, Redon and Rouault were printed along-side his own contribution in the catalogue. The publication, which attracted considerable attention, even in Paris, thus took on the character of a manifesto. This exhibition seemed to vindicate all that Jawlensky and Kandinsky and their friends and fellow artists had sought to achieve. Whereas Le Fauconnier called for 'a minimum of means to achieve a maximum of aims' the Burlyuk brothers were the only ones to address the concept of 'synthesis' in their paean on French painting, though what they meant by it was actually nothing more than simplification. In this context, Kandinsky's text is particularly interesting as an indication of the distance between him and the other painters. The contrast between objective natural impression and subjective perception, which Jawlensky sought to synthesize in the composition of an image, expands in Kandinsky's interpretation to a clash between the spiritual and the material. For Kandinsky, painting thus becomes 'speaking of mystery by mysterious means.' With such words, 'Kandinsky had undoubtedly left the territory on which he and Jawlensky had agreed during their work together in Murnau.' (Armin Zweite) By this time, Kandinsky had moved away from most of his fellow artists not only theoretically but also in his artistic work, and his *Composition II,* which already goes well beyond figurative portrayal, was not only singled out as a target of criticism at the exhibition, but was even a bone of contention for the more moderate members of the NKVM.

Once again, the second NKVM exhibition in the fall of 1910 triggered vehement and polemical criticism in the local newspapers, especially from the pen of the *Münchener Neueste Nachrichten*'s art critic M.K. Rohe, who dubbed the artist 'incurably mad,' 'shameless charlatans' and 'sensation-hungry' and went

36   Vladimir Bekhteyev,
Battle of the Amazons, 1909
Oil on canvas, Bayerische
Staatsgemäldesammlungen, Munich

beyond the pale of insult in ridiculing them as the 'Munich association of Eastern Europeans.'

Yet the NKVM found unexpected support, which was to have significant consequences for the future. Franz Marc, who had followed the activities of the NKVM right from the start, had visited the exhibition and welcomed the work he saw there as related to his own. In her recently published personal memoirs, Maria Marc insists that it was not this second NKVM exhibition, as was previously assumed, that first brought the group to Franz Marc's attention, but that the first exhibition in late 1909 had already made an important impression on him and helped him to come out of his own artistic isolation in early 1910. "In the fall of the year 1909, some very strange posters were to be seen in Munich – brightly colored and with extraordinarily striking forms – advertising an exhibition of the NKVM. F. M. was speechless to see that there was such a thing. His speechlessness soon turned into enthusiasm once he had seen the exhibition. He would have liked to go straight up to the people to meet them. But bitter experience of his colleagues had made him more reserved – so he waited, and was incensed at the stupid critiques printed in the newspapers. It was the first exhibition of the NKVM with Kandinsky, Jawlensky, Werefkin, Bekhteyev, Kanoldt, Erbslöh, Münter, and Bossi – the impact was enormous – as was the enthusiasm it generated for Franz, giving him enormous inspiration and encouraging him to give more space to the ideas that he had already being pursuing for so long."

When the second exhibition a year later was also attacked by the press in the most derogatory terms, Franz Marc felt he had to write his own positive portrayal, and he sent the manuscript to the gallery owner Heinrich Thannhauser, who passed it on to Adolf Erbslöh, secretary of the group at the time. Delighted at such a positive reaction, the NKVM asked permission to publish Marc's review together with the article by Rohe in a small brochure to be inserted in the catalogue for the further stations of the exhibition's tour to Karlsruhe, Mannheim, Hagen, Berlin, Dresden, and Weimar. The highly interesting art theoretical implications of Marc's text, which has been described as a "passionate plaidoyer" can only be touched upon briefly here. In his essay, Marc endeavored to describe to the public the still unfamiliar and enriching aspect of the NKVM paintings, whose particularity he had immediately grasped: "The totally spiritualized and dematerialized inwardness of perception, which our fathers, the artists of the nineteenth century, never even attempted to render visually. This bold undertaking to spiritualize the very 'matter' in which impressionism has been bogged down is a necessary *reaction* that began in Pont-Aven under Gauguin and has already spawned countless experiments. What is new about the Neue Künstlervereinigung, and what seems to us so promising, is the fact that their pictures contain extremely valuable examples of spatial structure, rhythm and color theory, as well as a highly spiritualized significance." He makes special mention of Kandinsky, in particular: "What artistic insight this rare painter possesses! The enormous consistency of his handling of color holds the balance with his free draughtsmanship – is this not, at one and the same time, a definition of painting?" – but also Vladimir Bekhteyev.

His praise for Bekhteyev's *Battle of the Amazons* the previous year is further evidence that Marc had indeed seen the first NKVM exhibition, which featured Bekhteyev's *Amazons* (fig. 36). For Marc, such a painting, too, with its ornamental, independent handling of line, structuring of plane and mysterious color tonality, seeks to "generate spiritual moods that have little to do with the matter of that of which is portrayed, but which prepare the ground for a new and highly spiritualized aesthetics."

Franz Marc, son of the painter Wilhelm Marc, was born in Munich in 1880 and had studied at the Munich academy under Gabriel Hackl and Wilhelm von Diez, who taught their students moderate naturalism and plein air painting. Soon afterwards, however, like the early Kandinsky, he began to work from nature himself, and spent a lot of his time in the Alpine foothills of Bavaria – from 1902 in Lenggries, and later on the Staffelalm above Kochel. Until he finally settled in Sindelsdorf in the spring of 1910, he worked in relative isolation in Munich, apart from his contacts with a few of the *Scholle* artists and members of private art schools and schools of applied art, where he taught during those years to better his chronic financial situation. At an early stage, Franz Marc concentrated on paintings of animals, which for him were a metaphor of purity and innocence through which he hoped to find purity for his artistic and compositional approach. From his naturalistic beginnings, adopting some of the achievements of Impressionism, and influenced from 1903 by Van Gogh, Marc had come somewhat closer to his aim of "animalising art" in his paintings and sculptures around 1909/10. Marc uses this expression in his first publication, an essay for a 1910 book entitled *Das Tier in der Kunst* (The Animal in Art) published by Reinhold Piper, which also contains his famous and often quoted remark: "I seek to heighten my sense of the organic rhythm of all things, I seek a pantheistic empathy with the trembling and flowing of blood in nature, in the trees, in the animals, in the air." His *Two Horses* sculpture of late 1908 already indicate Marc's endeavors and his ability to render visible the "inner" organic life of the animals' bodies and their harmonious relationship with the environment through sweeping strokes and parallels (fig. 37).

Once Marc had contacted the NKVM in writing, he soon met Adolf Erbslöh, Alexei Jawlensky and Marianne von Werefkin personally. As Maria Marc writes in her memoirs: "They now quite naturally met in person. F. M. visited Erbslöh, Jawlensky; and met the other members – except Kandinsky, who was traveling. They were delighted with one another and enjoyed each other's company." Wassily Kandinsky was on an extended journey to Moscow and Odessa from October to December 1910, setting up contacts and organizing exhibition opportunities for the NKVM with a number of Russian artists' associations such as the Jack of Diamonds and the Salon Isdebsky. Kandinsky and Franz Marc eventually met on New Year's Eve 1910 at the salon of Jawlensky and Werefkin. Impressed and inspired by this first personal encounter, Marc wrote to his friend Maria Franck in Berlin on 2 January 1911, "Yesterday Helmuth [Macke] and I went to Jawlensky's and I talked all evening to Kandinsky and Münter – wonderful people. Kandinsky excels them all, even Jawlensky, in his personal appeal; I was quite enchanted by this fine and innerly distinguished person who is outwardly pleasant down to the very tips of his fingers. The fact that young Münter, whom I liked very much, simply adores him, is something I can well understand." Looking forward to future meetings, which were to continue with remarkable intensity, he adds, "Now they all want to visit me and Helmuth at Sindelsdorf, and we shall visit Kandinsky and Münter in Murnau. Oh how I am looking forward to meeting them with you; you will feel at ease immediately, even with Münter, I think." With these almost prophetic words, the year 1911 began, and with it a great artistic friendship that was to change the course of twentieth century painting and lead to the formation of the Blue Rider even before the year was out.

37   Franz Marc, *Two Horses*, 1908/09
Bronze, Städtische Galerie im Lenbachhaus, Munich

The Blue Rider Almanac

1911 began with intense exchanges between these artist friends. On 2 January, the day after they had spent the evening together, the members of the NKVM and Franz Marc attended a concert by Arnold Schoenberg in Munich, which prompted Kandinsky to create his famous painting *Impression III (Concert)* (see plate 18). Kandinsky's enormous interest in Schoenberg's new music prompted him to write a letter to the composer somewhat later, in which, although they did not know each other personally, he immediately struck up a discussion, presenting his own theories of the relationship between 'dissonance in art' in contemporary painting and musical composition, to which Schoenberg replied in equally lively terms. Franz Marc, too, sensed the relationship between the new painting and the new music, and set forth his impressions in detail in letters to his musically versed partner Maria, to whom he also reported his discussions with Kandinsky. On 4 January, back in Sindelsdorf, he wrote to her that "the Schoenberg concert entirely fulfilled all my expectations, right down to the shortcomings that I so often sense in this association and which are of no consequence whatsoever in terms of evaluation. At any rate, the art of both belong closely together." This relationship of the music to the avant-garde and its most important contemporary representatives was to be of even greater significance later.

One month later, on 4 February 1911, a delegation of the NKVM consisting of Jawlensky, Werefkin and Erbslöh, arrived in Sindelsdorf to see the paintings by their new artist friend in his studio. As a result of this extraordinarily enthusiastic and friendly visit, Marc was immediately elected 'unanimously as a member and third chairman' of the group. In this function, he soon became a close associate of Kandinsky, who had resigned from his post as first chairman of the NKVM a few weeks before, on 10 January, submitting a formal letter to Jawlensky in which he stated, "The last year (1910) has made it all too clear to me that my views regarding the activities of our association and the form of its structuring are not shared by the remaining members of the committee and the majority of the ordinary members. This principal difference on fundamental views naturally precludes my continued activity as chairman." In these turbulent weeks of early 1911, when the smoldering conflicts between the moderate and progressive members of the group were exacerbated, Kandinsky and Marc became much closer, and their deep mutual understanding of their artistic endeavor became evident. In a letter dated 10 February, for instance, Marc wrote to his friend Maria, shortly after his acceptance in the NKVM, telling of another visit to Munich, when he had lunch with Alexander Kanoldt at the home of the wealthy Erbslöh: "Next morning I strolled to Kandinsky's! The hours with him are among my most thought-provoking experiences. He showed me many works, old and new. The latter are incredibly powerful. I immediately felt the vast joy of his strong, pure, fiery colors, then the brain started to work; there is no escaping these images even though one feels one's head will burst ... Kandinsky is hoping for good neighborly relations this

summer in Murnau – Sindelsdorf, and so am I." Indeed, the contact between these two artists intensified further, and they visited one another in Sindelsdorf, Murnau and Munich (fig. 38).

In the meantime, tensions were heightening in the NKVM between the 'conservatives' around Erbslöh, Kanoldt and Wittenstein on the one hand and Kandinsky, Münter and Marc, on the other hand. On the face of things, at least, the debate focused on questions of jury rights, the establishment of a members' club on Franz-Josef-Strasse (which Kandinsky opposed) and the inclusion of foreign guests and non-members in the planned third NKVM exhibition (which Erbslöh and Kanoldt opposed).

In a crucial letter to Franz Marc on 19 June 1911 which goes into considerable detail about the differences of opinion in the group, Kandinsky closes with an initial outline of his plan to publish an art almanac with Marc, reflecting various aspects of contemporary art: "Well, now I have a new plan. Piper will have to do the publishing and we two shall be editors. A kind of almanac (annual) with reproductions and articles by artists only. The entire year has to be reflected in the book, enlivened by a link with the past and a pointer to the future." In this letter, Kandinsky also specifies a heterogeneous and interdisciplinary approach involving the juxtaposition of "high art" and "primitive" art as an underlying principle of the planned book. "We'll put an Egyptian work next to a child's drawing, a Chinese work next to Rousseau, folk prints alongside Picasso and that kind of thing. We'll get writers and musicians. The book could be called *Die Kette* (The Chain) or maybe something else."

Klaus Lankheit, who published a new, annotated edition of the almanac in 1965, is not exaggerating when he writes: "This letter dated 19 June 1911 is the birth certificate of the Blue Rider." Since then, much has been written about the plans for the Almanac and the publication itself, whose creation can be reconstructed in detail in the correspondence between Kandinsky and Marc. Yet Klaus Lankheit's preface outlines in essence what made this long-planned publication so special when it finally appeared in May 1912: "It was Kandinsky, older and more experienced than Marc, who had the original idea for the almanac. Right from the start, he had determined the fundamental concept of the publication: both painters would act as editors, artists would contribute essays, the latest foreign works would be presented alongside Egyptian and East Asian art, folk art, children's art and amateur painting. The principle of a comparative juxtaposition of works from different fields and eras was particularly important." Lankheit also stressed the innovative aspect of including all manner of different works of art in a lavishly illustrated almanac which has lost none of its vitality and unconventional impact even today: "It was to no small degree the fact that it so provocatively equated the visual arts of various eras and cultures that made the Blue Rider seem revolutionary when it was published. Yet even this aspect is not without precedent. In the Romantic age, old German prints and medieval and Persian miniatures were rediscovered and, more recently, nineteenth century French artists had been inspired by 'l'art japonais' and by 'l'art primitif et l'art populaire'. Finally, Picasso and the Brücke group, independently of each other, had hailed the art of Africa and other treasures in ethnographic museums as unexpected confirmation of their own 'urge to abstraction'. The lasting achievement of the Blue Rider, however, was that it presented a diversity of expression of past epochs and foreign cultures diametrically opposed to the academic naturalism of the official art world." They also included Egyptian silhouettes, French and Russian folk prints – the so-called *lubki* that so incensed the public at the second Blue Rider exhibition of graphic arts – as well as drawings by children and a selection of Bavarian and Bohemian paintings on glass, presented in an art historical context for the first time.

In the course of the summer, the plans for the almanac matured. Franz Marc welcomed the idea with enthusiasm and identified with it avidly. On 8 September 1911, in a letter to his friend August Macke, he described the ambitious goals and how far the idea had been developed: "We want to found an 'almanac' that will be the organ of all new authentic ideas of our times. Painting, music, theater etc. It is to be published in Paris, Munich and Moscow with lots of illustrations. In Paris, Le Fauconnier and Girieud will work on it for a start. As for musicians, we have Schoenberg, and we also have some people in Moscow apart from the Burlyuks. Comparative material is to be used to explain a lot. Your old plans for a comparative history of art would fit in well here. We mean to present old paintings on glass, French and Russian folk prints, foreign works and our own new stuff, with some 'modern Munich painting' as well by way of comparison. We expect it to bring so much that is healing and inspiring, for our own work as well, and for the clarification of our ideas, that this almanac has become our greatest dream." Some of these ideas never actually came to fruition, among them the plan to make a revealing comparison between 'Munich modernism' and the 'real avant-garde' – a concept that Franz Marc had already proposed in the spring of that year as a counterblast to the conservative painter Carl Vinnen's polemical *Antwort auf den Protest deutscher Künstler* (Reply to the Protest of German Artists). At any rate, the friendship between Franz Marc and Auguste Macke, who had first met in January 1910, brought another important artist to the circle of what was soon to become the Blue Rider. Macke had previously looked mainly towards modern French painting, the Impressionists and Matisse, developing his own style of compact, homogeneous color planes around 1909. In the fall of 1909, the young August Macke, who was only twenty-two, moved from Bonn to Tegernsee with his wife Elisabeth in order to devote himself entirely to his painting. Another reason for leaving the Rhineland was the fact that Elisabeth had become pregnant before their marriage, and their families had pressured them to go to far-away Bavaria to have the child. Elisabeth Macke came from a wealthy Bonn family. Her uncle, Bernhard Koehler (1849–1927), the Berlin industrialist and art collector, had become a patron of Macke, and Macke in turn would accompany Koehler on trips to Paris, where he helped him to build up his considerable collection of important works of the French and German avant-garde. The crucial role that Berhard Koehler would later play as a patron of the Blue Rider, for Franz Marc especially, could not yet be foreseen. In early January 1910, his son Bernhard Koehler Jr. visited August Macke at Tegernsee with Macke's cousin, Helmuth Macke, who was also a painter. Together, they visited some art dealers in Munich, where they came across a number of lithographs by Franz Marc and were so impressed by them that they paid a visit to the artist's studio on Schellingstrasse in Schwabing. Franz Marc wrote a vivid description of this first meeting in a letter to Maria Marc, to which she refers in her memoirs, adding: "They had so much in common, including their love of Paris, which they both knew well. . . . It was a stroke of fortune for FM, for it meant that he was no longer alone. What is more, the young Koehler arranged for his father to buy some works, which also alleviated FM's general situation. Macke had also taken a keen interest in the NKVM exhibition, and so there was always plenty for them to talk about when they met, and they inspired each other with new ideas for their work." Soon, Franz and Maria Marc were visiting the Mackes at Tegernsee and a close and mutually inspiring friendship grew up between the two artists. On Macke's return to Bonn in the fall of 1910, they kept up a regular correspondence which gives some extremely interesting insights into their artistic and theoretical discussions. Maria Marc goes on to relate that it was not long before Franz Marc was introduced to Bernhard Koehler Sen., who helped him to mount his first solo exhibition at Josef Brakl's gallery in February 1910, and bought some works as well. A year later, in January 1911, shortly before joining the NKVM, Marc also arranged for his new patron to visit some of the other members, with gratifying results: "And then on to Erblöh! Lots of works by Kanoldt and Bossi had been brought along; Erslöh and Kanoldt were most tactful and sociable – the impression was immediately pleasant and promising. We spent hours there, going through everything. Koehler warmed to them more and more, becoming genuinely enthusiastic, and leaving with handshakes all round. He is already looking forward to coming back in May (for my exhibition!) and visiting Jawlensky and co. He wants to buy a (very good) Kanoldt and has asked me to speak to him about the price, etc.," wrote Marc in a letter to Maria on 28 January 1911. As for Franz Marc himself, his financial situation had already been settled by this stage, for Koehler, who had hardly been able to contain his enthusiasm on his visit to Marc's Sindelsdorf studio at the artist's "enormous progress in the space of just one year," had offered to pay him a monthly allowance to be offset by regular acquisitions.

In the course of the following six months, during which Marc had a joint exhibition with Pierre Girieud at Galerie Thannhauser in May 1911, Kandinsky and Marc drifted further from the NKVM, and the gap between them was widened even more by their plans for the almanac. The NKVM, however, was still in existence, and when Gabriele Münter spent the summer months visiting relatives in Berlin and the Rhineland, Kandinsky and Marc wrote many letters to her, urging her with almost youthful fervor to 'advertise' the NKVM to the progressive institutions in Essen, Wuppertal, Barmen, Düsseldorf, and Cologne. In Berlin, Münter called on Bernhard Koehler, and when she visited her brother in Bonn, she also met August Macke. They liked each other immediately and traveled to Cologne together to Emmy Worringer's progressive Greens-Club gallery, where the first Blue Rider exhibition would be shown six months later. Macke's thoroughly positive impression of Münter and Kandinsky's work is recorded in a letter to Franz Marc on 1 September 1911: "Münter did me good. I think Kandinsky is a very important inspiration in her painting, so much so that I cannot quite agree with her assertion that it is entirely her own personal work – no more than I can imagine my own work without a strong French influence. I have the impression that she tends very much towards the enigmatic (still life, saints, lilies in a corner of the garden, sharply lit thunderclouds, lamps and old chairs). There is something very 'German' in it, something of the romanticism of altars and families. I like her very, very much. But I like Kandinsky even more. The picture by him that we have here constantly radiates something wonderful. He is a romantic, a dreamer, a teller of fairy tales. But he is also something else, and that's what counts. He is full of boundless life.... The mysterious thing about him is his infinite vitality – he is so full of joy and yet so very serious. I often wish I had a picture from his current period. I gain so much pleasure from the one I have. I do feel sorry for the people who cannot appreciate him."

Kandinsky had spent most of the exceptionally hot summer of 1911 in Murnau, tending the garden and exploring the subject of Resurrection and The Last Judgment in his work – in paintings on glass, woodcuts and large paintings. In September, on Münter's return, work on the almanac began to get beyond the planning stage. Letters were written to the Burlyuk brothers in Russia, to Max Pechstein of the *Brücke* group, to Alfred Kubin in Zwickledt, Upper Austria, to Le Fauconnier asking him to set up suitable contacts in France, and to Girieud asking him to write an article and provide some examples from his collection of *Images d'Epinal* as illustrations.

Steps were also taken to ensure the inclusion of contemporary music, on which Kandinsky had always insisted. Among the articles in the finished almanac – some had to be dropped because the authors did not meet their deadlines –

there are no fewer than four important contributions on the subject. They are Arnold Schoenberg's *Das Verhältnis zum Text* (The Relationship to the Text), Thomas von Hartmann's *Über die Anarchie in der Musik* (Concerning Anarchy in Music), an essay by Leonid Sabaneiev on Scriabin's *Prometheus* and one by Nikolai Kulbin on *Free Music*. There were also inserts of scores with compositions by Arnold Schoenberg and his students Alban Berg and Anton von Webern as well as Kandinsky's own famous *Der Gelbe Klang* (The Yellow Sound) in which he published for the first time his vision of a *gesamtkunstwerk* of painting, music and stage in a text that still seems highly unconventional, even today. Kandinsky was particularly keen to have Arnold Schoenberg editorially involved in the almanac, and wrote to him at his summer residence on Lake Starnberg, inviting him to visit Murnau, "... where my good friend Franz Marc (painter) and his wife live, who are very interested in you." After some initial difficulty in setting a suitable date, Kandinsky and Schoenberg did meet at Lake Starnberg in early September. In his last letter to Schoenberg on 1 July 1936, Kandinsky vividly recalls the meeting. "Remember, dear Mr Schoenberg, how we met at Lake Starnberg – I came with the steamer, in short *lederhosen*, and saw a black-and-white print – you were dressed entirely in white and only the face was deep black." They talked about the plans for the almanac and Schoenberg's part in it. Gabriele Münter's request in a letter of late September, "eagerly awaiting article and illustrations" was to be repeated in the following weeks and months with increasing urgency. In his first reply to Kandinsky at the very beginning of their correspondence, Schoenberg had mentioned that he also painted and later sent some photographs of his works, which Kandinsky liked very much. So the editors of the almanac were not only waiting for an essay on music theory, but also for some paintings by Schoenberg which they hoped to publish and also include in the third NKVM exhibition. Schoenberg, however, had moved from Vienna to Berlin after the summer holidays to take up a teaching post at the Stern'sches Konservatorium, and was slow to deliver the requested text. It finally arrived in Munich in early 1912 (fig. 39).

A letter from Kandinsky to Franz Marc dated 9 October, mentioning reproductions of works by Robert Delaunay for the first time, echoes the climate of feverish activity that prevailed during these months and the wealth of inspiration that the editors had grasped: "Really nice reply from Matisse – I can reproduce whatever I want – says he can't write, makes a cross and swears never to do it again ('you have to be a writer to do that kind of thing'). Délonné [sic] has sent a 'Tour Eiffel'. We'll include that. I want to order all the reproductions so that I can head for Murnau with a clear conscience. I'm quite sure you'll agree (on Délonné): it is certainly interesting and expressive, even though it smacks a little too much of theory. We have to take note of things like this. Met Klee yesterday through [Louis] Moillet. Now there's a man with soul. [Eugen von] Kahler collection at Thannhauser very interesting! Vibrant! I do wish you could see it! But the exhibition ends this week. It is wonderfully fine that so many different notes are now being struck. Together they are the symphony of the twentieth century."

39   Arnold Schoenberg, portrait photograph with dedication to Kandinsky, 12.12.1911
Photograph: Musée National d'Art Moderne, Centre Georges Pompidou, Paris, Fonds Kandinsky

It must have been during these few weeks in the fall of 1911 that the name *Der Blaue Reiter* was found for the publication. Of the eleven or so watercolors that Kandinsky created in rapid succession for the cover of the almanac, ten of which are now in the Lenbachhaus, two bear the title *Der Blaue Reiter*. Almost all of them feature a rider leaping triumphantly, arms outstretched, a cloth fluttering above his head, with a dynamic forward movement symbolising the triumphal power of the spirit (fig. 40). For the final version of the cover, however, Kandinsky abandoned these drafts in favor of a motif whose compelling symbolism visualizes the intentions of the publication. His last watercolor sketch, stylistically influenced by folk paintings on glass, features the figure of an armed rider in the guise of St. George the dragonslayer, who stands in Christian iconography for liberation and the triumph of good over evil (see plate 37). In this final choice of motif, Kandinsky looks to traditional religious iconography and makes clever use of the aura associated with this particular figure. Yet the distinctive stylization and the predominance of blue – the color of yearning and spirituality since the Romantic age, and regarded by Kandinsky as "the archetypal heavenly hue" – imbues this figure with a significance that goes beyond the religious associations of popular glass paintings and makes him the bearer of a universal meaning. In many ways, the almanac bore a message of redemption heralding a new spiritual era – a vision that Kandinsky in particular, and Marc as well, had nurtured before World War I. In 1930, in a retrospective written for the periodical *Das Kunstblatt* at the request of its editor Paul Westheim, Kandinsky

40 Wassily Kandinsky, design for the cover of the Blue Rider almanac, 1911
Brush and ink drawing, watercolor, white highlights, Städtische Galerie im Lenbachhaus, Munich

41 Wassily Kandinsky, final design for the cover of the Blue Rider almanac, 1911
Woodcut, Städtische Galerie im Lenbachhaus, Munich

noted in a tone so casual that it verges on irony: "We came up with the name The Blue Rider while we were having coffee in the garden at Sindelsdorf; we both loved blue, Marc loved horses and I loved riders. So the name was an obvious choice. And Mrs. Maria Marc's fairy-tale coffee tasted all the better for it."

Kandinsky created a number of color woodcuts for the cover on the basis of his final watercolor design which clearly bears the words *Almanach Der Blaue Reiter*. At an editorial meeting held at the publishing house of Piper-Verlag on 21 September 1911, when the structure of the almanac was more or less definitive, the first essays and photographs had already been submitted and Kandinsky felt "as though embarking on an exhilarating and enormously interesting mountain hike," the publisher Reinhard Piper and his production manager emphatically rejected the use of the word "almanac" in the title. "Piper and Hammelmann are both very much against the word 'almanac', and with good reason. I want to cut that word out of the woodblock," Kandinsky reported to Franz Marc – and did exactly that for the final version (fig. 41). The decision to remove the word 'almanac', which indicates the plan for an annual publication, proved wise, for although a second issue was still in the planning until 1914, it never got off the ground. The first almanac, published in May 1912, was a stroke of genius, never to be repeated.

At this stage, however, the editors and their colleagues were still involved in the preparations. At the end of October, the now legendary editorial session was held over a period of several days at the Murnau home of Gabriele Münter and Wassily Kandinsky. Franz Marc and August and Elisabeth Macke were also there. "We four [the Mackes and the Marcs] traveled there," writes Elisabeth Macke-Erdmann in her occasionally rose-tinted memoirs, "and were comfortably accommodated by Kandinsky in a large house nearby. And now the Blue Rider was born in lengthy meetings with debates on art, demands, suggestions for prefaces, etc. These were unforgettable hours, with each of the men working out his manuscript and we women then faithfully transcribing it. Contributions arrived from the artists who had been invited to take part. Everything was viewed, discussed, accepted or rejected, but not without arguments and discord." According to Franz Marc, whose major contributions *Geistige Güter* (Spiritual Goods), and *Die 'Wilden' Deutschlands* (The 'Savages' of Germany) were already all but finished, August Macke now finalized his own essay *Die Masken* (The Masks) whose melodically rhythmic first lines indicate the lyrically associative character of the text: "Ein sonniger Tag, ein trüber Tag, ein Perserspeer, ein Weihgefäss" (A sunny day, a dull day, a Persian spear, a censer). Yet Macke, too, agreed with Kandinsky's thesis that true artistic form, however different it might be among all peoples and eras, was "the expression of mysterious powers."

Shortly after the Murnau meeting, when the guests from the Rhineland were still staying at the home of Franz and Maria Marc in Sindelsdorf, Reinhard Piper sent Kandinsky a book showing works by the 'naive' customs officer Henri Rousseau. It made an enormous impact. The book in question was a publication by Wilhelm Uhde, a German collector and art critic living in Paris, who had been one of the first to discover Rousseau and Picasso. He was also on good terms with Sonia Terk, his ex-wife, who had married Robert Delaunay following her divorce from Uhde in 1905. On 29 October, Kandinsky wrote exuberantly to Franz Marc: "What a wonderful person this Rousseau was! And naturally in touch with the 'Beyond'. And what profundity in his pictures! Just a few days ago, I was thinking, The first BR and no Rousseau! The editors should turn puce with embarrassment! And the last thing – that cigar box painting! I wrote to Delonnay [sic] immediately yesterday and asked him whether he thought Uhde might give us some clichés."

Marc, who not only had August and Elisabeth Macke but also Helmuth Macke and Heinrich Campendonk staying at his house in Sindelsdorf, sent word back to Murnau that there was a "great general glass painting production" going on, and otherwise eagerly agreed with Kandinsky on Rousseau: "My (that is to say our) thoughts are constantly with Rousseau. I have immortalized his self-portrait in a glass painting, though it is just as well that poor Rousseau cannot see it" (fig. 42). The painting on glass with an silver foil backing, on which the yellow glow of a lamp stands like a halo above the head of the customs officer, is based on Rousseau's *Self-Portrait with Lamp* in the book by Wilhelm Uhde, which Kandinsky had immediately sent on to Marc. This self-portrait by Rousseau was one of six works by this artist to be included in the Blue Rider Almanac, giving a prominent place to this French 'father of naive painting.'

In his text *Über die Formfrage* (Concerning the Question of Form) which takes the title *Konstruktion* (Construction) in the provisional table of contents submitted to Reinhard Piper on 10 September 1911, Kandinsky outlines the two poles of abstraction and realism that he regarded as fundamental to the painting of the future, in which the question of outer form versus inner necessity became irrelevant. In speaking of what he terms "realists," for example, he writes to Franz Marc, "I find that Rousseau belongs in their company: Kahler, Kubin, Epstein, Schoenberg, Münter. My antipodes! Is that the reason why I love and respect them all so much?" In his essay on the Question of Form he also spoke of his empathy with Arnold Schoenberg's didactic *Nurmalerei* (pure painting) and with the immediate, almost raw directness of the new and emergent form of realism that succeeds in embodying the essence of an object. In 1911 Kandinsky wrote to Schoenberg on related matters in terms considerably less theoretical and complex than those he uses in either this essay or his seminal work *Über das Geistige in der Kunst* (Concerning the Spiritual in Art): "I am quite delighted by your paintings: a natural necessity and finely tuned sensibility are your sources. I have long suspected that this great age we live in will bring not one but many opportunities. In a treatise that some people seem to like, but for which I have yet to find a publisher [*Über das Geistige in der Kunst*] I propose, for example that the opportunities in painting could well become so rich that they will not only go to extremes, but may even verge on overstepping them. And these two extremes are the polar opposites of complete abstraction and pure realism. I for my part tend increasingly towards the former. But I welcome the second just as much. And I await its appearance impatiently. I believe it will come tomorrow!"

42   Franz Marc, *Portrait of Henri Rousseau*, 1911
Painting on glass, Städtische Galerie im Lenbachhaus, Munich

In their attitudes to what they regarded as the "authentically creative" aspect of works with different forms of expression, genres and eras, Kandinsky and Franz Marc invariably agreed. As second editor of the Almanac, Marc also made an important practical contribution to the project. It was Marc who had arranged negotiations with Reinhard Piper and paved the way for publication, and it was he who had persuaded Bernhard Koehler to underwrite the project – not to mention his tireless commitment to obtaining the photographs and manuscripts they needed. The Almanac in its published form presents outstanding works by contemporary artists in a context that deliberately and provocatively juxtaposes diverse forms of expression. It includes Van Gogh's *Portrait of Dr. Gachet*, Kokoschka's *Portrait of Elsa Kupfer*, *La Danse* and *La Musique* by Matisse, Picasso's Cubist *Woman with a Guitar*, Münter's *Still Life with St. George* and, finally, the famous juxtaposition of Delaunay's *Tour Eiffel* with El Greco's *St. John* – both from the collection of Bernhard Koehler. Other works in Koehler's collection that were presented in the Almanac were a Rhenish Gothic wood sculpture, a Spanish *Death of the Virgin*, Girieud's *Semi-Nude* and a still life by Cézanne (fig. 43).

In recent art historical discussions of the almanac, there has been a renewed emphasis on the principle of comparing works of old and new art, which the editors may well have adopted from contemporary exhibitions.

If, as the two editors claim in the foreword, the Almanac is meant as an "organ of all the new and authentic ideas of our times," then, what, asks art historian Magdalena Bushardt, is the preponderance of comparative material meant to explain, and what image of modernism is the non-modern art supposed to project? She goes on to maintain that there were two sides to this comparative approach: on the one hand, it provided the traditional backdrop that would cover for the formal experiments of modernism. On the other hand, paradoxical as

43 Robert Delaunay, *Eiffel Tower*, 1911; El Greco, *Saint John*, 1600/10 Double page from the Blue Rider almanac

it may sound given the rejection of a consistent notion of style, it set a standard – albeit a standard of content as opposed to one of form. It was the art that could not be explained in terms of historical development, free from the 'external' influence of the past and observing only its own inner laws – in short, the "authentic" aspect of the new art – that was behind the comparative examples.

Some may tend to agree with this view that the editors were driven by idealism and irrationality in seeking the "authenticity" of all art, and that their efforts, as Armin Zweite and others have maintained, were in a sense "misplaced." Others may subscribe more generously to the enormous impact of this book, which is revolutionary still, seeing in it, as Klaus Lankheit did, utopian tendencies and a benchmark of modern aesthetics. Its publication was undeniably an extremely modern act. By embracing the notion of the "essentially artistic," its editors followed on from the traditions of Idealism and the Romantic age, as opposed to the materialism of the nineteenth century, and in doing so they emancipated the expressive value of an art work from all formal canons. In this respect, they paved the way for the pluralism of twentieth century modernism and the blurring of boundaries between genres and disciplines. In 1936, Kandinsky once more summed up their endeavors, saying that they had wanted to make a book "that would bring down the barriers between the arts and prove once and for all that the question of art is not a question of form, but a question of creative content."

The First Blue Rider Exhibition in 1911

Preparing the almanac highlighted and even exacerbated the artistic differences between the progressive and moderate factions of the NKVM, and tension within the group mounted as they squabbled over the statutes. Their views on what new art should entail and how it should be defined diverged increasingly. A split, as predicted by Franz Marc in a now famous letter to his friend August Macke on 10 August 1911, had already begun to seem increasingly inevitable. In the letter, Marc describes with vivid regret the latest "Cubist" paintings by Alexander Kanoldt, for which he reserves a criticism that betrays the intimacy and consensus between the writer and the addressee: "I had to go to Munich the other day for a board meeting – Erbslöh, Kanoldt, Dr. Wittenstein and myself – and had the opportunity of seeing Kanoldt's 'summer works.' You cannot imagine how depressed I was when I came home. Not so much the lack of quality – this tropical summer may well have affected his powers of production – but the direction of his ideas; such a ridiculous and banal imitation of faddish Cubist ideas that it would be simply embarrassing to exhibit the stuff. I saw nothing by Erbslöh, but I feared the worst when he began gushing enthusiastically about Kanoldt's work. (Of course, I didn't say *a thing*)." The very strong criticism leveled at Kanoldt's paintings, which clearly refers to the *Eisacktal* landscapes he had produced that summer in South Tyrol, is more easily understood in the light of the deeper underlying conflict that Marc and Kandinsky saw between "external imitation" and the "modernist program" on the one hand,

and "inner necessity and true perception" on the other hand. This central tenet of the Blue Rider overrode any form of apparently superficial adoption – even of new avant-garde stylistic forms – unless motivated purely by the inherent expressive force of the artwork itself. This evidently applied to Kanoldt's geometrically reduced "landscapes with houses" (fig. 44). Further on in the same letter, Marc urges his friend to join the NKVM to lend more support to the party around him and Kandinsky: "I am writing all this to you so that you can see things clearly, and not just to make it even easier for you to *stay away*. On the contrary – see that you join us as soon as possible, for the following reason: I clearly foresee, like Kandinsky, that the next jury (in late fall) is going to prompt a dreadful argument and that sooner or later there is going to be a split, or some are going to leave, and the question will be who *stays*. We don't *want* to give up the association, but incompetent members will have to go." He envisages allegiances between "Kandinsky, Münter, Marc, Jawlensky, Werefkin" on the one hand and "Erbslöh, Kanoldt, Dr. Wittenstein, Dr. Schnabel, Frl. Kanoldt," on the other hand, with "Kogan, Bekhteyev" undecided but tending towards the conservative. Yet Marc was not certain of the votes of Alexei Jawlensky and Marianne von Werefkin, suggesting that financial interests might sway them, since Adolf Erbslöh had purchased a considerable number of Alexei Jawlensky's paintings.

When the jury met several months later on 2 December 1911 to organize the third NKVM exhibition planned for the end of the year, the row Marc had predicted was unleashed. Even in the days running up to the meeting, when the works submitted had been set out for preview at the association's rooms on Franz-Josef-Strasse, the flames of the smoldering conflict about the jury's criteria had been fanned. Basically, the bone of contention was the fact that what Kandinsky and Marc wanted, short of jury exemption for their own works, was jury rights for artists only, but not for 'non-artists' as demanded by Wittenstein and Schnabel. Once again, their demands were refused. Moreover, at the actual meeting on 2 December 1911, one of the works Kandinsky had submitted – his *Composition V* – was rejected by the majority of the jury around Erbslöh, Kanoldt, Wittenstein and Schabel on grounds that it was "too big." This abstract painting on the theme of the Last Judgment has a black line whipped across it like the visual embodiment of a trumpet blast, with the blurred figures raised from the dead below, and in the center, on a kind of hilltop, a horseback rider before falling towers – an image that Kandinsky was soon to use for the cover of his book *Über das Geistige in der Kunst* (*Concerning the Spiritual in Art*) to signify the triumph of the spiritual over the material (fig. 45).

Composition V did in fact exceed the prescribed four square meters that Kandinsky himself had stipulated after the founding of the NKVM, partly to exclude the large works by Hugo Schimmel, who soon left the group.

When the jury voted to reject *Composition V*, a heated argument broke out, verging on the physical, and Kandinsky, Marc and Gabriele Münter resigned from the NKVM. On the evening of 2 December, Maria Marc wrote an angry and detailed letter to her friends August and Elisabeth Macke in Bonn. It clearly states that the group around Erbslöh and Kanoldt were not in a position to justify their general lack of understanding for Kandinsky's steps towards abstraction, and that Jawlensky and Werefkin, though artistically closer to Kandinsky than the others, had not resigned. "At that, Kandinsky, Münter and Franz declared their resignation and left. The opponents had got their way, but the baroness [Werefkin] said, when the three had left, 'Well, gentlemen, we have now lost our two most worthy members as well as a wonderful painting, and we ourselves shall soon be wearing dunce's caps.' The fact that Jawlensky and the baroness did not resign with the others is due to perfectly understandable personal reasons, which we respect. They expressed their complete solidarity with our views, and the baroness, who called on Kandinsky later in the evening, left him in no doubt that she felt the association no longer had any future." Speaking to August Macke as a fellow artist, Maria Marc continues, "Now the editors of the Blue Rider will be holding exhibitions. More details later. They will certainly be in for a surprise, those young ones who did not dare to take the step the more mature artists are taking. Now that's a first – the younger generation trying to hold back their elders."

44   Alexander Kanoldt, *Stone Desert*, 1911
Oil on cardboard, Städtische Galerie im Lenbachhaus, Munich
On permanent loan from the Gabriele Münter and Johannes Eichner Foundation, Munich

That same evening on 2 December 1911, Gabriele Münter wrote to Alfred Kubin, an external member of NKVM, at his home in Zwickeldt, informing him of the split and urging him to resign as well. "Dear Mr Kubin, Take heed! Allow me to present three fresh and refreshed non-members of the NKVM: Kandinsky, Marc, Münter. We have resigned following futile arguments arising from differences in our views on art and on the work of the jury. It is a matter of urgency that you should be informed, which is why I am writing to you, as Kandinsky has had to go out. We urge you to inform Kandinsky *by telegraph* of your *resignation* from the association in order to lend some force to the resignation. . . . It is *quite* possible that we shall soon be mounting our own *interesting* exhibition (at Thannhauser!) – by all means in the course of the winter." Kubin responded immediately and became one of the founding members of the Blue Rider along with Kandinsky, Marc and Münter. They wrote long letters to other colleagues, among them Henri Le Fauconnier and Pierre Girieud, in an attempt to persuade them to resign. Le Fauconnier submitted his resignation rather half-heartedly from Paris and undertook nothing further. Girieud declined to do so on grounds of his obligation of friendship to Erbslöh and Jawlensky, and from then on he rapidly broke away both artistically and personally from the leading figures and ideas of the almanac, to which he never contributed, though he was repeatedly invited to do so. Thomas von Hartmann, who had been a constant companion to Kandinsky in their exploration of experimental painting and music, soon resigned from the NKVM. The new group, still without a name, hurriedly issued the following newspaper announcement as soon as the official statements had been received from the members who had not been present at the jury meeting: "The following artists have resigned from the Neue Künstler-Vereinigung München: Hartmann, Kandinsky, Kubin, Le Fauconnier, Marc, Münter."

45 Wassily Kandinsky,
Composition V, 1911
Oil on canvas, on loan from
The Museum of Modern Art,
New York

Immediately after the argument on 2 December, the newly-formed group began thinking about organizing their own exhibition as a counterpoint to the third NKVM exhibition. On a now famous postcard from Marc to Kandinsky, the exhibition program is outlined with urgency and brevity, and already the choice of artists and exhibits clearly reflects an affinity with the tenets of the Blue Rider Almanac: "L.K., own room at Thannhauser for 2nd half December, next to NKVM, where we 2 can exhibit what we want. So let's *do it*, and get *serious*. Hurriedly, FzM." He added in a postscript: "My program: Burlyuk, Campendonk, August [Macke], some paintings on glass, Schoenberg, Bloch, if possible Rousseau (not too big). Then Delaunay and maybe two or three old works (woodcuts, paintings on glass, votive images). *It's got to be really good*." The postcard itself is not dated, but it bears a date-stamp of 4 November 1911, indicating that Marc and Kandinsky had been planning an exhibition of their own weeks before the jury row. This has long been a point of controversy among art historians. Yet the tone of urgency in the letters written by Maria Marc and Gabriele Münter on 2 December, together with a number of other factors, indicate that the main protagonists started to organize their own exhibition in a hurry only after that date. Marc's letter to his friend Macke on 7 December, for example, asking him to send pictures immediately for an "alternative exhibition" suggests that the date-stamp is very probably wrong. They urgently sought to win over like-minded artists who had already been envisaged for inclusion in the NKVM exhibition. Kandinsky first approached Albert Bloch, an American artist of German-Bohemian extraction, who had been working in Munich since 1909 and, like Marc, had learned of the NKVM through its exhibitions and catalogue. On studio visits, the Almanac editors had sensed an affinity between Bloch's laconic cityscapes and figural scenes and their own ideas of artistic synthesis, and had intended to invite him to take part in the third NKVM exhibition (fig. 46). In October, there had been an argument about Bloch with the NKVM chairman Adolf Erbslöh, who insisted that, in accordance with a motion tabled at their February 1911 meeting, the next exhibition should be "small and internal" – that is to say, without works by non-members. Nevertheless, ignoring this prior decision, Kandinsky in particular had continued to negotiate with Albert Bloch, Arnold Schoenberg, Elisabeth Epstein, Eugen von Kahler, the Burlyuk brothers, and Hans Bolz. On 11 October, Marc wrote to Kandinsky reporting that, "Bloch, Epstein and Bolz have been written off by Erbslöh – I'll write to him about it." Marc did just that, and in vain he commenced a formal correspondence lobbying for the inclusion of Albert Bloch in the exhibition.

Then, on 4 December – the day Marc presumably sent his postcard outlining the exhibition concept – Kandinsky wrote to his friend: "My dear Marc. The whole thing is very much on my mind, keeping me awake at night. I have two very strong sentiments rooted in two kinds of human and artistic forms of action. My disgust at the way our 'opponents' are behaving increases at the same rate as my joy and gratitude at what you are doing. It is becoming clearer than ever to me how selflessly you worked for the association and how well you managed, in your quest for truth, to forgo all that might be to your advantage. My 'advanced years' give me the right to say such things." At the end of the letter, he added, "I visited Bloch. He looked astonished. But he did say 'it isn't entirely unexpected.' He'll go along with us. Kindest regards to both of you from both of us. Kandinsky." Bloch was to present no fewer than six works at the first Blue Rider exhibition.

46   Albert Bloch, *Houses with Tower*, 1911
Oil on canvas, Städtische Galerie im Lenbachhaus, Munich
Gift of Mrs Anna Bloch, Lawrence, Kansas

They also contacted Elisabeth Epstein, a Russian painter and former student of Kandinsky who had married a Polish doctor in Munich and was now living in Paris. The surviving correspondence between Epstein, Kandinsky and Münter shows that she was not only considered for inclusion in the third NKVM exhibition as an external participant, but that she had actually been invited to take part in the first NKVM exhibition in 1909 and had been unable to do so on grounds of ill health. After the split, Kandinsky approached Elisabeth Epstein again, asking her to take part in the planned independent exhibition. Her paintings, which were predominantly still lifes and portraits, seem to have appealed to Kandinsky in much the same way as Arnold Schoenberg's did, as "pure painting" with a simple and almost magical effect. Kandinsky purchased her *Portrait* (current whereabouts unknown) which was one of the two paintings Epstein showed at the Blue Rider exhibition (fig. 48). Epstein was also an important mediating figure in the Almanac circle. As a close friend of Sonia Delaunay-Terk, she had sent photographs of Robert Delaunay's paintings to

47   Eugen von Kahler, *Rider in the Forest*, 1911
Formerly Bayerische Staatsgemälde-sammlungen, Munich
Confiscated in 1937, whereabouts unknown

48   Elisabeth Epstein, *Portrait*, c. 1910/11
Whereabouts unknown

Kandinsky, and had also introduced him to the work of Henri Rousseau, through Delaunay and Wilhelm Uhde. It was Epstein, too, who had set up the contact with Eugen von Kahler, a German-speaking Jewish painter from Prague who had studied in Munich in 1901/03 but barely knew the circle around Albert Weissgerber, Rudolf Levy, and Alfred Kubin that frequented Café Stefanie. Kahler was living in Paris in 1909 and Epstein recommended him for the second NKVM exhibition in 1910, with the result that four of his works on paper were included at short notice. Soon after the exhibition opened in the fall of 1910, while Kandinsky was away in Moscow and Odessa, Epstein also organized a personal meeting by sending him to see Gabriele Münter at Ainmillerstrasse. "I have taken the liberty, dear Miss Münter," she wrote from Paris on 15 November 1910, "of recommending that the painter Eugen Kahler, who is currently in Munich, should contact you, though I do not know whether he will call or when as his time seems to be taken up very much with his paintings. I trust I have not caused you any inconvenience, for he is a pleasant and intelligent person and painter, as you already know from his works."

What Kandinsky liked about Kahler's work was the visionary mysticism of a world brimming with fantasy figures, which linked the distinctive motifs rooted in mystic Judaism with a formal fabric of tropically luscious density. In October 1911, Kahler, frequently bed-ridden by pulmonary disease and unable to travel to Munich, had a solo exhibition at the Galerie Thannhauser which Kandinsky described to Marc in the most glowing terms. His enigmatic *Rider in the Forest* was also shown at the Galerie Thannhauser alongside other works with similar and related motifs (fig. 47). In the course of that year, contacts between the artists were intensified and news of preparations for the almanac had

49   Vladimir Burlyuk, *Trees*, 1911
Oil on canvas, Städtische Galerie
im Lenbachhaus, Munich
On permanent loan from the
Gabriele Münter and Johannes
Eichner Foundation, Munich

reached the sanatorium in the Rhenish spa of Hohenhennef where Kahler
was spending the summer of 1911. From there, he traveled to Bonn to meet
Gabriele Münter, and he wrote to Kandinsky to discuss the latest achievements
in a quest for a new "realism" that had been outlined to him by Elisabeth
Epstein. "I would like to hear more," he wrote, "about how you approach your
modern painterly ideas through the old stylists, painting on glass and woodcuts. It would be interesting if this kind of art that uses a limited means of expression could lead to a distinctly modern form of expression. . . ." Yet when
Kandinsky urged him to go into more detail about his approach to art and
perhaps even write a theoretical treatise for the almanac, Kahler declined,
claiming that, for him, "ignorance and composition" were so inextricably linked
that he was neither willing nor able to talk about his art.

Kandinsky's esteem for his work is reflected in the fact that, when Kahler
died on 11 December 1911, he wrote an obituary for him in the almanac, and
included two of his works posthumously in the Blue Rider exhibition. The
brothers David and Vladimir Burlyuk, who had been invited by Kandinsky to
participate as guest artists in the second NKVM exhibition, were represented
in the Blue Rider exhibition by works they had had sent from Russia in June
1911 at Kandinsky's suggestion in preparation for their possible inclusion in
the third NKVM exhibition – as documented in the correspondence between
the Burlyuks and Kandinsky. Their works are informed by a kind of radical
Cubism whose recourse to the plane leaves only the heavy framework of the
objects – sometimes in strong, contrasting colors, and sometimes "misty, planar,
matt," as Münter once described a work by Vladimir Burlyuk in comparison
with her own (fig. 49).

Franz Marc helped gain the involvement of August Macke, Heinrich Campendonk and Jean-Bloé Niestlé. The young Swiss artist Niestlé had been a friend of Marc's since 1904 and they shared a love of animal painting and rural solitude. They had undertaken painting excursions together since 1907, in the course of which they had discovered the moorlands of Loisachmoos near Sindelsdorf. A few years later, Marc left Munich to settle in Sindelsdorf, which is situated between Murnau and Kochel in the foothills of the Alps. In 1910, Niestlé and his companion, the French art student Marguerite Legros, also moved to Sindelsdorf to be near Franz Marc.

In Sindelsdorf, Niestlé perfected his own particular form of animal painting in which extreme precision and observation of nature are combined with a highly developed technique of "fine painting" reminiscent of Japanese miniatures. Niestlé's sensitive portrayals of animals as living creatures in their natural habitat bore certain affinities with the artistic objectives that Franz Marc pursued by very different pictorial means. The Rhenish artist Heinrich Campendonk, who had studied with Helmuth Macke, also moved to Sindelsdorf in October 1911, after Marc, whom he had never actually met, had lobbied art dealers and exhibition organizers on his behalf at the recommendation of August Macke. Like Niestlé, Campendonk and his future wife Adda lived in Sindelsdorf until 1914, in direct proximity to Marc, and was soon drawn into the Almanac circle and the Blue Rider exhibitions. When Franz and Maria Marc moved to Ried near Benediktbeuren in the spring of 1914, Niestlé and Campendonk and their respective partners moved to Seeshaupt on the shores of Lake Starnberg, where the tireless art patron Bernhard Koehler had given Niestlé the use of a small house. Even years after Franz Marc was killed in the war, his influence was still clearly evident in the work of both these artists. Campendonk, in particular, developed his own distinctive adaptation of the Blue Rider influence in his handling of new motifs and subject matters.

Officially, the first Blue Rider exhibition was held from 18 December 1911 until 1 January 1912 on the upper floor of Galerie Thannhauser, at the same time as the third NKVM exhibition on the ground floor. It was billed as *Die Erste Ausstellung der Redaktion der Blaue Reiter* (The First Exhibition of the Editors of the Blue Rider) and thus referred specifically to the almanac. It showed some fifty works by Albert Bloch, David and Vladimir Burlyuk, Heinrich Campendonk, Robert Delaunay, Elisabeth Epstein, Eugen von Kahler, Wassily Kandinsky, August Macke, Franz Marc, Gabriele Münter, Jean-Bloé Niestlé, Henri Rousseau, and Arnold Schoenberg. In actual fact it did not open its doors until 19 December – the effusive postcard that Kandinsky, Münter, Franz and Maria Marc, Albert Bloch, and Berhard Koehler wrote to Robert Delaunay from their opening-night party at the Restaurant Schottenhamel also bears this date. The four large paintings by Delaunay are documented as arriving in Munich on 18 December, as Kandinsky confirmed on the same day: "Fortunately everything is going well; we are hanging today – your four pictures just arrived today." According to a newspaper announcement, the exhibition was extended until 3 January 1912.

50   The first exhibition of the
Blue Rider, 1911/12
Room 1 (from left to right):
Jean Bloé Niestlé, *Birds* (top left)
Albert Bloch, *Head* (bottom)
Wassily Kandinsky, *Impression
Moscow*
Photograph: Gabriele Münter and
Johannes Eichner Foundation, Munich

This first, legendary exhibition by the "Editors of the Blue Rider" – a milestone in the development of modern art in Germany – is documented in six
detailed photographs by Gabriele Münter which allow us to reconstruct the
show fairly precisely on the basis of the works that can be seen in them. On
the basis of these photographs, as well as the handwritten lists of the artists
shown and works sold, Mario-Andreas von Lüttichau has painstakingly reconstructed the installation. He describes it as follows: "In the first room hung
Kandinsky's *Impression Moscow* which was purchased on the first day of the exhibition by the Berlin industrialist Bernhard Koehler, an uncle of Macke's
wife Lisbeth and the leading patron and collector of the Blue Rider. Koehler
had also been involved in hanging the exhibition. Next to it is *Birds*, which
has since been lost [now in a private collection in Berlin], loaned by Koehler,
and *Head* by Bloch (fig. 50). To the left of the door … hung *Evening*, a work
by Gabriele Münter which has also been lost since then, and below it Macke's
Still Life of Flowers with Agave and Bloch's *Houses and Chimneys*. On the long
wall is Schoenberg's *Landscape by Night* which is not listed in the catalogue, the
Frosty Landscape by Gabriele Münter and *La Ville No. 2* by Delaunay (fig. 51).
To the left of Delaunay is the "Rousseau Memorial Corner": a painting on
glass by Marc after Rousseau's *Self-portrait with Lamp*, which Marc gave to
Kandinsky for Christmas, and *La Basse-Cour* by Rousseau himself, which
Kandinsky had been able to purchase from Delaunay with Elisabeth Epstein's
intervention, and which was hung in the exhibition as a loan from his own
private collection. This small, unspectacular picture also graced the information

brochure for the Blue Rider almanac. Beneath these two pictures, a laurel wreath was hung as a sign of admiration and deep respect for the artist who had died in Paris in 1910. In the corner was a small table with brochures and, very probably, Kandinsky's book *Über das Geistige in der Kunst* (Concerning the Spiritual in Art) which is known to have been sold at the exhibition (fig. 52).

On the next wall leading to Room 5 were Campendonk's *Leaping Horse* and Bloch's *Three Pierrots*; on the right next to the door is Gabriele Münter's *Dark Still Life*, in the second room hung the now lost *Improvisation 22* by Kandinsky, and on the left of it two paintings on glass not listed in the catalogue: Marc's large *Landscape with Animals and Rainbow* at the top and Kandinsky's *With Sun* below it; over the door is *Horses* by David Burlyuk, next to it Macke's *Indians on Horseback*, which was purchased by Koehler, and *St. Séverin No. 1* by Delaunay (fig. 53). This painting, surprisingly, was purchased during the exhibition by Adolf Erbslöh, a member of the NKVM and one of Kandinsky's main opponents in the jury row. On the long wall there were three large paintings: a now lost *Still Life (Pink)* by Gabriele Münter, Kandinsky's *Composition No. V* – the bone of contention that had caused the split with the NKVM, and Marc's *Deer in the Forest I*. On the transverse wall was Vladimir Burlyuk's *Portrait Study* and Gabriele Münters *Country Road in Winter*; beside them, barely visible, another painting on glass not listed in the catalogue, Kandinsky's *Saint George II*. To the left of the door into Room 6 are Schoenberg's *Self-Portrait* and Marc's *The Yellow Cow* (fig. 54). Through the opening leading to Room 6 three paintings can be discerned: at the top Bloch's *Bearing of the Cross*, with the *Storm* by August Macke

below it, and to the left of that, almost hidden by the door frame, Delaunay's *La Ville No. 1.* This painting, now lost, was purchased by Alexei von Jawlensky, also a member of the NKVM, who had adopted a neutral stance in the jury argument. Next to it, from right to left, hung a now lost portrait by Elisabeth Epstein, which Kandinsky bought, a now lost painting by Campendonk entitled *Woman and Animal*, Delaunay's *Tour Eiffel* which Koehler bought right at the start of the exhibition, and Marc's *Landscape (Stoney Path)* (fig. 55).

Not visible in the vintage photographs are further works by Bloch, Burlyuk, Schoenberg, Epstein, and Kahler. In addition to the 43 paintings listed in the catalogue, there were at least five more, and possibly even seven, that were not listed. These included Schoenberg's *Landscape by Night* and the paintings on glass by Marc and Kandinsky, as well as the *Monkey Frieze* by Marc, which Bernhard Koehler had loaned from his private collection at short notice.

As in the almanac, the prevailing mood at the exhibition was one of confrontation, "in order to show an inner bond in diversity. Nevertheless the exhibition was hung in a way that emphasized the spectacular works by Delaunay, Kandinsky and Marc, with the more modestly sized paintings by the other exhibitors grouped around them." (Lüttichau). This expressly declared diversity, the heterogeneous nature of the exhibition with its aim of providing a platform for artistic innovation, was also stated in the preface of the little catalogue brochure, hurriedly printed by Bruckmann Verlag and delivered about a week after the opening. "In this little exhibition we do not seek to propagandize [sic; altered in subsequent editions to *propagate*] but aim to show the diversity of the forms represented, and how the inner desire of the artist takes many forms." This was a key tenet that Kandinsky and Marc had already formulated

53   The first exhibition of the
Blue Rider, 1911 / 12
Room 2 (from left to right): Gabriele
Münter, *Still Life (Pink)*, (cropped),
August Macke, *Indians on Horseback*
(top, see plate 101), Robert Delaunay,
St. Séverin No. 1 (below), David
Burlyuk, *Horses* (over the door),
Franz Marc, *Landscape with Animals
and Rainbow* (top), Wassily Kandinsky,
With Sun (bottom, see plate 40),
Wassily Kandinsky, *Improvisation 22*
Photograph: Gabriele Münter and
Johannes Eichner Foundation,
Munich

54 The first exhibition of the
Blue Rider, 1911 / 12
Room 2 (from left to right):
Franz Marc, *The Yellow Cow*, Arnold
Schoenberg, *Self-Portrait* (from
the back), Wassily Kandinsky, *Saint
George II*, Vladimir Burlyuk, *Portrait
Study* (top), Gabriele Münter, *Country
Road in Winter* (bottom), Franz Marc,
Deer in the Forest I (cropped at right),
Wassily Kandinsky, *Composition No. V*
Photograph: Gabriele Münter and
Johannes Eichner Foundation, Munich

more precisely in other writings. Shortly after the opening, the first sales were
made, among them three works by Robert Delaunay – *Tour Eiffel* to Bernhard
Koehler, *St. Séverin* to Adolf Erbslöh and *La Ville No. 1* to Alexei Jawlensky.

In all, eight paintings were sold at the exhibition, five of them to the collector
Bernhard Koehler. Kandinsky purchased two paintings by Henri Rousseau,
La Basse-Cour and *Le peintre et son modèle*, and the portrait by Elisabeth Epstein.
Delaunay made Kandinsky a gift of his small pencil drawing *La Tour*, which
was the only work on paper in the first Blue Rider exhibition. This is probably
the reason why neither Alfred Kubin nor Paul Klee, who had recently joined

the circle that winter, were included. The famous photograph showing several of the figures closely associated with the Blue Rider on the balcony of Kandinsky and Münter's apartment in Schwabing was probably taken during the exhibition, when Bernhard Koehler was still in Munich (fig. 56). Apart from some minor differences between the exhibitors – Jean-Bloé Niestlé withdrew his almost hyper-realistic *Birds* shortly after the exhibition opened because he did not feel comfortable in the presence of so many very different works by other artists – there was also some degree of reconciliation between the 'opposing' parties of the NKVM and the Blue Rider. One obvious expression of this détente was the fact that Erbslöh and Jawlensky bought works by Delaunay, while Maria Marc reported in one of her long and chatty letters to the Mackes that Werefkin and Jawlensky were now "running after Kandinsky in the most atrocious way." It may be said that the animosity lessened somewhat in the course of 1912 when the Blue Rider exhibition went on tour and further developments within the NKVM led to it being disbanded.

In his article *Die Wilden Deutschlands* (The 'Savages' of Germany) for the Almanac, Franz Marc had already written a kind of retrospective history of the NKVM before the split. In it, he distinguishes between the work of other 'savages' in Germany such as the *Brücke* or the New Secession in Berlin and endeavors to describe the special nature of the Munich group within the context of the avant-garde of the day. His text reads like a call to create a new movement which recognizes that "renewal should not be formal, but a rebirth of thinking" and it culminates in his frequently vision of an art based on the principle of mysticism and 'the spiritual' through which the Blue Rider then overstepped the mutual basis of the NKVM. "The first and only serious exponents of the new ideas in Munich were two Russians [Kandinsky and Jawlensky] who had been living and working there for many years before some Germans

joined them. With the founding of the NKVM, those beautiful and strange exhibitions began which made the critics despair. Typical for the artists of the NKVM was their strong emphasis on the program – they each learned from one another, and shared an ambition to grasp the ideas best. Sometimes the word 'synthesis' may have been used too often. The young French and Russian artists who exhibited as their guests were liberating. They provided food for thought, showing that art is about the most profound things, that renewal should not be formal, but a rebirth of thinking. Mysticism awoke in their souls and with it the ancient elements of art. It is impossible to explain the recent works of these 'savages' as a formal development and new interpretation of Impressionism.... The most beautiful prismatic colors and the celebrated Cubism are now meaningless goals for these 'savages.' Their thinking has a different aim: to create out of their work symbols for their own time, symbols that belong on the altar of a future spiritual religion, symbols behind which the technical heritage cannot be seen."

For all the heterogeneity of the Blue Rider movement and its first exhibition in the winter of 1911, even today we can still sense something of this missionary zeal and appreciate the innovative contribution to modernism that is so clearly reflected in the finest works of its exponents, among them Marc, Münter, Macke, and Delaunay.

1912-1914

In late December 1911, while the first Blue Rider exhibition was still showing, Kandinsky's book *Über das Geistige in der Kunst* (Concerning the Spiritual in Art) was published by Piper-Verlag in Munich. This seminal work containing the essence of his pre-war art theories has inspired artists and critics ever since. The vision of redemption and a new age dawning symbolized by the "standing and falling tower with rider" on the cover vignette is arguably less important than the unerring faith it expresses in the capacity of art to convey a spiritual message (figs 57, 58). Indeed, it is this that distinguishes the Blue Rider from other avant-garde movements such as Cubism or Futurism and even sets it apart from the Expressionism of the *Brücke* group.

Though Kandinsky and Marc agreed on this in principle, Kandinsky was particularly radical in propagating his credo. The second Blue Rider exhibition, which opened at the Hans Goltz gallery in Munich on 12 February 1912 and ran until mid-April, highlighted the differences between them. Under the official title of "The Second Exhibition of the Editors of the Blue Rider Black-and-White," the exhibition showed only works on paper – watercolors, drawings and prints. No fewer than 315 works were shown in all, representing a wide range of the contemporary international avant-garde by artists from France, Russia, Switzerland and Germany, apart from the members of the Blue Rider circle. Artists in the exhibition included André Derain, Pablo Picasso and Maurice Vlaminck, Natalia Goncharova, Michail Larionov and Kazimir Malevich, Hans Arp and Oscar Lüthy, and the *Brücke* artists Ernst Ludwig Kirchner, Otto Müller, Max Pechstein, Georg Tappert, and Emil Nolde. Franz Marc had been especially keen to include the *Brücke* artists and had visited a number of them personally when he and his wife Maria were in Berlin at the beginning of 1912. Kandinsky was wary of his friend Marc's interest in the Expressionism of the *Brücke*, which he saw as a betrayal of their own ideas. There were other quarrels, too, some of them triggered by Gabriele Münter's feeling that Franz Marc and August Macke did not treat her politely enough, and the atmosphere of discord briefly cast a shadow over the previously good relations among the Blue Rider artists. On a more positive note, the Black-and-White exhibition brought an important addition to the group. Alongside Alfred Kubin, seventeen works by Paul Klee were presented for the first time. Klee, who concentrated mainly on drawings and prints at the time, and did not begin to work in oils until 1914, lived near Kandinsky on Ainmillerstrasse and had been introduced to him in a Munich café in October 1911 by the Swiss artist Louis Moillet. "Then we took the tram home together and agreed that we would meet again. In the course of the winter I joined his Blue Rider," noted Klee in his diary. In his letter of 9 October 1911 to Franz Marc, Kandinsky writes, "Met Klee yesterday through [Louis] Moillet. Now there's a man with soul" (fig. 59). Though Klee was not included in the first Blue Rider exhibition, one of his works, the 1910 drawing *Man Breaking Stones II* was published in the almanac. Klee's profoundly intellectual and deceptively simple drawings corresponded

57   Wassily Kandinsky, cover of
Über das Geistige in der Kunst,
published by Piper-Verlag, Munich
1912 (issued in December 1911)

58   Wassily Kandinsky at his desk
at Ainmillerstrasse 36, 1913
Photograph: Gabriele Münter and
Johannes Eichner Foundation, Munich

in their own distinctive way to the notion of rendering visible "the spiritual" in art. His early works (fig. 60) point towards the rich later oeuvre in which he consolidates this approach by exploring a wide variety of compositional forms, making a seminal contribution to the art of the twentieth century. Constantly reflecting on his work, Klee wrote in his pre-war diaries about this aspect of apparent simplicity: "If my works sometimes give a primitive impression, this 'primitive' aspect can be explained by my discipline of reduction. It is sheer economy, the ultimate professional awareness. In other words, it is the very opposite of the truly primitive."

The first exhibition of the Blue Rider went on an extended tour, starting with the Gereons-Club in Cologne at the end of January 1912. It then went on to the Sturm Galerie in Berlin, run by Herwarth Walden, who had seen the show in Cologne and suggested taking it over as the inaugural exhibition for his new exhibition space on Tiergartenstrasse. There, it was shown from March to April 1912 in combination – "The Blue Rider, Franz Flaum, Oskar Kokoschka, Expressionists" – and with a new catalogue. Meeting Herwarth Walden, who had founded the periodical *Der Sturm* in 1910 and was to become a cutting-edge exhibitor in the following decade, was to prove a crucial turning point for the artists of the Blue Rider. It was Walden who organized most of the other venues to which the first Blue Rider exhibition toured – Bremen, Hagen, Frankfurt, and Hamburg in 1912, Budapest in 1913 and Oslo, Helsinki, Trondheim, and Goteborg in 1914 – and he included all the Blue Rider artists in his huge 1913 *Herbstsalon* exhibition. Moreover, Walden also organized Kandinsky's first major solo exhibition at the end of 1912, with a catalogue which in the full text of his now famous *Rückblicke* was published, and followed it up with Gabriele Münter's first solo exhibition. Over the next few years, Walden continued to mount group exhibitions featuring such artists as Paul Klee, Franz Marc and Albert Bloch. Shortly after showing the first Blue Rider exhibition at his Sturm Galerie, Walden held another Blue Rider exhibition that helped to smooth the troubled waters between the Blue Rider artists and their colleagues Alexei Jawlensky and Marianne von Werefkin, who had stayed with the NKVM. In May 1912, the now legendary *Sonderbund* exhibition opened in Cologne. It was the most important official exhibition of the international avant-garde to be held before World War I, and the Munch circle had also been invited to take part. Following some initial differences with the *Sonderbund* commissioners, which August Macke sought to resolve, the artists of the Blue Rider felt they were not adequately represented as a group, and were displeased by the rejection of some of their works. In response, primarily at the instigation of Marc and Kandinsky, they organized an exhibition of "refusés of the *Sonderbund*." It was shown under the simple title *Der Blaue Reiter* at Herwarth Walden's Sturm Galerie from June 1912 – and this time it included not only Paul Klee but, significantly, six major paintings by Alexei Jawlensky, including *Green Eyes*, *The Feather Hat* and *Prerov*, as well as three recent works by Marianne von Werefkin. Walden later integrated some of these works in the continuing tour of the first Blue Rider exhibition, for which an amended catalogue was published in late December. Their presence in the touring exhibition from 1912 onwards and their close association with the formative years in Murnau leading up to the creation of the Blue Rider would certainly justify including Alexei Jawlensky and Marianne von Werefkin in the circle of the Blue Rider.

Alexei Jawlensky and Marianne von Werefkin eventually joined the circle of the Blue Rider, albeit somewhat belatedly, on resigning from the NKVM a year after the argument that had originally led to the split by the Blue Rider group. The third NKVM exhibition had also gone on tour, first to Zurich and then to Bremen, where it was actually shown at the same time as the touring Blue Rider exhibition. Further stations were planned up to the summer, but

59 Paul Klee, Munich, 1916
"Sturm" postcard

60 Paul Klee, *Suburb (North Munich)*, 1913
Wash drawing with white highlights, Städtische Galerie im Lenbachhaus, Munich

68

not all of them materialized. Finally, in November 1911, the art historian Otto Fischer, who had joined the NKVM that same year, published *Das Neue Bild*, a lavishly produced book with an introduction outlining the history of the NKVM and presenting the individual artists by way of short texts and illustrations. It was Fischer's polemical introductory remarks about Kandinsky's "incomprehensible" and "abstract" works, and his unqualified comments on the other artists that prompted Werefkin and Jawlensky to leave the NKVM, followed by Vladimir Bekhteyev, Moisey Kogan, and Alexander Mogilewski. With that, the association more or less ceased to exist. In a lengthy letter to Richard Reiche, director of the Kunstverein Barmen and a key contact for the artists of NKVM and Blue Rider alike, Werefkin explained their resignation and reiterated the events of the previous year:

"Ever since our most brilliant artists had left us, any confidence we may have had in the authenticity of the artistic convictions held by the remaining members was crushed for ever. And then the rot set in. Our association, created in unity, … was now divided in two. On the one hand Jawlensky, Bekhteyev, Kogan, Mogilewski and myself continued to hold fast, with all the strength of our faith and knowledge, to immaterial things, to the necessity of freedom to search, to progress, irrespective of criticism and heedless of practical considerations. All our sympathies went out to those for whom art is not a question of good paintings that sell well. The other party proceeded to negate in word and deed all the goals and objectives that our association had set itself in the first place. With neither guest artists nor new talent, the exhibitions withered.... All that we had hoped and wished for – working energetically in the sunny atmosphere of comradeship and support – had become a sham. Erbslöh and Kanoldt, who had come to our studio as inexperienced young artists and who had learned all they know today from us, whose eyes we opened to an art they knew nothing of – these two, having succeeded in dismissing Kandinsky's art as 'bluff,' dared to puff themselves up as the ultimate authorities in aesthetic judgment." The inappropriate commentaries in Otto Fischer's book, she went on, had hit them "like a whiplash," whereupon they had sealed the fate of the group by resigning.

The Blue Rider, on the other hand, continued its activities until the outbreak of World War I. Many of their plans never came to fruition, and much of their early enthusiasm waned. The planned second almanac – in which, in the words of Andreas Hüneke, they intended to "continue the approach of juxtaposing diverse cultural expressions from different eras and from all over the world" – was postponed several times, although a number of articles were submitted. Kandinsky, in particular, procrastinated, repeatedly reassuring Marc of his plans, while writing to him yet again in June 1913 to say: "I hardly believe we shall be able to produce the second volume by the coming winter season. Where is the material to be found, especially good articles? … And illustrations? So far, I have only one idea, which I would ask you, in the meantime, to keep to yourself and tell no one – except, of course, your wife. Old commercial signs and advertising images, including painted fairground stalls (such as those at the

Oktoberfest). I would like to try to go to the limits of kitsch (or perhaps, some might say, beyond the limits). Together with pictures from nature, especially individual objects and parts of objects. But what about new pictures? New art?" Kandinsky claimed that he could see little in the way of original and vital new approaches, apart from "the work of the young Dutchman," Adriaan Korteweg, who was working in Munich at the time and who was to die in Indonesia in 1917. Though Marc agreed with Kandinsky on the state of the contemporary art scene, he was eager to get on with publishing a second volume of the almanac, for which he had already written a foreword. In March 1914, he wrote to Kandinsky: "I have the feeling that *today*, especially, something has to be *said by us*, precisely *because* the material is lacking. Once it is no longer lacking, others will show the material, and will have more right to do so."

Herwarth Walden's groundbreaking *Herbstsalon* exhibition in Berlin in September 1913 once again united the members of the Blue Rider with a number of other avant-garde artists from Germany and other countries. Among them, for the first time, was Lyonel Feininger, who had been introduced to Walden and the Blue Rider circle by Alfred Kubin. This exhibition, which Franz Marc and August Macke helped to hang, strengthened the sense of opposition that Macke had harbored against Kandinsky ever since the first Blaue Reiter exhibition to the same extent as it fuelled his enthusiasm for Robert Delaunay's latest works – his series of *Fenêtres* and *Formes circulaires*. It was in connection with the *Herbstsalon* that Macke created his watercolor *Satire on the Blue Rider*, showing Franz Marc as the driver, with Kandinsky seated regally in the carriage, Herwarth Walden perched nervously behind him, and Macke himself an insignificant little figure on the sidelines. The entire picture is covered in flowing lines and blotches of color in a caricature of Kandinsky's abstract painting (fig. 61). Notwithstanding internal squabbles and artistic differences, Kandinsky and Marc, in particular, achieved a real breakthrough to public recognition and positive press reviews from art critics with the large works they showed at the *Herbstsalon*, including *Composition VI*, *Painting with a White Edge*, *Improvisation 31* and the *Animal Fates*, *Tower of the Blue Horses*, and *Tyrol*.

In the spring of 1913, there were plans to issue a bible illustrated by Blue Rider artists. Kandinsky, Marc, Alfred Kubin, Erich Heckel, Oskar Kokoschka, and Paul Klee were to be involved. Once again, Marc's correspondence in preparation for the project was prolific. He wrote to Paul Klee, "Kubin has written to say that he would take the prophet Daniel. Kokoschka would take Job, Heckel one of the Gospels, Kandinsky the Apocalypse. I would take the Book of Moses – and the rest of the world is free for you to choose!" Klee chose the Psalms and, like the other artists involved, began preparing a number of works on biblical themes. It was in connection with this bible project that Marc created his last prints, the *Creation I* (fig. 63) and *Creation II* woodcuts of 1914. By the time war broke out, only Alfred Kubin had completed his twelve illustrations, which was published separately by Georg Müller Verlag in Munich in 1918.

Finally, in the spring of 1914, some of the Blue Rider artists, most notably Kandinsky, Marc and Kubin, joined the young author and playwright Hugo

61 August Macke, *Satire on the Blue Rider*, 1913
Watercolor, pencil, chalk, Städtische Galerie im Lenbachhaus, Munich

Ball in an attempt to revive the Münchner Künstlertheater (Munich Theater of Artists). They soon withdrew from actively implementing the plans and stage sets, however, which they felt were not progressive enough. There were plans for the envisaged stage reform to be presented in a publication entitled *Expressionistisches Theater* or *Das Neue Theater,* featuring a list of authors distinctly reminiscent of the almanac. According to Andreas Hüneke, although the book was never realized, the project indicates that Hugo Ball "had begun to study the stage ideas of the Blue Rider more closely. . . . At first, Ball wanted to involve Bekhteyev, but later there is no mention of him, and the provisional table of contents lists mainly members of the Blue Rider. Texts by Kandinsky on the *gesamtkunstwerk*, by Hartmann on the anarchy of music and by Jewreinov on psychology, as well as designs by Marc for *The Tempest* [Marc had created two figurines for a performance of Shakespeare's *Tempest*], by Klee for the *Bacchantes* of Euripides and by Kubin for a play called *Der Floh im Panzerhaus* (Flea in a Carapace), as well as scenes and dramas by Kokoschka, who was represented in the Blue Rider almanac. Michail Fokin was to write on ballet, Ball himself on Expressionism and the stage, and Erich Mendelsohn on stage sets. It would appear that there was also some thought of using Hartmann's texts from the almanac as well as Kandinsky's notes on stage composition and *The Yellow Sound*."

The outbreak of war in August 1914 put an end to all these activities and tore the Blue Rider circle apart. Kandinsky and Münter hurriedly returned to Munich from Murnau and left for Switzerland on 3 August. A few months later, in November 1914, they separated in Zurich. Kandinsky, unable to stay in Germany as an 'enemy alien,' returned to Russia, and spent the years of war and revolution in Moscow. He left almost his entire pre-war oeuvre and many works by his artist friends in the care of Gabriele Münter in Munich. In the spring of 1915, Münter traveled to Berlin and from there to Stockholm, to wait for Kandinsky in a neutral foreign country. But it was only after a lengthy wait and some dramatic letters that Kandinsky eventually came to Stockholm where he stayed until March 1916. Kandinsky and Münter never saw each other again. In 1917, Kandinsky married Nina von Andreyevskaya in Moscow and returned to Germany with her in 1921 when Walter Gropius invited him to teach at the Bauhaus in Weimar. There, he met Paul Klee and Lyonel Feininger once more, both of whom had also taken up teaching posts at the Bauhaus. From around 1929 onwards, Kandinsky, Klee, Feininger and Jawlensky formed a loosely-knit association called *Die Blaue Vier* (The Blue Four), primarily at the suggestion of Emmy 'Galka' Scheyer who found it a convenient vehicle for organizing exhibitions and promoting the work of the four artists in America.

By 1925, the changing political climate in Germany made the Bauhaus move from Weimar to Dessau. Paul Klee was the first to leave the Bauhaus under mounting National Socialist pressure in 1931, taking a professorship at the Düsseldorf Academy instead, only to return to his native Switzerland in 1933 when he was finally barred from teaching altogether. Kandinsky moved with the Bauhaus from Dessau to Berlin before emigrating to Paris in 1933. In an essay for the 1931 issue of the *bauhaus* periodical, dedicated to Paul Klee to mark his departure from Dessau, Kandinsky outlined their shared experience in Munich, Weimar, and Dessau, and highlighted the spiritual and intellectual bond between them: "I wish to speak on a personal note. More than 20 years ago, when I moved into the Ainmillerstrasse in Munich, I soon learned that the young painter, Paul Klee, who had caused such a stir with his first exhibition at Galerie Thannhauser, was living next door. We were neighbors right up to the

63   Franz Marc, *Creation I (Monkeys)*
Woodcut, 1914
Albertina, Vienna

outbreak of war, and our friendship goes back to those days. The war drove us apart. Eight years later, fate brought me to the Bauhaus in Weimar, where Klee and I became neighbors a second time. Our studios at the Bauhaus were almost side by side. Then we were torn apart again when the Bauhaus was wrenched out of Weimar at the speed of a zeppelin. Klee and I owe our third period as neighbors [in Walter Gropius' so-called master-houses] to that flight. For more than five years, we lived close together. Only a party wall separated our apartments. We could visit one another without even leaving the building if we went through the cellar. Bavaria – Thuringia – Anhalt. And now? Even without the connecting cellar, we remain spiritual and intellectual neighbors."

Alexei Jawlensky and Marianne von Werefkin had also left Munich hurriedly, together with Helene Nesnakomoff and Andreas, her son by Jawlensky. They emigrated first to St. Prex on Lake Geneva, later moving to Ascona, where Jawlensky and Werefkin finally separated. Jawlensky married Helene Nesnakomoff and moved to Wiesbaden with her and their son. In Wiesbaden, Emmy Scheyer organized an exhibition for him, attracting a number of collectors who provided a much-needed source of income. Marianne von Werefkin, like Kandinsky, had lost almost her entire wealth as a result of the Russian revolution. She spent the rest of her life in Ascona, in the artists' colony there. August Macke and Franz Marc were both called up for military service. Macke was killed in September 1914 on the western front in Champagne and Franz Marc died on a patrol ride near Verdun in March 1916.

Gabriele Münter stayed in Scandinavia until the early 1920s and, after years of personal crisis, moving between Murnau and Munich, Elmau, Cologne, Berlin and France, she finally settled permanently in Murnau in 1931. Münter was the only one of the original group to return to the birthplace of the Blue Rider in Murnau and Munich. With the gift of the works cared for by her, she left the city of the Blue Rider a unique heritage.

Plates

with commentaries by Annegret Hoberg

Wassily Kandinsky

b. 1866 in Moscow – d. 1944 in Neuilly-sur-Seine, France

At the age of thirty Kandinsky gave up his promising university career as a lecturer in law and moved to Munich in order to take up painting. After studying for a while at a private school of painting and at the Academy, where he was a pupil of Franz von Stuck, he founded his own *Phalanx* art school in 1901. One of his first pupils, Gabriele Münter, was his companion for many years. From 1904 to 1909 the couple traveled extensively. When they returned to Munich and Murnau in 1909, Kandinsky became one of the founding members of the progressive *Neue Künstler-Vereinigung München* (New Artists' Association, Munich). Only two years later a rift arose between Kandinsky and the more moderate members of the group. Together with Marc, Münter, and Alfred Kubin, Kandinsky left the *Neue Künstler-Vereinigung* to form the Blue Rider circle, the Munich equivalent of the revolutionary *Brücke* group in Berlin and Dresden. The year 1912 saw the publication of the famous almanac *Der Blaue Reiter* (*The Blue Rider*) and of Kandinsky's *Über das Geistige in der Kunst* (*Concerning the Spiritual in Art*), whose common message was that inner, spiritual experience should take precedence over the representation of reality. For Kandinsky, this meant moving systematically toward abstraction.

At the beginning of World War I Kandinsky returned to Moscow, where he played a leading role in the debate on the politics of art which followed the Revolution. In 1922 he was appointed to a teaching post at the Bauhaus in Weimar. After the Nazi seizure of power in 1933 he left Germany and moved to Neuilly-sur-Seine, where he remained for the rest of his life, painting the late pictures of the "Paris years."

Wassily Kandinsky

1   **MUNICH – THE RIVER ISAR**
(München – Die Isar)   1901

Oil on canvas board, 12³⁄₄ x 9¹⁄₄" (32.5 x 23.6 cm)
Inscribed "Kandinsky" (lower right)
GMS 7

Wassily Kandinsky, the great pioneer of modern art, only began
painting at the age of 30. He proceeded to explore and experiment for over a decade before arriving at what is usually
termed the "breakthrough to abstraction," an accomplishment
that was to pave the way of the future. After several years of
teaching at Anton Ažbe's private art school and a year of studies
at the Munich Academy under Franz von Stuck, Kandinsky
chose to paint not only on his own, but also to paint directly
from nature, free of academic restraints. At first he painted various
places in Munich, soon on outings in the surrounding countryside as well and later on trips abroad. *Munich – The River Isar* is
one of the first of the numerous pictures painted outdoors between 1901 and 1907 that Kandinsky himself called "small oil-
studies." To begin with, his plein air painting follows the Post-
Impressionist tradition. However, instead of further dissolving the
picture's subject matter, his apparently randomly chosen views
of nature and his highly individual way of applying the paint
serve to intensify the colorful effect. A characteristic feature of
all of Kandinsky's early landscape paintings is the use of the
palette knife to apply the paint, sometimes with more impasto,
sometimes more liquid, but always showing the direction of
the palette knife's stroke. The composition of this small view of
the Isar, with its pictorial structure creating a certain illusion of
depth and its reflections of the bridge pier in the water, is still
rather traditional. Yet the coherence of the motif is broken up
by the powerful, clearly distinct and differently colored strokes
of the palette knife, especially in the foreground. In some
places the unprimed grey canvas shows through between the
different areas of color. Kandinsky's use of the palette knife
brings to mind one of his great predecessors and one of the
"fathers of modern art," Van Gogh. However, each artist creates
a different effect with this technique: while Van Gogh aimed
to heighten expressiveness by showing the artist's touch with
circular, emphatically communicative strokes, Kandinsky was
trying to underscore the power of artistic means and the artistic process as such. Though they herald a central concern of
Kandinsky's, when seen on their own, the early landscapes do
not even begin to suggest the complexity of his later works.

Wassily Kandinsky

2 IN THE PARK OF SAINT-CLOUD
(Im Park von Saint-Cloud) 1906

Oil on cardboard, 9¼ x 14⅞" (23.6 x 37.7 cm)
GMS 23

In the Park of Saint-Cloud, painted during Kandinsky's one year
stay in Paris with Gabriele Münter in 1906, exhibits basically the
same style and palette knife technique as the "small oil-studies"
he had been painting since 1901. Here, however, the application
of these artistic means has been taken considerably further. In
the landscapes painted towards the end of this period up to 1907,
which are classed as Kandinsky's early works, the conspicuously
formed, extremely pastose strokes and dabs of the palette knife
tend to take on a life of their own. The subject matter depicted is
almost concealed by the paint. The colorful autumnal avenue
can only be distinguished in the underlying structure of the
trees and the ground. While the orange, old rose and yellow-
green dots in the foreground and the longer blue streaks can still
be associated with natural forms such as foliage and shadows,
the yellow, vermilion and dark brown on the left thicken into
a glowing 'abstract' accumulation of paint.

In connection with this striking little painting, whose unique-
ness also becomes clear upon comparison, for instance, with
Gabriele Münter's *Avenue in the Park of Saint-Cloud* (see plate 60),
has us recall Kandinsky's position in relation to the art of his
day and its preconditions. Seurat's Neo-Impressionism and
the Pointillist technique have often been cited as his sources.
Kandinsky himself expressed the nature of his interest in Neo-
Impressionism in a statement of principle: "The Impressionists'
'problem of light and air' interested me very little.... The theory
of the Neo-Impressionists, which was essentially about the effect
of color and left the air in peace, seemed more important to me."
In the continuation of Impressionism, which had separated colors
optically mainly in order to depict natural light and atmospheric
conditions as perceived by the eye, its heirs – especially Van
Gogh and the Neo-Impressionists – absorbed light in their
paintings through color. They gave color an independent role
based on rules of its own in the context of the picture.
Kandinsky began to build upon the division and isolated use
of colors that they had arrived at. He is no doubt acknowledg-
ing this particular achievement of his most recent forerunners
when he notes that Neo-Impressionism, despite the dogmatics
of its color theory and its ultimate realism, "ranges into abstraction at the same time." Kandinsky's last oil-studies in the
palette knife technique, such as *In the Park of Saint-Cloud*, show
that the subject of a nature study matters less to him than the
paint he captures it in and the increasing artistic independence
of the materials used.

Wassily Kandinsky

3   RIDING COUPLE (Reitendes Paar) 1906-07

Oil on canvas, 21⅝ x 19⅞" (55 x 50.5 cm)
Inscribed "Kandinsky" (lower right)
GMS 26

Riding Couple is one of a large group of early works, done before 1907, in which Kandinsky conjures up a world of poetic, fairy-tale images. Set in a long-vanished past, the pictures are surrounded by an air of mystery and unreality. They feature groups of nineteenth-century figures, medieval knights in ancient German streets, and, above all, motifs from Russian history, which play a particularly prominent part in Kandinsky's early work and also provide the key to many of the ideas and associations in his later pictures.

Riding Couple was painted in the winter of 1906–07 while Kandinsky was staying in Sèvres, near Paris. The final version was preceded by a tempera study and a number of pencil sketches. Using small, delicate particles of color, the artist depicts a young couple on horseback, dressed in Russian costume and locked in a tender embrace; the stylized birch trees above their heads are covered with a net of golden leaves. In the middle distance a calmly flowing river winds through the picture; the water is a mosaic of varied colors in which it is just possible to discern the white sails of two Viking ships, reminders of a remote historical past. On the far side of the river the brightly colored domes and towers of an old Russian city stand out like a shining vision on the horizon.

One detects a number of different influences in this picture, as in other early works by Kandinsky. The poetic character of *Riding Couple* owes an obvious debt to the aesthetics of Art Nouveau and to Symbolism, with its emphasis on the abstract, spiritual content of art and the necessity of dematerializing physical reality. The style also echoes that of contemporary Russian fairy tale illustrations, which in turn were influenced by the highly artificial forms of Art Nouveau and Symbolism. In addition, Kandinsky profited from the innovations of Neo-Impressionism, whose exponents had invented Pointillism, a technique of breaking up colors into a multitude of elements.

Kandinsky uses color as a means of disguising the content of the picture. This is one of the major features of his aesthetic approach; in one of his early notes for the publication *Concerning the Spiritual in Art* he wrote: "The rich coloring of the picture must exercise an irresistible fascination on the viewer and at the same time obscure the underlying content." The individual motifs of *Riding Couple* – the horse's bridle and decorative apparel, the clothes of the young couple, the forms of the earth and the sky – are fragmented into myriad particles of color, in which the external contours of reality dissolve and merge.

Wassily Kandinsky

4　**MOTLEY LIFE (Das bunte Leben)**　1907

Tempera on canvas, 51 ¼ x 63" (130 x 162.5 cm)
Inscribed "Kandinsky 1907" (lower left)
On permanent loan from the Bayerische Landesbank
FH 225

With its teeming variety of human figures, the large tempera painting *Motley Life,* executed in Sèvres at the beginning of 1907, is the last of Kandinsky's early cycle of poetic pictures; its format and general ambitiousness make it the main work in this series. Depicting a broad panorama of different human situations, Kandinsky draws once more on the nostalgic, fantastic motifs of his early work. The picture is an enamel-like, glowing mosaic composed of individual particles of color, in which the human figures appear as symbols of birth and death, belief and struggle, love and separation, against a black background that conveys a sense of spatial uncertainty. In the distance a Russian city stands out on a dark, humplike hill on the other side of the river.

A number of the archetypal Russian figures in the picture appear in earlier paintings and woodcuts, such as *Bewegtes Leben* (*Bustling Life,* 1903). In his autobiographical *Reminiscences,* Kandinsky himself speaks of the resemblances between *Motley Life,* the tempera painting *Ankunft der Kaufleute* (*Arrival of the Merchants,* 1905), and the later *Composition II* (destroyed); according to the artist, all three works lend expression, in different ways, to an early, feverish vision which exercised an initially unconscious influence on his painting. While *Arrival of the Merchants* shows a similarly varied group of Russian figures, albeit with a lesser degree of narrative definition than in *Motley Life,* the link between the latter picture and the virtually abstract *Composition II* may seem somewhat surprising. But this picture too is dominated by conflicting images of happiness and impending doom, of life's contradictions, evoked by scantily outlined figurative symbols. *Motley Life* is evidently a step on the road toward the discovery of new means of formal expression. Kandinsky later wrote: "In *Motley Life,* where the task which charmed me most was that of creating a confusion of masses, patches, lines, I used a 'bird's-eye view' to place the figures one above the other. To arrange the dividing-up of areas and application of the brushstrokes as I wished, on each occasion I had to find a perspective pretext or excuse." This proves that, when working on the richly varied colors of tempera paintings such as this, Kandinsky was experimenting with new, semiabstract ways of seeing. The dreamlike disparity and isolation of the figures also contributes to the dissolution of traditional notions of form and content. However, it is important to realize that in the work of Kandinsky, dissolution of form is accompanied by a symbolic complexity which is evident in both his early and his later pictures. A number of the motifs found in his early work – the horseman, the boat, the Russian city, and the mysterious encounter, for example – recur in his abstract pictures, transformed into cryptic signs which imbue these meticulously composed and highly suggestive works with an aura of mystery and wonder.

Wassily Kandinsky

5   **BEFORE THE CITY (Vor der Stadt)** 1908

Oil on cardboard, 27⅛ x 19¼" (68.8 x 49 cm)
Inscribed "Kandinsky 1908" (lower left)
GMS 35

After several years of traveling around from one country to the next, Kandinsky and Münter returned to Bavaria in 1908. In August of that year they stayed for the first time in the small town of Murnau in the foothills of the Bavarian Alps, where they were joined by Jawlensky and Marianne von Werefkin. For Kandinsky and Münter in particular, working in Murnau meant the end of a long period of experimentation and the beginning of a decisive breakthrough in the discovery of new means of artistic expression. Shortly afterward, the couple settled in Munich and rented an apartment together in Schwabing, the artists' quarter of the city.

Before the City was one of the first pictures to emerge from this new phase in Kandinsky's creative development. Painted in strong, almost explosive colors which betoken a highly individual artistic approach, the work is a view of Kandinsky's new surroundings on the outskirts of the old city. The viewer's eye moves upward from the wavy lines of royal blue, green, yellow, and red in the lower section to the glowing deep blue of the sky and the brightly colored architecture, which is in turn offset by the darker tones at the bottom of the picture. The reckless, carefree manner in which Kandinsky applies the paint evidently owes a good deal to the influence of Fauvism, which he had heard all about from Jawlensky after the latter's visit to Henri Matisse's studio. The Fauvist preference for strong, pure colors, applied in flat, unbroken lines and patches, was fully compatible with Kandinsky's aim of exploiting the intrinsically expressive attributes of artistic materials, sealing off the surface of the picture and eliminating all sense of atmospheric illusion.

In the small plein air oil studies which he had been doing for several years in addition to his lyrical colored drawings, Kandinsky had already allowed himself the maximum possible degree of freedom in the use of color. He later wrote: "In my studies, I let myself go. I had little thought for houses and trees, drawing colored lines and blobs on the canvas with my palette knife, making them sing just as powerfully as I knew how." However, these early works, up to 1907, were painted with small strokes of the palette knife in a late Impressionist style that offered no possibilities for further development. Kandinsky's first stay in Murnau, and the pictures which followed, brought him closer to the fulfillment of his artistic aims. More than any of its predecessors, this picture conveys a sense of what Kandinsky referred to as "the brightly colored atmosphere of Munich, saturated with light, its scale of values sounding thunderous depths in the shadows."

Wassily Kandinsky

6   KOCHEL – GRAVEYARD AND RECTORY
(Friedhof und Pfarrhaus in Kochel) 1909

Oil on cardboard, 17½ x 12⅞" (44.4 x 32.7)
Inscribed "Kandinsky" (lower right)
GMS 43

Following their first period of residence in Murnau in 1908,
Kandinsky and Münter entered a phase of exceptional productivity and rapid creative development. Up to the outbreak of
World War I in 1914, the two artists made a habit of spending
the summer in Murnau and of retreating there for occasional
weeks during the rest of the year. Especially in the years 1908
to 1910, but also later, until 1913, Kandinsky painted a large
number of landscapes in Murnau which document the way in
which he was advancing toward a new way of seeing and
toward the discovery of new forms.

Kochel – Graveyard and Rectory was painted in February
1909, during a visit to the small, nearby town of Kochel. What
strikes one in particular is the fascinating interplay of color
between the brilliant yellow facades of the houses, the bold, if
thinly applied, blue of the sky, the bluish-tinged snow, and
the hues of the bushes in the foreground. Modifying and
experimenting with colors and forms of the various winter
motifs, Kandinsky was moving away, step by step, from realism and representational conceptions of painting.

Wassily Kandinsky

7   RAILROAD AT MURNAU
(Eisenbahn bei Murnau) 1909

Oil on cardboard, 14¼ x 19¼" (36 x 49 cm)
GMS 49

In the late summer of 1909, at Kandinsky's prompting, Münter bought a house in Murnau which soon became known among the locals as the *Russen-Haus* (*The Russians' House*; plate 75). Here the couple spent their most productive months together, paying frequent visits to Marc in the nearby village of Sindelsdorf. It was in Murnau that Marc and Kandinsky edited The Blue Rider almanac in 1911. The Munich–Garmisch railroad ran right past the end of the garden, and the occupants of the house saw trains steaming by every day. Together with *Landschaft bei Murnau mit Lokomotive* (*Landscape near Murnau with Locomotive;* Solomon R. Guggenheim Museum, New York), *Railroad at Murnau* is one of the few pictures by Kandinsky with a technological or industrial theme. Unlike the North German Expressionists or the French Impressionists, whose work he knew well, Kandinsky depicts the train as a kind of toy, pro-

pelled by some supernatural force: the picture strikes a naive, almost comical note. The train resembles a huge black snake; its dark silhouette stands out clearly against the surrounding fields of color. The flickering red of the sunlight under the wheels of the train, the white steam, and the handkerchief of the waving girl create an impression of dynamic movement which extends to the two stylized telegraph masts.

In this picture one detects the subliminal influence of primitive art and the Bavarian folk art of painting on glass. Primitivism and the antidescriptive conception of images in popular art were an important stimulus to the imagination of Kandinsky, Münter, and the other members of the Blue Rider circle. Kandinsky did not see the realistic intentions of popular art as conflicting with his own aim of reducing the materiality of the object. In his essay "On the Question of Form" in The Blue Rider almanac, he argued that "the truly artistic" could be either realist or abstract; citing the naive painter Henri Rousseau as an example of what he called "great realism," he put the latter approach to art on a par with "great abstraction." Looking at pictures such as *Railroad at Murnau,* it becomes easier to understand this equation of two apparently opposed stylistic positions.

Wassily Kandinsky

8   **MURNAU – GRÜNGASSE**
(Grüngasse in Murnau)   1909

Oil on cardboard, 13 x 17½" (33 x 44.6 cm)
Inscribed in Münter's hand "Kandinsky" (reverse)
GMS 42

Kandinsky painted *Murnau – Grüngasse* in the summer of 1909. The brilliant, deliberately artificial colors appear at first glance to correspond naturalistically to the sun-soaked stillness and the deep shadows of the street. However, the use of color has a deeper significance: the strong, triumphantly glowing, yet subtle contrasts of variegated yellows, blue, and warm, straw-berry red structure the image of the street in such a way as to lend the picture an exceptional formal presence. As in so many of Kandinsky's landscapes from 1908 onward, the main elements of the picture are thinly edged in black, so that their contours are clearly recognizable. But here too we find Kandinsky playing visual games with the forms constructed by color, such as the blue shadows on the ground and the colored shadows on the walls of the houses. The hedge in the foreground and the arrangement of the houses lend the picture a certain sense of spatial depth, but the laws of perspective and three-dimensional perception are suspended in favor of a carefully structured, homogeneous treatment of all the individual components.

Wassily Kandinsky

9   NATURE STUDY FROM MURNAU III
(Naturstudie aus Murnau III) 1909
Oil on cardboard, 12⅜ x 17⅝" (31.5 x 44.7 cm)
Inscribed "Kandinsky" (lower left)
GMS 40

Kandinsky painted numerous pictures of Murnau, with its
church, medieval castle, and brightly colored houses, as seen
from the window of the house where he lived with Münter.
As in *Murnau with Church I* (plate 16), which was painted the
following year, the avenue of trees in the foreground opens up
the space of the picture and makes its forms intelligible. The
most striking feature of *Nature Study from Murnau III* is the
power of the colors, the mixture of dark and bright, warm
and cold, pure and mixed tones in the autumn landscape. By
cutting off the horizon at the top of the picture, in a manner
that is reminiscent of his earlier small-format studies in oil,
Kandinsky deliberately weakens the sense of perspective and
reduces the element of representational illusion. The effect
and the expressive dimension of the landscape are evoked
solely by the spontaneous brushwork and the resonance of the
colors.

Wassily Kandinsky

10   **NATURE STUDY FROM MURNAU I**
(Naturstudie aus Murnau I) 1909

Oil on cardboard, 13 x 17½" (32.9 x 44.6 cm)
GMS 45

Nature Study from Murnau I exhibits a greater degree of formalization than any of Kandinsky's previous pictures. A light blue road leads straight through the middle of the picture toward a dark blue triangular mountain, whose sharp-peaked outline is echoed by the silhouettes of a number of further mountains, painted in royal blue and a complementary yellow. The forms of the landscape are reduced to a set of basic geometric structures.

The resemblances between the work of Kandinsky and that of Münter and Jawlensky are closer in the Murnau pictures than at any other point in the three artists' development. Their landscape studies in particular were influenced by Jawlensky's notion of "synthesis," a principle of formal and stylistic economy whose aim was to render what Münter called the "extract" of things. *Nature Study from Murnau I* can be compared with Jawlensky's *Murnau Landscape* (plate 82), which was painted in the same year, and Münter's *Gerade Strasse* (*Straight Road;* private collection), painted in 1910. In all three pictures dark lines are used to emphasize the contour of the motifs; however, Kandinsky takes this technique a stage further by using similar lines as graphic abbreviations for the trees along the road and the two laborers working in the field. This double function of line as descriptive contour and independent figure anticipates Kandinsky's later reversal of its role in the pictorial process. In the free application of color, which subverts the rigid organization of the forms, there is a certain element of irrationality which distinguishes Kandinsky's landscape studies from those of his friends. The proximity of his landscapes to his more cryptic, abstract works is demonstrated by the main motif which dominates the painting: the blue mountain rearing up in the distance, with its slightly asymmetrical shape and the tip of its peak cut off at the edge of the picture. The same motif is found in a similarly dominant form and position in a number of further Murnau landscape studies, as well as in the enigmatic painting *Mountain* (plate 13) and the famous *Impression VI – Park* (Centre Georges Pompidou, Paris), painted in 1911.

Wassily Kandinsky

11 MURNAU – FOOTPATH AND HOUSES
(Murnau – Fussweg und Häuser) 1909

Oil on cardboard, 12⅞ x 17½" (32.7 x 44.5 cm)
Inscribed "Kandinsky" (lower left)
GMS 36

Throughout the Murnau period up to 1914 Kandinsky continued painting some of his work outdoors, yet the majority of
these now famous landscapes were produced in 1909–10. Like
many of these Murnau views, *Murnau – Footpath and Houses* is
painted on the art cardboard measuring approximately 13 x 18"
(33 x 45 cm) that Kandinsky and Münter found convenient to
carry around and easy to handle when working outdoors. This
painting's effect derives from the daring use of straight lines
dissecting the picture asymmetrically and from the fascinating
combination of colors. It cleverly plays with the vibrant contrast
between blue and green, toned down by being mixed with
white and by a larger whitish plane on the foreground. The
dominant color is blue in every kind of shade from blue-grey to
turquoise, interspersed with central accents of unmixed glowing
ultramarine in the middle ground. Even the dark brown of the
fence along the narrow footpath, introduced into the picture
by vertical straight lines on the left, is reflected on the opposite
side in dark blue. In the foreground the dark horizontal of a
wooden fence closely and decisively cuts off the rest of the
picture zone, where the composition leads you to expect the
green of a meadow. Instead, there is a thin and restless coat of
white-yellow, probably partly finger-painted, leaving parts of
the ochre cardboard exposed.

Like many of Kandinsky's Murnau nature studies, this painting
radiates an unusual vitality. The artist had evidently discovered
the 'free hand' with which he pursued the continuing development of his objectives. When Kandinsky blends elements from
his earlier figure and landscape paintings into the imaginary
conceptions of the larger compositions he painted from 1909
onwards, the character of his Murnau studies also contributes
to the lively mystique of this new kind of painting.

12 **STUDY FOR IMPROVISATION 2 (FUNERAL MARCH)**
(Studie zu Improvisation 2 [Trauermarsch]) 1909

Oil on cardboard, 19⅝ x 27⅜" (50 x 69.5 cm)
GMS 50

From 1909 onward, Kandinsky began to divide his more important new works into three categories: "impressions," "improvisations," and "compositions." He explained this distinction in *Concerning the Spiritual in Art.* "Impressions," in Kandinsky's terminology, are "direct impressions of 'external' nature"; "compositions" are pictures in which "reason, the conscious, the deliberate, and the purposeful play a preponderant role" (see plates 29, 30); and "improvisations" are "chiefly unconscious, for the most part suddenly arising expressions of events of an inner character, hence impressions of 'internal' nature." *Study for Improvisation 2 (Funeral March)*, the finished version of which is in the Moderna Museet, Stockholm, is one of the first of a series of improvisations which Kandinsky created in the period from 1909 to 1913.

The scene, which incorporates elements of landscape, has an unreal quality. Three women of vaguely Russian appearance are seated in the center of the foreground, with a fourth woman in the bottom right-hand corner; a rider on a white horse enters the picture from the left. One detects a certain Symbolist influence. As in several of the later "improvisations," Kandinsky uses Russian folk-art motifs, whose form is modified but which nevertheless determine the entire character of this "impression of inner nature." The subtitle *Funeral March* indicates a general mood rather than a specific action. The subdued tone of the painting, which is fraught with significance, is echoed in *Bild mit Kahn (Painting with Skiff)*, also dating from 1909, and the earlier *Mit drei Frauen (With Three Women)*. The composition and some of the motifs of these two works provide a number of clues to an understanding of *Improvisation 2*.

Referring to *Painting with Skiff* and *With Three Women,* it is possible to identify the deep blue band which separates the figures from the background as a stream or river; the large blocks of color behind them are mountains, with a white cloud floating between the twin peaks. However, these two blocks of color, especially the orange one to the right, with its light blue "back," also have an organic appearance: the carefully differentiated use of color fills them with restless life. The schematic female figures are cowed and static; three of them directly face the viewer, while the fourth turns to welcome the approaching rider. The latter is one of Kandinsky's favorite symbolic figures: it frequently appears in the "improvisations," anticipating the "blue rider" on the cover of the almanac.

Wassily Kandinsky

13   MOUNTAIN (Berg)   1909

Oil on canvas, 42⅞ x 42⅞" (109 x 109 cm)
Inscribed "Kandinsky 1909" (lower left)
GMS 54

In 1909 Kandinsky painted this astonishing picture, whose
hallucinatory, emotionally charged, and near-abstract form
appears to anticipate his tempestuous "experimental" phase
shortly before the outbreak of World War I. It is only with
some difficulty that the viewer recognizes the deliberately
blurred outlines of two figures in front of a cone-shaped mountain, the main body of which is green, inlaid with white, and
framed by a dominant strip of blue, which in turn is surrounded
by a red zone of energy. On closer inspection, one realizes that
the enigmatic figures allude to symbols familiar from other
works by Kandinsky. A rider on a white horse is approaching
a second figure, whose identity is uncertain; the two figures
are attended, or threatened, by a sharply pointed zigzag shape
on the extreme left of the picture and by a dark, inclining form
on the far right. The form integrated into the mountain at the
top of the picture echoes the familiar motif of the Russian city.

In this case, as in many others, one's understanding of the
picture may be enhanced by comparing it with other works
by Kandinsky, in particular with *Der Blaue Berg* (*The Blue
Mountain,* 1908/09; Solomon R. Guggenheim Museum, New
York). In this work, the mountain occupies a similarly central
position, towering over, and visually dominating, the three
riders on white horses in the center. Two figures stand at each
edge of the picture: the one on the right leans slightly to the
left like the dark form in *Mountain.* The coloring of *Mountain*
is also echoed in the New York picture.

Although the figures are more clearly recognizable, the
theme of *The Blue Mountain* is just as enigmatic as that of
Mountain. All one can definitely say about the latter is that the
landscape and the rider are endowed with an intense spiritual
quality, to an even greater degree than in Kandinsky's previous
work. This is to some extent a function of the colors. Kandinsky regarded blue as the color of infinity, the "typical heavenly
color," which arouses a longing for purity and transcendence.
Red is a warm, mature color full of power and purposive
energy. White, on the other hand, which dominates the figures
in *Mountain,* is the color of absolute silence. However, Kandinsky writes, when we have "looked beyond the wall," we find
that white is full of unsuspected possibilities.

The mountain initially appears to be a highly formalized
depiction of a real landscape: it is interesting to compare its
form with the hierarchical, almost symmetrical shape of the
mountain in *Nature Study from Murnau I* (plate 10) and *Herbst-
landschaft* (*Autumn Landscape,* 1911; private collection, Chi-
cago). However, it is important to realize that in this picture,
the landscape and the figures merge into one another and
are unified in a new way. Two formerly separate areas of
Kandinsky's painting – the plein air landscape studies in oil
and the enigmatic depictions of the human figure in other
techniques – are brought together for the first time and integrated in a large-format work. Kandinsky had finally succeeded in liberating his technique from the traditional constraints with which he had long since broken in theory, but
not as yet in practice.

Wassily Kandinsky

14   IMPROVISATION 6 (AFRICAN)
(Improvisation 6 [Afrikanisches]) 1909

Oil on canvas, 42⅛ x 37⅝" (107 x 95.5 cm)
Inscribed "Kandinsky 1909" (lower left)
GMS 56

Improvisation 6 (African) differs from the other "improvisations" dating from the same period in respect of its clearer composition and the greater definition of its motifs. Its theme almost certainly derives from the impressions which remained in Kandinsky's mind after his visit to Tunis with Münter in 1905. Two figures with turbans and voluminous caftan-like robes stand in the foreground; to the left, one sees a white, rectangular shape resembling the wall of a North African house. The robes, with their narrow black borders, create an ornamental play of lines. Kandinsky uses a variety of glowing colors – reds, yellows, greens, and blues – which contrast with the dull white in the left-hand section of the picture.

As in *Study for Improvisation 2 (Funeral March)* (see plate 12), the foreground vaguely echoes the atmosphere of Symbolist painting: Kandinsky himself referred to the Symbolists, in particular to Arnold Böcklin and Giovanni Segantini, as "seekers of the spiritual in the material." His stylized use of line in this painting is also reminiscent of Munich *Jugendstil*. The background, however, is quite different. Here, the forms become increasingly blurred; the colors merge into one another and cease to have any representational function. The two bowed forms behind the central figures also appear to be human, but the seemingly organic colored shapes in the background are entirely enigmatic.

In this "improvisation," which is admittedly less abstract than some of the others, it would seem that Kandinsky was nevertheless trying partially to hide the objects, in order to allow the viewer to discover their inner "resonance" for himself. As he later wrote, "I dissolved objects to a greater or lesser extent within the same picture, so that they might not all be recognized at once and so that these emotional overtones might thus be experienced gradually by the spectator, one after the other."

Wassily Kandinsky

15　**ORIENTAL (Orientalisches)**　1909

Oil on cardboard, 27 ⅜ x 38" (69.5 x 96.5 cm)
GMS 55

In painting *Oriental* Kandinsky drew on the same set of memories as in *Improvisation 6* (plate 14): the inspiration for the picture, with its exotic colors, was supplied by his visit to Tunisia in 1905. To an even greater extent than in *Improvisation 6* the dominant color is a powerful, sensuous red, combined with yellow and blue; green, however, is absent. Kandinsky also uses white to provide additional highlights, which stand out like jewels on the surface of a work whose broad format lends it a frieze-like quality. The crouching and moving figures are linked together by their long, awkward, intertwining limbs. In the background, behind the two white minarets, we see four cone-shaped mountains, crowned by Russian castles of the kind so frequently seen in Kandinsky's work. Thus, impressions of the Orient are fused with Russian motifs, via the intense experience of color of which Kandinsky so often spoke in connection with his native country. The same set of motifs is also used in a color woodcut, in which the distribution between figure and ground is deliberately blurred, thereby transforming the picture into a vibrant, near-abstract pattern.

Wassily Kandinsky

16   MURNAU WITH CHURCH I
(Murnau mit Kirche I)   1910

Oil on cardboard, 25½ x 19¾" (64.7 x 50.2 cm)
GMS 59

Murnau with Church I is one of the best known views which Kandinsky painted of the small market town in southern Bavaria. It stands out from the rest of the Murnau landscapes painted in the period up to and including 1910: while remaining faithful to the motifs and the genre of landscape, Kandinsky follows a less naturalistic approach and uses color in the freer, more spontaneous manner with which he was experimenting in his "fantasy" paintings. It is just possible to recognize individual pictorial signals which distinguish the objects in the flow of color: the tall white church steeple, for example, and the vague outlines of a cluster of houses to the left. Kandinsky painted a number of similar pictures, such as *Murnau with Church II* (Stedelijk Van Abbemuseum, Eindhoven), in which the view is outlined more clearly and the dark silhouette of the mountains behind the church steeple lends the landscape a sense of spatial definition. In *Murnau with Church I* the only sense of depth is provided by the conglomeration of colors in the center of the picture. The color is freely and spontaneously applied: here and there, the bare surface of the cardboard shows through. This use of paint, together with the dynamic tilt of the steeple and the houses, creates an effect of movement and energy. Despite its apparent immediacy, *Murnau with Church I* is composed with meticulous care: this is evident in the balanced distribution of blue and white in the picture.

It may have been this picture, or a similar one, which occasioned an experience described by Kandinsky in his autobiographical *Reminiscences*. One evening in his studio, shortly after dusk, he suddenly saw "an indescribably beautiful picture, pervaded by an inner glow. At first I stopped short and then quickly approached this mysterious picture, on which I could discern only forms and colors and whose content was incomprehensible. At once, I discovered the key to the puzzle: it was a picture I had painted, standing on its side against the wall." He sensed that the impression generated by this picture was closely akin to his idea of "true" abstraction, but realized that he still had a long way to go before achieving his goal of devising purely abstract pictorial forms by eliminating perspective, introducing graphic elements into oil painting, and liberating color from any descriptive function.

Wassily Kandinsky

17 THE COW (Die Kuh) 1910

Oil on canvas, 37 ¾ x 41 ⅜" (95.5 x 105 cm)
Inscribed "Kandinsky 1910" (lower left)
GMS 58

In painting *The Cow,* Kandinsky employed dissolved structures of the kind seen in *Murnau with Church I* (plate 16), with the difference that in *The Cow* these structures are used as a means of deliberately blurring the image, thereby producing an effect of alienation. In the foreground a large white-and-yellow cow, facing to the right, is being milked by a young peasant girl. The outlines of the cow are obscured by the white and yellow of the surrounding area. One is particularly struck by the white mountain, which seems to follow and extend the line of the cow's back. The pointed conical shape of the mountain, framed by a strip of blue, is typical of the Murnau mountain form (see plate 13) which occurs in so many of Kandinsky's pictures in the period up to 1913. Its peak is crowned by a white wall, which may be a reference to the city wall of Murnau, although behind it one sees a number of Greek Orthodox onion-shaped domes. Once again, we find Kandinsky painting a vision inspired by a specifically Russian quality of feeling, but set in the countryside of southern Bavaria, whose churches and chapels aroused in him, as he later wrote, a similar resonance to that evoked by Russian church architecture.

Like the form of the cow, these walls and towers are integrated into the colors of their surroundings. In this picture Kandinsky was evidently more concerned with creating structural analogies and dissolving the contours of the motifs than with concealing some deeper meaning.

Wassily Kandinsky

18   IMPRESSION III (CONCERT)
(Impression III [Konzert]) 1911

Oil on canvas, 30½ x 39⅜" (77.5 x 100 cm)
Inscribed "Kandinsky 1911" (lower right)
GMS 78

Impression III (Concert) was painted shortly after a concert of music by Arnold Schoenberg which Kandinsky attended on January 2, 1911, together with Marc and several other members of the *Neue Künstler-Vereinigung München*. Kandinsky was deeply impressed by Schoenberg's boldly innovative use of the twelve-tone scale and began to correspond with the composer, who took part in the Blue Rider exhibition at the end of the year.

Kandinsky numbered this fascinating picture among his "impressions," whose aim was to convey "a direct impression of 'external nature'." By this, he meant not only visual impressions but sense impressions of all kinds, which he attempted to translate into visual terms in a nonrepresentational manner. *Impression III (Concert)* is based on an acoustic experience, for which Kandinsky found a highly complex pictorial equivalent.

Yellow and black, accentuated by white, are the dominant colors in the picture. Under the dynamic area of black in the top section, the yellow unfolds with a broad, sweeping gesture. It seems to flood back and forth across the picture, almost engulfing the brightly colored patches and the linear arabesques on the left. On closer inspection, one sees that the picture conveys the essence of a musical experience, blending acoustic and visual impressions in a revolutionary way. The black area is a highly schematic representation of a grand piano; the colored shapes edged in black are concertgoers listening intently to the music. Two preparatory pencil sketches, now in the Centre Georges Pompidou in Paris, clearly depict the listeners sitting at the front of the auditorium and standing by the left-hand wall; in both painting and sketches, the piano is bisected by a vertical white column which, in the painting, seems to metamorphose into a white pillar of sound.

The main impression, however, is of a yellow "sound," which fills the concert hall and makes the picture itself into an almost symphonic experience. In Kandinsky's imagination the color yellow had a specifically musical connotation: as early as 1909 he wrote a stage composition entitled *Yellow Sound,* which was subsequently published in The Blue Rider almanac.

Impression III (Concert) is a particularly striking exploration of the phenomenon of synaesthesia, the analogy between music and painting, which played a major role in early twentieth-century art. Critics have repeatedly pointed to Kandinsky's interest in synaesthesia, as evidenced by his book *Concerning the Spiritual in Art,* in which he discussed the correspondences between colors and particular instruments and tones. However, Kandinsky emphasized that painting and music each have their own specific resources. Only to the extent that it is inherently abstract, emancipated from nature, can music serve as a model for the new painting of the coming era of the "great spiritual." "In this respect," Kandinsky writes, "painting has caught up with music, and both assume an ever-increasing tendency to create 'absolute' works, i.e. completely objective' works that, like works of nature, come into existence 'of their own accord,' as the product of natural laws, as independent beings."

Wassily Kandinsky

19 IMPRESSION IV (GENDARME)
(Impression IV [Gendarme]) 1911

Oil on canvas, 37 3/8 x 42 1/4" (95 x 107 cm)
GMS 85

Like *Impression III (Concert)* (plate 18), *Impression IV (Gendarme)*
belongs in the category of "direct impressions of 'external
nature'." Altogether, Kandinsky painted six of these "impressions," all of them in 1911, two years after the first "improvisations" and a year after beginning work on the "compositions."
This shows that the distinction between "impression," "improvisation," and "composition" does not imply any kind of value
judgment: Kandinsky did not regard the depiction of "external"
nature as inherently inferior to the abstract, spiritualized form
of the "compositions." Some of the impressions, such as *Concert*
and *Impression V (Park)* (Centre Georges Pompidou, Paris),
themselves tend toward the abstract. As Johannes Langner has
indicated, the salient point about the distinction between the
three groups of works is the fact that Kandinsky categorized
his pictures in a new way, according to the manner and circumstances of their genesis rather than to their content. This
practice constituted a radical departure from traditional concepts
of iconography and genre. In this respect, as in so many others,
Kandinsky was a truly revolutionary artist.

The six impressions are subtitled *Gendarme, Fountain, Moscow,
Concert, Park,* and *Sunday,* titles which point to a world of
bourgeois leisure and civilized, genteel amusement. In the foreground of *Impression IV (Gendarme),* which at one time was mis-
takenly titled *Impression III (Fackelzug)* (*Torchlight Procession*), one
sees the powerful black contours of a huge horse facing from
right to left and the black outline of a rider. The two diagonal
lines on the left and right extend the structures of the horse
over the plane of the picture. On the left, next to the horse's
head, two passersby dressed in black are doffing their hats. In the
right-hand section of the picture one recognizes the blurred
outlines of a crowd of people; above their heads a mass of
brightly colored lanterns is framed by energetic strokes of dark
color. In the center, behind the rider, there is a kind of portal
with three pillars, the outlines of which are also boldly painted.
It would seem to be part of a pseudo-classical building in a public place in which a crowd, controlled by mounted gendarmes,
has gathered on some form of official occasion.

It is thought that *Impression IV (Gendarme)* was inspired by a
procession to the Königsplatz in Munich to mark the 90th birthday of the Bavarian Prince Regent on March 12, 1911. The
participants in the procession carried lanterns, and tall pylons
with torches were erected in the square: one of these pylons
can be seen at the top of the picture, to the right of the rider's
head.

Wassily Kandinsky

20   IMPRESSION VI (SUNDAY)
(Impression VI [Sonntag]) 1911

Oil on canvas, 42 ⅜ x 37 ⅜" (107.5 x 95 cm)
GMS 57

To an even greater extent than the fourth impression, *Impression IV (Gendarme)* (plate 19), the motifs of *Impression VI (Sunday)* belong to the world of middle-class leisure. A couple dressed in their Sunday best, the man in a dark suit with a round, bowler-type hat, the woman in a long dress with a cinched waist, walks toward the viewer. A small white dog gambols in front of them; in the background one sees a brightly colored park scene with what appears to be a child on a swing. The whole exudes French chic and elegance.

The couple's clothes, although seen only in outline, hark back to the Belle Epoque, the last decade of the nineteenth century. Right from the beginning of Kandinsky's development as a painter, this period, together with the so-called Second Empire, was one of his major sources of themes in painting the human figure. Motifs of this kind can be seen in some of his earliest oil and tempera paintings, such as *Helle Luft (Bright Air,* 1901; Centre Georges Pompidou, Paris), with its promenading ladies in crinoline skirts, and *Im Park (In the Park, c.* 1902; Lenbachhaus), which features a lady dressed in the fashion of the Belle Epoque and accompanied by a small dog. Similar scenes are depicted in a number of Kandinsky's early woodcuts.

One of the most striking general features of the "impressions" is the way in which Kandinsky reduces the figures to a set of more or less bold, black outlines. Deprived of their materiality, they take on a transparent quality: the color appears to pass through them. In this way they merge with their surroundings, while at the same time retaining their identity. They function as graphic ciphers of the kind which played an increasingly important part in Kandinsky's pictures from 1911 onward.

Wassily Kandinsky

21 ALL SAINTS I (Allerheiligen I) *c.* 1911

Oil on cardboard, 19⅝ x 25⅜" (50 x 64.5 cm)
Inscribed "K", in a triangle (lower left)
GMS 71

From 1910 onward, Kandinsky increasingly turned his attention to Christian motifs, such as the figure of St. George (see
plates 24, 41) and the eschatological themes which played an important part in a number of his major pictures from the pre-1914
period, including *Composition* (private collection, Switzerland),
painted in the fall of 1911, and the two subsequent "compositions," VI and VII (see plates 30, 31). These motifs are not only
central to the meaning of the pictures themselves, they also offer
a key to the understanding of Kandinsky's work as a whole
and of the Blue Rider movement, with its message that a new,
"spiritual" age was dawning.

One of the earliest pictures based on biblical themes is *Jüngstes
Gericht (Last Judgement,* 1910; private collection, New York),
whose motifs include the kneeling figure of a resurrected soul
with severed head, an angel blowing a trumpet, and the crumbling towers of a city on a hill. *Last Judgment* was followed in
1911 by a similar painting, this time on glass (Lenbachhaus), on
which Kandinsky painted the Russian word for "resurrection."
In a further painting on glass entitled *Grosse Auferstehung (Great
Resurrection;* Lenbachhaus), Kandinsky introduced a number of
additional motifs, including a boat with a triangular sail and a
group of Christian believers bearing lighted candles. These
features also appear in a colored woodcut with the same title.

All Saints I, too, was based on a painting on glass (plate 42).
It modifies and partly disguises the theme, which the "naive"
painting on glass presents in a more direct fashion. By comparing the two works it becomes possible to recognize the figures
of two saints embracing each other in the center; they are
surrounded by a group of smaller figures, which includes a
female saint in a yellow habit sitting in the foreground with
one arm outstretched. To the left of the two central figures
one sees a knight in armor on a white horse; in front of them,
there is a small boat with a blue sail and, at the top of the
picture, a city on a hill, with collapsing towers. The picture is
dominated by the figures of two angels with golden trumpets;
the angel on the left with long yellow hair is especially prominent. This motif is particularly significant: it serves to combine
the theme of All Saints with that of the Last Judgment, thereby
adding an apocalyptic connotation – Kandinsky's alternative
title for the picture was *Day of Judgment.* It is possible that
Kandinsky's intention in partially disguising the theme was to
lend an additional emphasis to the "ultimate truth" of the
work.

Wassily Kandinsky

22 ALL SAINTS II (Allerheiligen II) 1911

Oil on canvas, 33⅞ x 39" (86 x 99 cm)
GMS 62

In 1911 Kandinsky created a large number of paintings, water-colors, and woodcuts based on eschatological themes. In these pictures, religious figures are combined with images from the artist's earlier symbolic vocabulary – for instance, the images of the rider and the city on the hill – to create an iconographical repertoire which is unique in modern art. *All Saints II,* which is closely related to *All Saints I* (plate 21), explores the possibil-ities of this new stock of images. With their black outlines, the figures in the picture have a simplicity which reminds one of Kandinsky's paintings on glass (see plate 42), but they are drawn in a freer, more expressive manner. The three saints in the center gesturing toward the right have been identified as St. Basil, St. Gregory, and St. John Chrisostom. The female figure in front of them is said to be St. Walburga, the patron saint of Bavaria. St. Vladimir, the patron saint of Russia, stands with out-stretched arms above the group of candle-bearing believers, the sailing boat, and the whale – a reference to the story of Jonah. At the top of the picture, the prophet Elijah is ascending to heaven in a fiery chariot drawn by three golden horses. This image, known as the *troika* motif, often recurs in Kandinsky's abstract pictures, where the outlines of the horses are suggested by three wavy lines. On the right, St. John the Evangelist, the chronicler of the Apocalypse, stands next to a resurrected soul with severed head, looking up at one of the trumpet-bearing angels floating high above the scene. In the center, we re-encounter the familiar motifs of the rider and the collapsing city on the hill. This image of the rider and the crumbling tower, which Kandinsky used in the frontispiece for his book *Concerning the Spiritual in Art,* is a kind of symbolic shorthand for the idea of the coming apocalypse and the dawning of a new, "spiritual" age.

Wassily Kandinsky

23 **ROMANTIC LANDSCAPE**
(Romantische Landschaft) 1911

Oil on canvas, 37¼ x 50¾" (94.3 x 129 cm)
Inscribed "Kandinsky 1911" (lower right)
GMS 83

Romantic Landscape stands in a class of its own: it is neither an "impression" nor an "improvisation," nor is it a true landscape. The form of the picture is breathtakingly open and spontaneous, casting a kind of hermetic spell. An impression of immediacy is generated by the three horsemen emerging from a zone of dense color and galloping downhill from right to left. The blue slant of the hill, the blood-red sun, and the two forms rearing up in the foreground are hastily sketched in bare outline. The blobs of color in the top right-hand corner evoke the dynamic power of the landscape; their almost untamed, disparate energy is collected and concentrated in the elongated forms of the three horses with their violet-colored riders. The color of the front two horses is echoed by the blue-green contours of the yellow one at the rear, which emphasize the power and speed of the group. Their rushing, downhill movement is highlighted by the diagonal brushstrokes in the rest of the picture, which impart a sense of kinetic urgency to the surrounding landscape. The steep, light-brown hill toward which the riders are galloping seems to pose a kind of threat, which is counterbalanced by the dark form from which the group has escaped. This form is in turn offset by the openness of the white into which the elements of the landscape are nonchalantly strewn, by the graphic economy of the work, and by the harmony of the colors.

Some twenty years later, in a letter written in 1930, Kandinsky commented once more on the picture: "In 1910 I painted a *Romantic Landscape* which had nothing to do with earlier Romanticism. I intend to use a title of this kind again.... Where is the dividing line between the lyrical and the Romantic? The coming Romanticism is indeed deep and rich in content; it is a lump of ice in which a flame burns. If people only see the ice and not the flame, then so much the worse for them." In *Romantic Landscape,* which was in fact painted in 1911, Kandinsky transposed the flickering puzzles of the "improvisations," based on inner impressions of nature, into the spacious realm of lyrical freedom.

Wassily Kandinsky

24   ST. GEORGE NO. 3 (St. Georg Nr. 3)   1911

Oil on canvas, 38⅜ x 32⅜" (97.5 x 107.5 cm)
Inscribed "Kandinsky 1911" (lower left)
GMS 81

From 1911 onward, the Christian motifs of All Saints and
the Last Judgment occupied a central position in Kandinsky's
symbolic vocabulary. At about the same time, the figure of
St. George, the dragon-killer and vanquisher of evil, took on
a particular significance for the artist. For a discussion of the
symbolism of the saint – a close relative of the figure of the
rider, which had always been one of Kandinsky's favorite
motifs – the reader should refer to plates 37 and 41. In addition
to three paintings on glass, one of which is almost identical
with the woodcut on the cover of The Blue Rider almanac,
Kandinsky made three oil paintings depicting St. George, in
which this Christian theme is varied in a number of ways. The
pictures have an almost hallucinatory quality. *St. George No. 1,*
owned by a Swiss collector, shows a schematic figure enve-
loped by white, amorphous clouds, stabbing his lance into
the dragon beneath him. *St. George No. 2* (The Hermitage,
St. Petersburg) is an almost abstract representation of the horse
and the rider behind the expressive diagonal of the sacred
lance. In *St. George No. 3* the knight, on the extreme left of the
picture, is scarcely recognizable. He thrusts his lance vertically
into the maw of the dragon at his feet. The dragon's light-
colored body, with its lashing tail, seems to dissolve into its
surroundings. The image is deliberately obscured by the prolific use of the color white: St. George himself, the dragon, and
the background are mainly white, which is relieved only by
the weapon, the pink and yellow section of the dragon's body,
and the dark lines distributed through the picture.

Here, as in a number of Kandinsky's other major works, the
formal makeup of the picture takes on a meaning of its own,
which is almost more important than the motif. According to
Kandinsky, white is a color which does not occur in nature
and which the artist only uses to translate nature into an "inner
impression." In *St. George No. 3* there seems to be some form
of secret relationship between the dominant zone of white and
the picture's aura of struggle, death, and salvation. In *Concerning
the Spiritual in Art* Kandinsky wrote: "As a closer definition, *white,*
which is often regarded as a noncolor . . . is like the symbol of
a world where all colors, as material qualities and substances,
have disappeared. This world is so far above us that no sound
from it can reach our ears. We hear only a great silence, that,
represented in material terms, appears to us like an insurmount-
able, cold, indestructible wall, stretching away to infinity. For
this reason, white also affects our psyche like a great silence,
which for us is absolute . . . . It is a silence that is not dead, but
full of possibilities. White has the sound as of a silence that
suddenly becomes comprehensible." The schematic image of
St. George recurs once more in one of Kandinsky's major
abstract pictures, *Bild mit weissem Rand* (*Picture with White Border;*
Solomon R. Guggenheim Museum, New York), painted in 1912.

Wassily Kandinsky

25   IMPROVISATION 18 (WITH TOMBSTONE)
(Improvisation 18 [mit Grabstein]) 1911

Oil on canvas, 55½ x 47¼" (141 x 120 cm)
Inscribed "Kandinsky" (lower right)
GMS 77

The *Improvisations* offered Kandinsky a further field for experimenting with the blurring of images, which for him was an important means of exploring the possibilities of abstraction. Rather than adopting the more obvious course of painting in a geometrical or ornamental style, Kandinsky moved toward abstraction through a complicated process of dissolving the object. Even pictures such as *Improvisation 18 (With Tombstone)* retain a certain figurative element, although the motifs are divested of their meaning and external form and rendered almost unrecognizable. Only their "inner sound" remains – as a kind of absurd echo, as if a single word were being repeated over and over again – and fills the picture with a wealth of barely perceptible but nevertheless highly intriguing implications.

The picture contains a disturbing jumble of vague forms piled up on top of each other in diagonal layers; the pale, empty zones between the forms appear to represent the rudiments of a landscape. The three tombstones, barely discernible in a dirty patch of gray in the bottom right-hand corner, are echoed by the three bowed figures at the top of the picture. A further group of figures stands huddled together in the center. One is reminded of the medieval topos of the Meeting of the Three Living and the Three Dead, with which Kandinsky was undoubtedly familiar. What is important, however, is not the iconographical content of the picture, but the way in which the statement that it makes is modified by the obscuring of form. A year later, Kandinsky wrote: "My personal qualities consist in the ability to make the inner element sound forth more strongly by limiting the external. Conciseness is my favorite device. For this reason I do not carry even purely pictorial means to the highest level. Conciseness demands the imprecise (that is, no pictorial form – whether drawing or painting – that produces too strong an effect)." In many of the "improvisations" and "compositions" which he painted during this phase of his development, Kandinsky successfully employed this technique of reduction, deliberately blurring motifs and even allowing the effects of different colors to cancel each other out.

Wassily Kandinsky

26 IMPROVISATION 19 1911

Oil on canvas, 47¼ x 55¾" (120 x 141.5 cm)
GMS 79

To a greater extent than any of the other pictures included here, *Improvisation 19* points to a further important aspect of Kandinsky's liberation of painting from traditional notions of representation. Sixten Ringbom and other scholars have shown that in the period before World War I Kandinsky took a marked interest in theosophy and spiritualism. It is known that he was familiar with the ideas of the anthroposophical thinker Rudolf Steiner and that he had connections with the Munich circle of the poet Stefan George; his library contained a number of theosophical treatises featuring illustrations of occult manifestations and parapsychological phenomena. The revolutionary discoveries of psychology in the early years of the century also opened up new avenues of thought which tied in with Kandinsky's search for a means of conveying inner experience. The influence of these various areas of thought can be detected in his secret language of abstract forms.

Improvisation 19 depicts two groups of figures whose attention appears to be focused on some unknown event. The figures huddled together on the left seem to be advancing toward the front edge of the picture. The colors of the background shine through their flat, hollow bodies. Behind them one sees the vague outlines of a further group of figures, edged in white: the color of hidden, as yet uncertain possibilities.

The central section of the painting is dominated by a variety of vivid blues, illuminating the figures on the right, which seem to be moving toward some goal at the edge of the picture. These larger figures, in an attitude of spellbound concentration, appear to be closer to the moment of being "chosen" than the group advancing from the background on the right. Between the two groups an elongated form with rounded contours enters the picture from the top: its diaphanous play of colors is bordered by a thick black line.

These evidently represent a form of aura, the visible emanation of a particular mode of thought and feeling; and the round form at the top of the picture can be seen as a kind of occult manifestation. Whereas the figures on the left are characterized by "earthly" colors, the blue is the color of a higher, spiritual realm; the violet heads of the "initiated" convey the idea of transition to a higher plane of consciousness. In *Improvisation 19* Kandinsky attempted to translate spiritual phenomena into pictorial terms, a task to which he saw semiabstract forms as well-suited. The mysterious ritual of the picture lends expression to an almost Messianic hope of salvation, which Kandinsky connected with art and which was one of the main factors in the dawning of that "epoch of the great spiritual" of which he spoke in *Concerning the Spiritual in Art*.

Wassily Kandinsky

27 IMPROVISATION 19a 1911

Oil on canvas, 38¼ x 41¾" (97 x 106 cm)
GMS 84

Improvisation 19a is a further demonstration of the extent to which Kandinsky's painting had succeeded in freeing itself from the external appearance of nature in order to construct its own pictorial system. In the bold but indeterminate movement of the colors the elements between body and space are impossible to pin down. Despite the variety of bright colors, the overall tone of the picture is dark and brooding, conveying an atmosphere of struggle that is underlined by the conflict between the different color effects. Kandinsky had finally succeeded in developing a technique adequate to the task of expressing the transcendental spirit of nature, thereby overcoming his previous doubts about his ability to solve this problem. In *Reminiscences* he wrote: "Years had to elapse before I arrived, by intuition and reflection, at the simple solution that the aims (and hence the resources too) of art and nature were fundamentally, organically, and by the very nature of the world different – and equally great, which also means equally powerful."

However, what Rose-Carol Washton-Long calls the "hidden imaginary" still continues to play an important part in this process of transmission. It gives the almost abstract picture its "inner vibration" and lends it a suggestive charm. The overall structure of *Improvisation 19a,* with the sharp peaks of the "mountains" in the background and the division of the "hills," may be based on a recollection of the landscape in Murnau. Two stooping figures can be seen on the edge of the "hill" in the top right-hand corner; below them, two further figures seem to be passing something from hand to hand. The most striking feature of the picture is the dark yellow, domed form in the foreground, which appears to shoot up and then cascade down like a mountain stream; the black aperture also allows it to be read as a conical body turned toward the right.

Comparisons with other works by Kandinsky, such as *Improvisation 7* (Tretiakov Gallery, Moscow), in which the movements follow a similar direction, are of only limited use. The motifs would seem to evoke an animated landscape in which people are wandering aimlessly, driven by fate. The salient features of the picture, however, are the overall impression of disorder and the deliberate distortion of the image, which is elevated onto another, more universal plane. The nexus of meaning is broken up by the indeterminacy of the individual forms and the chaotic manner in which they are juxtaposed, in accordance with a principle of planned disorder which can already be seen in Kandinsky's early work. Johannes Langner has aptly characterized the development of Kandinsky's work toward the open, abstract picture as follows: "In a concatenation of motifs which is no longer founded in action or verifiable fact, but only in meaning and mood, free association replaces causal connection."

Wassily Kandinsky

28 IMPROVISATION 21a 1911

Oil on canvas, 37¾ x 41⅜" (96 x 105 cm)
Inscribed "Kandinsky 1911" (lower left)
GMS 82

Improvisation 21a was inspired by the small painting on glass
With Sun (plate 40). It is closely related to the picture *Kleine
Freuden* (*Simple Pleasures;* Solomon R. Guggenheim Museum,
New York), which Kandinsky painted some eighteen months
later, in the summer of 1913. Kandinsky himself described how
the delicate colors of *With Sun* gave him the idea of painting
a larger picture on the same theme. In *With Sun* the individual
pictorial elements are more clearly identifiable than in *Improvisation 21a* or *Simple Pleasures.* At the top, one sees the sun and,
in the center, two hills crowned by the familiar onion-shaped
domes of a Russian church; on the left there is a pair of figures
leaning backward at a sharp angle; above them, three riders are
racing up a hill. On the right there are two large curved forms:
a boat with three oars and a dark cloud in the sky above. In
Improvisation 21a, on the other hand, the motifs are to some
extent blurred; the bright, glowing colors of the painting on
glass are suppressed and overlaid with a whitish gray.

Nevertheless, the picture makes a bold general statement
whose intensity is heightened by the multiplicity of associations
to which it gives rise. Many Kandinsky scholars, especially Rose-
Carol Washton-Long, emphasize the importance of the dramatic
contrast between the two halves of the painting, the confrontation between the sun and the dark, menacing cloud
above the boat in the storm-tossed lake. Comparing the symbolic vocabulary of *Improvisation 21a* with that of such pictures as
All Saints II, the various paintings on glass of the *Last Judgment,*
and *Composition VI (Sintflut)* (*Deluge;* The Hermitage, St. Petersburg), Washton-Long and Sixten Ringbom see the work as embodying an apocalyptic vision of despair and hope, destruction
and renewal.

However, in his account of the genesis of *Simple Pleasures,*
which draws on a similiar set of motifs, Kandinsky makes no
mention of such visions, concentrating instead on the formal
properties of the picture, its "balance" of heterogeneous elements. Describing the basis of the work as "spiritual," he
writes: "My aim . . . was to let myself go and pour a quantity
of simple pleasures over the canvas." The dark cloud struck a
more serious note, in the form of a "subtle inner simmering,"
an "overflowing." However, this melancholy note remains in
the background, as a muted "vibration": as Kandinsky says,
"it all remains in the area of simple pleasures and does not
take on a painful overtone." Once more, one is surprised by
Kandinsky's complex mode of thinking, which deals with
individual elements of pictures in a new and contradictory
manner and renders them inaccessible to closer analysis.

Wassily Kandinsky

29 IMPROVISATION 26 (ROWING)
(Improvisation 26 [Rudern]) 1912

Oil on canvas, 38¼ x 42⅜" (97 x 107.5 cm)
Inscribed "Kandinsky 1912" (lower left)
GMS 66

The subtitle *Rowing* indicates the motif of this intriguing picture. The viewer who is familiar with the visual ambiguities of Kandinsky's painting recognizes the outlines of a boat with laid-out oars, gliding weightlessly over the iridescent surface of the work. The motif of the boat is an integral part of Kandinsky's figurative cosmos; it appears, in a variety of contexts, in some of his earliest works, such as *Motley Life* (plate 4). As Armin Zweite has pointed out, its connotations change from one picture to another: in some instances it can be taken to mean farewell and the anticipation of new pastures, in others it is a metaphor of liberation or of an apocalyptic vision of doom.

It may well be possible to discover connotations of this kind in *Improvisation 26 (Rowing),* which is unusual in respect of its single motif: Kandinsky's pictures frequently combine several forms in a complex whole. Perhaps the most interesting feature of the picture, however, is its formal appearance, which places it among the true masterpieces of this revolutionary period in Kandinsky's work. Line and the spread of color have separated in order to form a new unity. The open curve of the rounded boat is painted in the same shade of madder as the undulating line in the upper section of the picture, which can be identified, by reference to one of Kandinsky's watercolors, as a chain of hills. The powerful black diagonals of the oars and the bent backs of the rowers convey a sense of disembodied psychic energy. Some scholars have interpreted the black lines at the top as trees or birds, but they can also be read as a collision between swift, conflicting movements.

In this picture Kandinsky succeeds in evoking a dreamlike, floating sense of space between plane and depth, which is based entirely on the choice and juxtaposition of the colors. In *Concerning the Spiritual in Art* he discusses the experiments of the Cubists in abandoning traditional perspective and constituting the picture on a new, ideal plane. He points out that there are alternative possibilities to those envisaged by the Cubists, "possibilities offered by the correct use of color, which can recede or advance, strive forward or backward, and turn the picture into a hovering in mid-air, which signifies the same as the pictorial extension of space." In this way, although the colors are laid side by side with no fixed borders, Kandinsky creates an impression of depth, of an independent pictorial space. He discussed this technique, which often involves a calculated use of contradictory effects, in his 1914 Cologne Lecture: "The colors which I employed later lie as if upon one and the same plane, while their inner weights are different. Thus the collaboration of different spheres entered into my pictures of its own accord. . . . This difference between the inner planes gave my pictures a depth that more than compensated for the earlier, perspective depth. I distributed my weights so that they revealed no architectonic center. . . . I would treat the individual color-tones likewise, cooling the warmer tones, warming the cold, so that even one single color was raised to the level of a composition."

Wassily Kandinsky

30   IMPROVISATION DELUGE
(Improvisation Sintflut) 1913

Oil on canvas, 37⅜ x 59" (95 x 150 cm)
GMS 76

Improvisation Deluge is one of several preparatory studies for *Composition VI* (The Hermitage, St. Petersburg), which is also based on the theme of the Deluge. Kandinsky describes the genesis of the latter picture in some detail. His starting point was a painting on glass "that I had done more for my own satisfaction. Here are to be found various objective forms, which are in part amusing (I enjoyed mingling serious forms with amusing external expressions): nudes, the Ark, animals, palm trees, lightning, rain, etc." However, some eighteen months elapsed before the artist was able to detach himself from the concrete image of the Deluge and find a form which would convey the "inner sound" of the theme, rather than its "external impression." In the major paintings from the year 1913 Kandinsky at last fully achieves his aim of dissolving the object and transforming the individual elements of the picture into a complex system of internal contradictions.

Improvisation Deluge is a raging whirlpool of colors. White rays of light shoot down from the top into the center of the picture. The work evokes an impression of drama and catastrophe, although there is no immediate figurative basis for such an interpretation. Here, as in the finished version of *Composition VI,* there are two centers, which Kandinsky describes thus: "1. On the left the delicate, rosy, somewhat blurred center, with weak, indefinite lines in the middle; 2. On the right (somewhat higher than the left) the crude, red-blue, rather discordant area, with sharp, rather evil, strong, very precise lines."

Nevertheless, there are a number of major differences between *Improvisation Deluge* and *Composition VI.* The paint in the "composition" is thinner and the dominant color is green, in various shades. A number of graphic signs, some of which are easily decipherable, continue the drama on a second level. On the left a large round boat with three laid-out oars floats in space; above it, one sees an angel blowing the Last Trumpet and, in the center, the body of a fish. The sharp diagonal lines in the center, which are now black instead of white, can be interpreted as representing either rain or the sound of the trumpet. These elements point once more to the themes of the Apocalypse and the Last Judgment, which occur frequently in Kandinsky's pictures from 1911 onward.

However, according to Kandinsky, "nothing could be more misleading than to dub this picture the representation of an event." In his estimation, the most important new element in *Improvisation Deluge* was the third center in the middle, which is missing in *Composition VI.* In the words of the artist, the "hovering" appearance of this center, its "feeling of 'somewhere . . . determines the 'inner sound' of the whole picture." The work is deliberately obscure: the objects are dissolved but nevertheless retain a subliminal presence, and Kandinsky uses a variety of contradictory formal devices in order to clothe "the greatest disturbance . . . in the greatest tranquility." It embodies an element of irrationality which, according to Wilhelm Worringer, contradicts "the rationalism of seeing that educated Europeans regard as the natural form of seeing."

Wassily Kandinsky

31 STUDY FOR COMPOSITION VII (VERSION 2)
(Studie zu Komposition VII [Entwurf 2] 1913

Oil on canvas, 39⅜ x 55⅛" (100 x 140 cm)
GMS 64

Composition VII is one of Kandinsky's most important paintings from the pre-1914 period: it marks the culmination of his attempts to stimulate "the capacity to experience the spiritual in material and abstract things" by creating a new art based on revolutionary principles of construction. In the course of his entire career Kandinsky painted only ten pictures with the grand title *Composition*. In *Concerning the Spiritual in Art* Kandinsky defined the "composition" as the expression "of feelings which have been forming within me . . . over a very long period of time, which, after the first preliminary sketches, I have slowly and pedantically examined and worked out. . . . Here, reason, the conscious, the deliberate, and the purposeful play a preponderant role. Except that I always decide in favor of feeling rather than calculation." These highly complex works are indeed the result of a synthesis of reason and creative intuition. The detailed planning which went into the pictures is demonstrated by the numerous sketches and studies for the 78-by-118-inch (2 × 3 m) final version of *Composition VII,* which is now in the Tretiakov Gallery in Moscow. In addition to some twenty drawings and watercolors, Kandinsky made six oil studies; the final work was produced in four days, from November 25 to 28, 1913.

The present work is one of the preparatory oil studies. Like *Improvisation Deluge* (plate 30), it seems at first sight to be a turbulent chaos of colors and forms, lacking any intelligible structure. Hence, one is surprised to learn that eschatological motifs play a significant part in the conception of the painting. Kandinsky deliberately obscures and breaks up the semantic content of the work, whose entirely abstract form is nevertheless pregnant with meaning.

In the numerous sketches and studies for *Composition VII,* the concentric circle of colors in the middle, traversed by two black lines, was established right from the outset. A striking feature of the present study is the vague emptiness at the bottom edge. In the final version, the dynamic force of the vortex in which the colors float above the chaos beneath is more sharply emphasized, and one clearly sees a large rowing boat in the left-hand bottom corner – an obvious piece of apocalyptic symbolism.

Composition VII has often been interpreted as a dramatic vision of impending doom and of the dawning of a new age. There can be no doubt that eschatological ideas of this kind were uppermost in Kandinsky's mind when he was painting this and other works from the pre-1914 period; however, rather than expressing these ideas in figurative terms, he translated them into a revolutionary form of pictorial thinking. "Painting," Kandinsky wrote in 1913, "is like a thundering collision of different worlds that are destined, in and through conflict, to create that new world called the work. Technically, every work of art comes into being in the same way as the cosmos – by means of catastrophes, which ultimately create out of the cacophony of the various instruments that symphony we call the music of the spheres. The creation of the work of art is the creation of the world."

Wassily Kandinsky

32   LARGE STUDY FOR A MURAL FOR EDWIN R.
CAMPBELL (SUMMER) (Grosse Studie zu einem
Wandbild für Edwin R. Campbell [Sommer]) 1914

Oil on canvas, 39 x 23⅜" (99 x 59.5 cm)
GMS 75

In 1914 Kandinsky was commissioned by Edwin R. Campbell,
the founder of the Chevrolet Motor Company, to produce a
series of murals for the entrance hall of his New York apartment. The commission was negotiated by the art dealer Arthur
J. Eddy. In a letter to Kandinsky, Campbell described the
proportions of the hall, which was almost round, with three
doors leading off it. In Murnau in the spring of 1914, the artist
created four paintings in the shape of a tall rectangle, two of
which were relatively narrow, while the others had a broader
format. The outbreak of World War I initially made it impossible to deliver the pictures; eventually, however, they left
Europe via Stockholm in 1916 and were hung in Campbell's
apartment on Park Avenue. All four works are now in the
Museum of Modern Art, New York.

   Since the publication of Kenneth C. Lindsay's seminal article
on the Campbell series in 1956, the four pictures have been
given the subtitles *Spring, Summer, Fall,* and *Winter* and been
seen as a cycle depicting the seasons. It must be emphasized
that these subtitles were not used by Kandinsky himself: their
sole function is to differentiate between the four puzzlingly
abstract works, which cannot be interpreted by reference to
traditional categories. Within the series, however, it is possible
to detect certain principles of order. *Fall* and *Winter,* the two
broader works, are the scene of a drama of dynamic colors,
while *Spring* and *Summer* are characterized by a fine structure
of lines; their floating surfaces of color are larger but less
obtrusive, and the individual elements more clearly isolated.

   The picture under discussion here is a study for *Summer.*
The long white tubular forms reach upward like tentacles; the
sprinkling of colors ("an inner seething in an unclear shape")
fills the center form with additional, subtle life. The other
colors in the painting are yellow, red, and blue; near the top
of the picture one sees a black patch with a white aperture.
This patch recalls the structures of meaning in Kandinsky's
Bild mit schwarzem Bogen (*Picture with a Black Arch,* 1912; Centre
Georges Pompidou, Paris), in which red and blue stand in an
antithetical relationship and traces of black lines dominate the
work. The study for *Summer* in the Campbell series is full of
overlapping graphic signs, all of which appear to be dim reflections of something else. The streaky black patch in the center
of the picture brings to mind the angel blowing the Last
Trumpet; the steep upward curve of the lines in the top left-
hand corner refers to the fiery chariot of the prophet Elijah;
and the strange blue angular shape at the bottom right with
the "eye" in the center possibly alludes to the face of St. John
on the island of Patmos. Paradoxically, the important thing
about these references is the fact that the remaining fragments
of lines have taken on an expressive value in their own right.
Although the delicate black structures of *Summer* embody the
tense quality of erstwhile graphic abbreviations, they have
liberated themselves entirely from any representational function. Thus the picture constitutes an important step on the
road toward an autonomous form of painting.

Wassily Kandinsky

33   IMPROVISATION GORGE
(Improvisation Klamm) 1914

Oil on canvas, 43¼ x 43¼" (110 x 110 cm)
GMS 74

Like many of Kandinsky's pictures from 1913–14, *Improvisation Gorge* conveys the impression of a tumultuous conglomeration of natural phenomena. Looking more closely at its jumble of forms, one sees a variety of meticulously executed figurative elements, drawn with a degree of realism which one would scarcely expect to encounter at this stage of Kandinsky's creative development. Hans Konrad Roethel characterizes the remnants of figurative motifs in the work as follows: "In deciphering the images, it is helpful to know that Kandinsky painted the picture immediately after an excursion with Gabriele Münter to the Höllental gorge near Garmisch-Partenkirchen on July 3, 1914. In the foreground one clearly recognizes a man and a woman dressed in Bavarian costume, standing on a landing-stage, beneath which two canoes are passing, with their oars jutting up into the air. From the landing-stage and the canoes the eye is drawn upward to the lake occupying the center of the composition. The surface of the water is defined by fine brushstrokes, like little waves; in the middle of the lake there is a yacht with a red sail. The lake is set in the majestic landscape of a mountain valley. A chain of mountain peaks, the sky, and streaks of cloud mark the upper limit of the picture." The form on the far right is a waterfall; "to the right of the center, on what would appear to be the shore of the lake, there is a red house with black windows. To the left of the house one sees a railroad line. On the left-hand side of the picture the motif of the Russian chapel seems to have merged with that of the church in Murnau, which can be recognized by the three domed towers." In the top left-hand corner a dark green fir tree bends in the wind. All these figurative elements, which lack any sense of proportion or perspective, seem to be caught up in a whirlwind whose vortex is marked by the structure resembling a rope ladder in the upper section of the picture. Roethel contributes a further clue to the interpretation of the work by pointing to the outlines of the white horse on the left, with the clearly visible set of beam scales above its head. This motif recurs, together with the couple on the landing-stage, the boats, and the waterfall, in a pencil sketch by Kandinsky dated June 22, 1914, on which he wrote the Russian word for "sunset." The visit to the Höllental gorge would appear to have supplied the impetus to execute the painting. Seen as a "sunset" and in relation to images of the Four Horsemen of the Apocalypse, the work echoes the fantasies of doom and destruction found in many of Kandinsky's prewar pictures.

Wassily Kandinsky

34 UNTITLED IMPROVISATION
(Unbenannte Improvisation) 1914

Oil on canvas, 48⅞ x 28⅞" (124.3 x 73.5 cm)
GMS 69

In 1913–14 Kandinsky painted a series of pictures, including *Untitled Improvisation* and *Schwarze Striche* (*Black Lines;* Solomon R. Guggenheim Museum, New York), in which fine calligraphic lines, mostly black but in some instances colored, take on a puzzling life of their own against a blurred background of color. In *Untitled Improvisation* one also sees transparent hermaphrodite shapes which document the living, organic quality of Kandinsky's abstract forms with exceptional clarity. A transparent, amoebalike form, which appears to have surfaced from the black, centrifugal depths, floats in the center of the picture. The small, light-colored waves above it and the curving, dark-blue edge on the right recall, like a distant memory in the hidden recesses of the mind, the shore of a lake, an impression which is reinforced by the storm-tossed zone in the foreground. However, the revolutionary perspective of the work is wholly oriented toward that "impression of inner nature" which Kandinsky had sought to convey in his "improvisations." The colors, which have a milky, translucent quality, retreat from the edge of the picture in a manner characteristic of Kandinsky's work during the war years. The concentration of the picture's action in the center, which in many of the paintings from this period is surrounded by a light-colored border, eventually leads to the reinforcement of the individual elements. A calmer, more restrained mood replaces the seething chaos of colors in Kandinsky's "classic" abstract phase up to 1914. In the 1920s the artist carried on painting in an abstract manner, using a quite different vocabulary.

Wassily Kandinsky

35 RED SPOT II (Roter Fleck II) 1921

Oil on canvas, 51⅝ x 71¼" (131 x 181 cm)
Inscribed "K 21", in a triangle (lower left)
FH 233

When World War I broke out, Kandinsky left Germany and returned to Russia via Switzerland. During the years of the war and the Revolution he painted very little and devoted the major part of his energies to the politics of culture. *Red Spot II* is listed in Kandinsky's personal catalogue as his first painting of the year 1921, in which he created a mere eight pictures. The technique is quite different from that of his earlier work and marks the beginning of a new phase in his creative development. The influence of such Constructivist artists as Kazimir Malevich, Vladimir Tatlin, and Lyubov Popova, with whom Kandinsky taught for a time in Moscow, is clearly evident in the clarity and precision of the work, the geometrical arrangement of the individual elements, and the smoothness of the surface. The expressive vehemence of the prewar pictures has given way to a more detached, seemingly rational mode of composition, using pure, simple forms.

However, despite the apparent influence of Constructivism on his work, Kandinsky was strongly critical of the new Russian art. In an article published in 1935 in the French journal *Cahiers d'Art,* he characterized the Constructivists as mere "mechanics," rather than abstract artists in the proper sense of the term, and it is indeed possible to detect certain differences between pictures such as *Red Spot II* and the work of the Revolutionary artists. Although Kandinsky uses geometrical forms, such as triangles, circles, and arcs, they are juxtaposed in an irregular, nongeometrical manner and used as elements in a more complex composition. The picture lacks the logical structure of Constructivist art. Behind the red patch, with its painterly texture, two arcs collide with a collection of smaller forms; at the edge of the white central zone one sees a number of colored circles of varying sizes. During the time when he was working at the Bauhaus the circle became a crucial element in Kandinsky's formal vocabulary. In 1929 he described his fascination with the "inner force" of the circle, declaring, "I love circles today in the same way that previously I loved, e.g., horses." Kandinsky evidently took a positive decision to follow the trend of the time in using geometrical forms, thereby continuing his quest for pure forms with no distracting associations.

Wassily Kandinsky

36 PARTIES DIVERSES 1940

Oil on canvas, 35 x 45⅝" (89 x 116 cm)
Inscribed "VK 40" (lower left)
On permanent loan from the Gabriele Münter and Johannes Eichner Foundation
FH 208

Parties Diverses is characteristic of the works which Kandinsky painted in Paris, where he lived from 1933, after the Bauhaus was finally closed down by the Nazis, until his death in 1944. Once again, his formal vocabulary underwent a decisive change. Numerous commentators have described the amoeba-like, semiorganic microorganisms and miniature structures which began to populate his pictures after the constructive, geometrical Bauhaus phase. These forms are seen with a certain detachment and inserted in an artificial, floating frame of reference, using equally artificial, "Asiatic" colors. *Parties Diverses* is divided up into a number of differently colored geometrical fields whose structure is ultimately symmetrical. In a somewhat muted form, the work once more invokes the principle of dualism, the sense of opposition and contradiction which had been one of the most prominent features of Kandinsky's art ever since his pre-1914 abstract-expressive phase. The oppositions in pictures such as *Parties diverses* and *Wechselseitiger Gleichklang* (*Mutual Harmony,* 1942; Centre Georges Pompidou, Paris) are anticipated by the "constructive" structures of, for example, *Entwicklung in Braun* (*Development in Brown,* 1933; Centre Georges Pompidou, Paris). As Serge Vonboult has pointed out, "Kandinsky's art can be defined, as a whole, as the synthesis of divided, conflicting forces." This conflict is shaped not only by archetypal, microcosmic forms and colors that convey "something of the spirit of the East," but also by the artificial colors and decorative forms of modern industry and the contemporary world.

Wassily Kandinsky

37 FINAL DESIGN FOR THE COVER OF THE BLUE RIDER ALMANAC (Endgültiger Entwurf für den Umschlag des Almanachs Der Blaue Reiter) 1911

Ink and watercolor, 11 x 8⅝" (27.9 x 21.9 cm)
Inscribed "K", in a triangle (lower right)
GMS 608

In 1911 Kandinsky and Marc, whose status in the *Neue Künstler-Vereinigung München* was growing increasingly precarious, conceived a plan to publish an almanac with the title *Der Blaue Reiter*. The publication, whose aim was to formulate the goals of a new art, featured contributions by painters, writers, and musicians from Germany and elsewhere. With its fourteen major articles and wealth of illustrations, the almanac endeavored, in a highly modern fashion, to break down the barriers between different periods and genres, in order to prove, as Kandinsky put it, that "the truly artistic is not a question of form, but of artistic content."

Kandinsky made, in quick succession, a total of eleven sketches for the cover illustration of the almanac, ten of which are in the collection of the Lenbachhaus. Almost all of them show a triumphant rider holding up a fluttering banner in his outstretched hands, symbolizing the victory of the spirit. For the final version, however, Kandinsky discarded the sketches and made a woodcut whose striking, eloquent symbolism neatly encapsulates the statement which the almanac intended to make. The rider in the final sketch, illustrated here, recalls the figure of St. George, the dragonkiller and conqueror of evil. Wearing a somewhat strange form of headdress and carrying a shield, the knight is mounted on a rampant horse. The dragon writhes on the ground beneath him; its scaly tail lashes upward, following the line of his back. On the right, in the foreground, one sees the diminutive figure of the captive princess turning to greet her liberator.

The form of the image is clearly influenced by the tradition of Bavarian painting on glass, whose naive, antinaturalistic style was an important source of inspiration to Kandinsky and his fellow members of the avant-garde. This influence is documented by a painting on glass by Kandinsky which is almost identical with the sketch for the cover illustration of the almanac and which is also in the collection of the Lenbachhaus. In the cover illustration itself, the figure of St. George, which appears in a number of Kandinsky's pictures from 1911/12 (see plates 24, 41), is drawn in a manner which largely conforms to traditional iconographical models; at the same time, however, the picture succeeds in conveying a universal meaning by dint of its original stylization and "spiritual" coloring. The figure of the Blue Rider becomes a symbol of a movement of spiritual renewal, struggling to purify the world and to rescue it from the dead forces of materialism. This message of salvation, proclaiming the dawning of a new spiritual epoch in which art and culture will play a major part, is one of the central themes of The Blue Rider almanac. The title Blue Rider became the name of the movement associated with Kandinsky and Marc when, at the end of 1911, the two artists organized the first exhibition of the group.

ALMA=
NACH
DER
BLAUE
REITER

R. PIPER & Cº MÜNCHEN VERLAG

Wassily Kandinsky

38   **WITH THREE RIDERS (Mit drei Reitern)**   1911

Ink and watercolor, 9⅞ x 12⅝" (25 x 32 cm)
Inscribed "K", in a triangle (lower right)
GMS 153

This famous watercolor once again uses the motif of the rider, which, after its adoption by Kandinsky, became one of the key symbols of modern art. The six bold lines of the galloping horses and their riders evoke a sense of concentrated movement and energy. Kandinsky draws the elongated lines of the horses' backs with smooth, powerful brushstrokes; the impression of speed is heightened by the bowed figures of the riders. The black ink lines are superimposed on the economically distributed colors, which, as in Kandinsky's major compositions, merely hint at specific forms and bodies: the three patches of

color – blue, red, and yellow – behind the three riders can be seen as an echo of their aura.

There are obvious parallels between *With Three Riders* and several other pictures by Kandinsky, including *Romantic Landscape* (plate 28), which was painted in the same year. Here again, three riders are depicted galloping from right to left. Kandinsky was especially intrigued by movement in this direction, which he saw as conveying a particular sense of intensity and dynamism, whereas movement from left to right, as he wrote in his book *Point and Line to Plane* (1926), induces a feeling of calmness or even tiredness. He included a woodcut based on *With Three Riders* in his poetry album *Sounds,* published in 1913. The watercolor has a fleeting charm of its own: rarely in Kandinsky's work does the line incorporate such a degree of autonomous psychological power, while at the same time fulfilling a representational function.

Wassily Kandinsky

39   LYRICAL (Lyrisches)   1911

Color woodcut on paper, 5¾ x 8½" (15.4 x 21.7 cm)
Inscribed "K", in a triangle (lower right)
GMS 303

Lyrical belongs to the same group of stylized and powerful "rider" pictures as *With Three Riders* (plate 38). Kandinsky also produced an oil painting with the same title, which is in the Boymans-van Beuningen Museum, Rotterdam. In both works the motif of the rider is sketched with brief, economical lines; the woodcut, however, is more powerful and compact than the painting. The contours of the horse and the rider bending low over its neck merge into an organic unity which vividly conveys the idea of swift forward motion. Whereas in the painting the colors in the vicinity of the finely drawn trees vaguely suggest the outlines of a landscape, the trees in the woodcut have vanished into the substratum of two-dimensional colored patches. A crucial feature of the woodcut is the white patch surrounding the rider, which lends his movement a sense of continuity.

The woodcut and painting illustrate yet again the extent to which Kandinsky regarded these two media as equally valid, mutually fructifying genres which facilitated his experiments in the reduction of form. In some instances, the woodcut, with its innate tendency toward stylistic exaggeration, precedes the painting.

Wassily Kandinsky

40   WITH SUN (Mit Sonne) 1911

Painting on glass, 12 x 15⅞" (30.6 x 40.3 cm)
Frame painted by the artist
GMS 120

With Sun is the model for *Improvisation 21a* (plate 28) and the later picture *Kleine Freuden (Simple Pleasures;* Solomon R. Guggenheim Museum, New York). It employs the same set of motifs, but uses the stylized, almost naive language of painting on glass. In the center of the picture one sees a group of overlapping hills, two of which are crowned by the silhouettes of a Russian city; on the left, three brightly colored riders are galloping up the hills. A menacing black cloud hangs over the right-hand section; beneath it, a purple boat with three occupants is tossing in the dark waves of a lake; in the foreground, two semiorganic forms project into the picture. The glowing colors of the figures – red, blue, and yellow – are muted by the grubby whitish tones of the hills and the landscape.

The attempts to interpret these images in terms of an apocalyptic vision have already been mentioned in connection with *Improvisation 21a.* Angelica Zander Rudenstine writes: "Ringbom too places the work in the context of Kandinsky's notion of the Apocalypse, announcing a new spiritual era. Although he does not discuss the imagery of the painting as a whole, he sees the ubiquitous hill with the 'onion dome towers' – also used on the cover of *Concerning the Spiritual in Art* – as a direct reflection of that passage in the book where 'a large city, solidly built according to the rules of architecture and mathematics, [is] suddenly shaken by an immense force,' the towers crumble and fall, the sun glows dark, and one searches in vain for the power with which to battle the darkness. . . . This central image of the collapsing or threatened city is, Ringbom argues, a metaphor for a shattered material world on the eve of spiritual regeneration."

However, Kandinsky's later comments on the picture *Simple Pleasures* have a quite different, ironic tenor; they are guided by the aura of the various pictorial elements, which are evidently divorced from the object, in terms of both form and ideas, and loosely distributed through the work.

Wassily Kandinsky

41   **ST. GEORGE I (Heiliger Georg I)**   1911

Painting on glass, 7½ x 7⅝" (19 x 19.5 cm)
Frame painted by the artist
GMS 105

St. George I is one of Kandinsky's best known paintings on glass. Influenced by the style of folk art, the figure of the saintly knight is an early version of the more abstract figure which was to become the herald of the Blue Rider. The brightly glowing painting is dominated by the diagonally slanting forms of the horse and rider. The saint bends down from his shying horse to thrust his massive lance into the dragon's body on the ground. Behind the horse, which is colored in a deep, "spiritual" shade of blue with gold flecks that echo the color of the knight's armor, one sees a dark red sky and the round form of a tree, which often appears in Kandinsky's pictures in connection with the rider motif. The picture is a drama of struggle and victory in a confined space.

Through his choice of colors for the picture and the frame Kandinsky further emphasizes the innate antinaturalism of Bavarian folk art, whose "primitive" character – its simplicity and directness, its boldly contrasting colors, and its genuine emotional fervor – was a continuing source of inspiration to Kandinsky and several of his contemporaries. During the summer that they spent in Murnau in 1908 he and Münter had discovered the charms of Bavarian folk art and, in particular, of its paintings on glass, a technique which they copied and adapted for their own purposes. Kandinsky, Marc, and Münter attributed an almost magical power to these folk-art pictures, a dozen of which were included among the illustrations reproduced in The Blue Rider almanac.

With the figure of St. George, a saint particularly revered in Bavaria, Kandinsky added a new dimension of meaning to the figure of the rider, which plays such a central part in his œuvre. The personal metaphor of the rider, which evokes a sense of the quest for a new art and a new spiritual awakening, acquires a religious connotation: St. George symbolizes the victory of good over evil. Kandinsky's particular interest in this theme is documented by three oil paintings of St. George (see plates 24, 37), in addition to which he made two further paintings on glass and a number of watercolors and woodcuts.

Wassily Kandinsky

42 ALL SAINTS I (Allerheiligen I) 1911

Painting on glass, 13⅜ x 16" (34.5 x 40.5 cm)
Frame painted by the artist
GMS 107

The painting on glass *All Saints I,* which formed the basis of the paintings *All Saints I* and *All Saints II* (plates 21, 22), features a wide variety of religious motifs that played a prominent part in Kandinsky's pre-1914 pictures. These motifs were drawn partly from Bavarian and Russian folk art and partly from early German Bible illustrations, whose naive expressive power was a source of inspiration to Kandinsky. Using simple forms and bright colors, and ignoring questions of proportion or logical connection, the artist assembles the figures under the yellow trumpet of the giant angel. The figures include St. George, with shield and lance, mounted on a white horse; St. Vladimir; a female saint bearing a lighted candle; and two saints piously embracing each other, whose identity is uncertain: it is possible that they are meant to represent either

St. Boris and St. Gleb, the first two martyrs of the Russian Orthodox Church, or St. Cosmas and St. Damian, two saints who are particularly revered in Bavaria. To their right, three mourners stand over the flat, curving figure of a dead monk, at whose feet a haloed figure sits in the foreground. The group is overshadowed by an opposition between light and dark, salvation and damnation, which is clearly expressed by the contrast between the two halves of the picture. Whereas the Russian city on the hill in the top left-hand corner is lit up by the rays of the red sun, the upper right-hand section of the picture is dominated by the black moon and the darkness against which the figure of Christ on the cross stands out like a beacon.

This opposition between light and dark, which also plays an important part in such pictures as *Improvisation 21a, Improvisation Deluge,* and *With Sun* (plates 28, 30, 40), implies the idea of a possible salvation. In *All Saints I* the dove fluttering above Noah's Ark, the butterfly, and the phoenix symbolize the hope that the drama of the Apocalypse will be followed by an era of salvation and renewal.

Franz Marc

b. 1880 in Munich – d. 1916 at Verdun

Marc originally intended to study theology, but changed his mind and turned to painting. Until 1903 he attended the Munich Academy; in the course of the following years he made several trips to Paris, where he came into contact with all the latest developments in modern art. It was only in 1909, however, that these influences began to make themselves felt in his work. In 1910 he met and befriended Macke, who taught him the importance of pure color and helped him to find his own personal style. He also made the acquaintance of Kandinsky, who became his closest artistic collaborator. Marc and Kandinsky were the joint editors of the The Blue Rider almanac, which featured contributions from a wide range of artists and reproductions of works from different periods and genres: the aim of the publication was to show that each work of art had its own expressive core, its own distinct "inner sound." Between 1911 and 1914 Marc concentrated almost exclusively on the depiction of animals: he saw them as embodying a particular quality of innocence which corresponded to his own quasi-religious striving for spiritual purity. His artistic approach was considerably influenced by the rhythmic compositional techniques of Futurism and by the "Orphic" Cubism of Robert Delaunay, whom he visited with Macke in 1912. In 1914 he began experimenting with abstraction. He was killed in action in World War I.

Franz Marc

43 GRAZING HORSES I (Weidende Pferde I) 1910

Oil on canvas, 25¼ x 37" (64 x 94 cm)
G 12 576

1910 marks a decisive turning point in the work of Franz Marc.
One aspect of it is that the representation of animals, especially
of horses, becomes increasingly the focus of his art. After his
studies at the Munich Academy from 1900 to 1903, Marc had
striven for years to find his personal form of expression and had
repeatedly come up against the limits of naturalistic painting. On
a trip to Paris in 1903 he had been so impressed by the œuvre
of Van Gogh that he did not want to return to the Academy.
From then on he became self-taught, usually working outdoors.
Studies mainly of horses in the landscape, and in this early period
of human beings, especially female nudes, provided the pictorial
forms that served Marc as a means to penetrate into the essence
of appearances. It was a high theoretical goal, which he himself
did not feel he had met in these years of searching.

In this process of artistic development, the motif of *Grazing
Horses* in a landscape, worked like a catalyst to help him reach
his actual objective. For three years Marc struggled with this
motif in a series of large pictures, culminating in the famous
Grazing Horses IV (*The Red Horses*, Busch-Reisinger Museum,
Cambridge) of 1911. At the beginning of the series is *Large
Horses Lenggries I* (whereabouts unknown) of 1908. He arranged
the horses on the canvas in a naturalistic manner, almost life-
sized but remarkably crowded and cut off. For the next two
years, in Sindelsdorf by then, he continued working on this
composition. He even had a shed built in the horses' pasture in
order to store his oversized canvases. Some of these, however,
were destroyed by the artist or cut up into separate sections.
Even these *Grazing Horses I*, the animals' bodies still naturalistic,
reveal the thorough study of nature that went into them. Yet
they also demonstrate Marc's attempts to create a rhythmic order
and compositional unity. A new integration into the surroundings shows especially in the way the horse in the background
turns towards the landscape. A further development was
Grazing Horses III (private collection), also dated 1910, which
is very similar but more compact and with a more colorfully
subdivided landscape. Finally, by relating the rhythms of the
animals to the forms of the landscape, Marc attained a reduction
of forms and a completely new, non-naturalistic palette that led
to his famous masterpieces, such as the *Red Horses* mentioned
above or the *Blue Horse I* of 1911 (see plate 45).

Moreover, the depiction of the human being as a part of the
metaphysically interpreted natural world becomes increasingly
rare in Marc's work from 1910 on. Only the animal in its innocence and purity seems worthy of representing the spiritual
principle behind physical appearances – an objective that
made Marc, next to Kandinsky, a major representative of the
Blue Rider.

Franz Marc
44 DEER IN THE SNOW (Rehe im Schnee) 1911

Oil on canvas, 33⅜ x 33¼" (84.7 x 84.5 cm)
Presented in 1971 by Elly Koehler to Hans Konrad Roethel in recognition of
his services to the Blue Rider
G 14 641

Deer in the Snow is one of the first works in which Marc
succeeded in freeing himself from the Naturalism of his early
animal pictures and in jettisoning realist conventions in the
depiction of nature. Whereas *Rehe in der Dämmerung* (*Deer at
Dusk*), painted two years previously, uses late Impressionist
techniques of individual characterization, the delicate brown
arabesques of the two animals in *Deer in the Snow* are inscribed
in the closed, abstract world of a winter landscape. The lines of
their bodies, the curving back of the deer on the left, and the
arched neck of its companion on the right are echoed by the
deep blue and green shadows in the pyramid of snow behind
them. In this picture and others like it, the objects are transformed into pure, semiabstract blocks of color. Writing to
Macke, Marc described a similar procedure in a picture which he
painted of his dog Russi: "As the color grew purer, the outlines
of the dog gradually disappeared, until a pure relationship of
color finally established itself between the yellow, the cold
white, and the blue of the snow."

   Deer in the Snow is the first picture in which Marc manages
to bring together the rhythms of animals and landscape in a
coherent composition based on a set of carefully interwoven
formal relationships, thereby evoking the sense of a specific,
harmonious order within nature. Here, we find Marc moving
toward a conception of painting centered on expression rather
than representation. On February 22, 1911, at about the time
he was working on *Deer in the Snow*, Marc wrote to his fiancée
Maria: "I am working very hard and striving for form and
expression. There are no 'objects' and no 'colors' in art, only expression . . . . That, in the final analysis, is what really counts. I
already knew that, but in my work I was always distracted by
other things, such as 'probabilities', the melodious sound of the
colors, so-called harmony, etc. . . . But we should seek nothing
but expression in pictures. The picture is a cosmos governed
by a different set of laws from those of nature." There is, it must
be admitted, something of a contradiction between this last
statement and Marc's conviction that the "animalized" forms of
his art would enable him to capture "the symbolism, the pathos,
and the mystery of nature."

Franz Marc

45   BLUE HORSE I (Blaues Pferd I)   1911

Oil on canvas, 44 x 33¼ (112 x 84.5 cm)
Bernhard Koehler Donation, 1965
G 13 324

Blue Horse I, one of Marc's best known pictures, has an exceptional symbolic power. The blue foal, its limbs still gangling and awkward, stands with its head cocked slightly to one side, as if lost in thought. Its angular body is tinged with white, but its mane and hooves are deep navy blue. The proliferation of contrasts between complementary colors – from vermilion and green at the bottom of the picture, via carmine and yellow, to violet, blue, and orange at the top – illustrates with rare clarity the color theory which underlies much of Marc's mature work. In a famous letter to Macke, written in December 1910, Marc explained: *"Blue* is the *male* principle, austere and spiritual. *Yellow* is the female principle, gentle, bright, and sensual. *Red* is *matter,* brutal and heavy, the color which the other two have to fight against and overcome! For example, if you mix the serious, spiritual blue with red, you intensify the blue to the color of an unbearable sadness, and the conciliatory yellow, which is complementary to violet, becomes *indispensable.* (The woman as comforter, not as lover!) If you mix red and yellow to make orange, you give the passive, feminine yellow a 'shrewish' sensual power, so that the cool, spiritual blue becomes indispensable – the blue of the man, which immediately and automatically aligns itself with orange: the two colors love each other. Blue and orange, a thoroughly festive sound. If you then mix blue and yellow to make green, you bring red, matter, the 'earth', to life, but as a painter I always sense a difference here: with green you can never quite suppress the eternal brute materiality of red. . . . Blue (the sky) and yellow (the sun) have to come to the aid of green in order to *silence matter."* Thus Marc sets out his theory of the symbolic significance of blue as the "spiritual" color *par excellence.*

In *Blue Horse I* he finally abandons "natural" colors in favor of what Klaus Lankheit has termed "essential color." The horse, a traditional symbol of nobility, acquires an additional connotation: it symbolizes the same spiritual striving as the rider in Kandinsky's cover illustration for The Blue Rider almanac. Its particular expressive pathos derives not only from its "spiritual" color, but also from its form. The pensively lowered head conveys the impression of a sentient being, with human thoughts and feelings. Johannes Langner has convincingly shown that Marc modeled many of his animal pictures on traditional images – for example, that of the lone, contemplative individual in the pictures of Caspar David Friedrich – thereby endowing the animals with a human aspect. The sense of a spiritual presence evoked by *Blue Horse I* finds its most complex and formally convincing expression in *Turm der Blauen Pferde* (*Tower of the Blue Horses*), a picture of four horses whose fragmented bodies form a cathedral of the spirit. Unfortunately, this work, which is Marc's most famous painting, was lost during World War II.

Franz Marc

46 DEER IN THE FOREST II (Reh im Wald II) 1912

Oil on canvas, 43¼ x 31⅞ (110 x 81 cm)
Inscribed "Marc" (lower right)
Bernhard Koehler Donation, 1965
G 13 321

In April 1910 Marc had moved to Sindelsdorf in southern
Bavaria, where he was to devote himself almost exclusively to
the painting of animals. The first version of *Deer in the Forest*
was painted in the summer of the following year, after Marc had
returned from his honeymoon in London via Bonn, where he
visited Macke. *Deer in the Forest I* was included in the first Blue
Rider exhibition in December 1911. In 1912 Marc painted this
second version, in which the individual forms are more clearly
delineated and the black trunk of a tree falls diagonally across
the picture. A sleeping deer, its head tucked into the curve of its
body, lies in a hollow on the floor of a fairy-tale forest, whose
colors have a dull nocturnal glow. Enclosed in the interlinking
colored surfaces of the incline which rises up behind it, the
deer appears at once protected and vulnerable. The top section
of the picture is dominated by the deep blue of the night sky,
interrupted by the white twigs hanging down in the foreground. The black diagonals of the tree trunk and the branch
on the right are inclined toward the sleeping animal. This has
been interpreted by Frederick S. Lewine, who studied the
covert apocalyptic symbolism of Marc's pictures, as signifying
an implicit threat.

Formally, the picture owes something to Cubism, which
helped Marc to integrate the animal into its surroundings: the
forest is seen, as it were, through the eyes of the deer itself.
Marc himself commented on this shift of perspective in dealing
with nature, the aim of which was to attain an experience of
a previously unknown form of transcendence: "What can be
more mysterious to the artist than the idea of how nature is
mirrored in the eyes of an animal? How does a horse see the
world, or an eagle, a deer, a dog? How impoverished and
soulless our convention is of placing animals in a landscape
which belongs to our eyes, instead of empathizing with the
soul of the animal in order to understand its view of the
world." The gentle figure of the yellow deer in the rhythmic
forms of the nocturnal forest does indeed convey a certain
sense of how the world must appear when seen from the
perspective of an animal.

Franz Marc

47 **RED AND BLUE HORSE**
(Rotes und blaues Pferd) 1912

Tempera on paper, 10⅜ x 13½ (26.3 x 34.3 cm)
Inscribed "Fz. Marc" (lower left)
GMS 706

In the curse of 1912 Marc increasingly used splintered, crystalline forms which remove the animals in his pictures from their
natural surroundings and transpose them onto a higher plane
of being. The landscape in *Red and Blue Horse* has a petrified
appearance, with yawning gaps that suggest an infinite abyss.
The lowered heads of the horses and the confrontation between
the "material" red and the "spiritual" blue convey an impression of both resignation and contemplation. Klaus Lankheit
has emphasized that the forms of the animals in Marc's pictures
are the product, not of an abstract stylization, but rather of an
attempt to grasp the essence of the species – in this case, of the
horse. The modernization of artistic form results from Marc's
aim of "animalizing" art. In his first published essay, a contribution to a book published by Reinhard Piper with the title *Das
Tier in der Kunst* (*The Animal in Art*), Marc explained his
ambitious artistic program: "My concern is not with animal
painting as such. I am looking for a good, pure, and clear style
which can fully accommodate at least a part of what we
modern painters have to say. I seek to strengthen my feeling
for the organic *rhythm* of things in general, to identify pantheis-
tically with the trembling and the flow of blood in nature, in
the trees, in animals, in the air – to make that into a picture
with new movements and with colors that pour scorn on our
old easel painting. . . . I can think of no better means than the
animal picture for achieving what I would call the *'animaliza-
tion'* of art. That is why I have taken to painting animals. In
the pictures of a Van Gogh or a Signac everything is animal,
the air, even the rowing boat which floats on the water, and
especially painting itself. These works bear no resemblance
whatever to what used to be called 'pictures.' "

Franz Marc

48 THE TIGER (Der Tiger) 1912

Oil on canvas, 43¾ x 39¾" (111 x 101 cm)
Inscribed "Fz. Marc/12" (reverse)
Bernhard Koehler Donation, 1965
G 13 320

The Tiger is one of Marc's finest works from the period before
the end of 1912, when his style began to evolve in a new
direction, influenced by the *simultanéisme* of Robert Delaunay
and evincing more abstract, interwoven forms and rhythmically arranged blocks of color. The almost square picture is
dominated by the powerful, angular form of the tiger, with
his beautifully formed head. The yellow of his body merges
with the transparent, Cubist forms of his surroundings: Marc
deliberately obscures the distinction between organic and inorganic matter. Despite the semiabstract style of the picture, the
essential nature of the animal – its temporarily suppressed,
explosive energy, its power and litheness – is captured with
exceptional precision in a tightly organized network of formal
relationships. *The Tiger* is the fruit of Marc's attempts over
several years to synthesize the typical attitudes and movements
of animals, to grasp the secret of their essential form. The details of this mature work are anticipated in the small bronze
sculpture of a panther, also in the Lenbachhaus, which Marc
made in 1908 and which, despite the artist's lack of experience
in this medium, demonstrates an astonishing formal virtuosity.
Hence the formal vocabulary of Cubism, which Marc had
encountered in the works by Picasso and Braque shown in the
second exhibition of the *Neue Künstler-Vereinigung München*
and in the 1912 *Sonderbund* exhibition in Cologne, is used only
as an additional expressive element in the painting of a figure
that Marc had already conceived some years previously: his reception of Cubism is an expressive reworking of its techniques. In
his famous essay "Die Wilden Deutschlands" ("The Fauves of
Germany"), published in The Blue Rider almanac, Marc correspondingly emphasized the priority of "spiritual" values over
mere formal innovation in art: "The most beautiful prismatic
colors and the famous school of Cubism have ceased to hold a
meaning for these 'wild' painters. Their thinking has a different
goal: to create symbols for our time which belong on the altars
of the spiritual religion of the future and whose technical creator
vanishes into anonymity."

Franz Marc

49 COWS, YELLOW-RED-GREEN
(Kühe, gelb-rot-grün) 1912

Oil on canvas, 24⅜ x 34½" (62 x 87.5 cm)
Inscribed "Marc" (lower right), "Sindelsdorf Marc" (on the stretcher)
Donated by Gabriele Münter, 1961
G 13 140

There are two previous versions of this picture. One of them, *Die Gelbe Kuh* (*The Yellow Cow;* Solomon R. Guggenheim Museum, New York), was received with a mixture of disapproval and incomprehension by Marc's former colleagues from the *Neue Künstler-Vereinigung München* when it was shown in the first Blue Rider exhibition in December 1911. Alexander Kanoldt, for example, deemed it "an altogether deplorable work." However, the bizarre image of a leaping cow was greeted with enthusiasm by an avant-garde minority of Expressionist artists and, in particular, poets, such as Theodor Däubler, who spoke of the "drop of sunshine in the soul of the cow," and Walter Mehring, who praised the "bellowing cow-yellow." It would be hard to find a more apt commentary on the picture than Kandinsky's remarks on the color yellow in *Concerning the Spiritual in Art,* published at the time of the first Blue Rider exhibition. According to Kandinsky, yellow, orange, and red generate "ideas of joy;" yellow is "the typical earthly color," which "affects us like the sound of a trumpet being played louder and louder"; it is "eccentric . . . leaping over its boundaries and dissipating its strength upon its surroundings." Däubler poetically describes the consequences of this choice of color for the rest of the picture: "The cow sees the world in blue."

Color symbolism also plays a constitutive part in the later *Cows, Yellow-Red-Green.* Here, the yellow cow is joined by a red calf and a green bull, and the landscape replaced by nocturnal darkness, with vague lines of orange, blue, and carmine in the foreground. As in so many of Marc's animal pictures, the formal structure of the work follows the rhythm of the creatures' stylized bodies. Marc concluded his letter of February 22, 1911, to his fiancée (see plate 44) with the following remark: "Nature is lawless because it is infinite, an infinite coexistence and sequence. Our spirit gives itself strict, rigid laws which enable it to depict the infinity of nature." In the irrational picture of a leaping yellow cow Marc once again breaks with the traditional conventions of animal painting.

Franz Marc

50 THE MONKEY (Das Äffchen) 1912

Oil on canvas, 27¾ x 37⅜" (70.4 x 100 cm)
Inscribed "Marc" (lower left), "Marc Sindelsdorf" (reverse)
Bernhard Koehler Donation, 1965
G 14 664

The Monkey offers a further demonstration of the remarkable
speed with which Marc progressed from the subdued Naturalism
of his studies of deer and horses, which he was still painting in
1910, to the experimental style of this and similar pictures. In
his later pictures, as in his earlier work, he took his motifs from
nature but enriched them through his own imagination. In the
center of the picture a small gray monkey with a long curling
tail is depicted in profile perching on the diagonal branch of a
tree. Behind him, the jagged forms of jungle vegetation form a
kaleidoscope of coruscating colors. In contrast to *Mandrill*
(Staatsgalerie moderner Kunst, Munich), painted the following
year, the monkey stands out from its surroundings, in a manner
reminiscent of the earlier *Affenfries* (*Ape Frieze,* 1911; Kunsthalle,
Hamburg). Its softly rounded head and its expression of shy
vigilance lend it an almost human appearance. The flowers
amidst the dark green vegetation constitute one of those references to the work of Paul Gauguin that occasionally occur in
Marc's pictures; here, they have the effect of precious, exotic
mannerisms.

Adolf Behne, one of the few critics who unreservedly praised
Marc's 1913 one-man exhibition at the Galerie Der Sturm in
Berlin, wrote: "Marc's pictures are deeply and intimately
rooted in nature. Indeed, I must confess that I would be hard
put to name another contemporary painter with such an ability
to move us and to lead us into the innermost depths of nature.
The innermost depths – that is precisely the point! The outward appearance, the outward form, the outward correctness
of nature – they mean nothing to him. What concerns him is
the hidden presentiment, the inner life, the soul, the pulse of
nature! In terms of the intensity of feeling which his magnificent pictures evoke, Franz Marc is a worker of miracles!"
However, statements of this kind, which echo the words of
Marc himself, should not lead us to overlook the anthropo-
morphism of Marc's pictures, the tendency to confer human
features on animals, which stems from a deeply felt desire
for harmony and from a nostalgic urge to escape from the
materialism of the modern world.

Franz Marc

51 DEER IN A MONASTERY GARDEN
(Reh im Klostergarten) 1912

Oil on canvas, 29¾ x 39¾" (75.7 x 101 cm)
Inscribed "Marc" (lower right), "Marc Sindelsdorf" (reverse)
Bernhard Koehler Donation, 1965
G 13 323

It is possible that Marc hit on the motif for *Deer in a Monastery Garden* while taking an evening stroll in the garden of the monastery at Benediktbeuren, where he might suddenly have glimpsed the outlines of a deer in the moonlight. Compared with the artist's other pictures from 1912, its style is exceptionally advanced. To an even greater extent than in *The Tiger* (plate 48), the individual elements of the picture are broken up into narrow, opposing facets and reassembled to create a new reality. The rudimentary forms of nature play a mysterious role in generating the bundles and grids of intersecting lines, semicircles, and triangles which structure the composition. The deer in the center of the picture, enclosed in one of the abstract angular forms and yet retaining its physical integrity, stands with its raised head pointing toward the dull sphere of the moon, which, bounded by subdued orange and blue tones, is the calmest element in the agitated nocturnal landscape.

Unlike Kandinsky, Marc was receptive to parallel movements in modern art. Thus, *Deer in a Monastery Garden* is clearly influenced by the Futurist pictures which Marc first saw in the catalogue of the 1912 exhibition at the Galerie Der Sturm in Berlin. He takes up the techniques used by the Futurists to convey a sense of dynamic movement and adapts them to his own purposes. A further, possibly more important influence on his mature work of 1913 and 1914 was his encounter with the art of Robert Delaunay. In a letter to Kandinsky from Bonn, Marc gave an enthusiastic account of Delaunay's series of "window" pictures: "He [Delaunay] is working toward truly constructive pictures, eliminating representation altogether: pure fugues of sound, one might say." Even if Klaus Lankheit is correct in his contention that *Deer in a Monastery Garden* was painted before Marc and Macke visited Delaunay in Paris in October 1912, it is certain that Marc was already familiar with a number of Delaunay's pictures, including a painting of the Eiffel Tower which had been shown in the first Blue Rider exhibition and a work from the *La ville* series which had been reproduced, alongside an essay on the artist, in The Blue Rider almanac. However, whereas in Delaunay's transparent prisms, the formal energy, intervals, and contrasts of color constitute the actual subject of a painting, Marc uses these formal effects to mirror the inner being of nature: his stated aim of "seeing the world through the eyes of the animal" is no more than a paraphrase for an artistic viewpoint whose aim is to attain an experience of transcendence.

In *Deer in a Monastery Garden* the light comes not only from the moon, but also from a number of other, concealed sources. In this, Frederick S. Lewine detects a new sense of hidden menace, and indeed, the works that Marc painted in the last two years before the outbreak of World War I do evince an atmosphere of impending doom.

Franz Marc

52 IN THE RAIN (Im Regen) 1912

Oil on canvas, 31 $\frac{7}{8}$ x 41 $\frac{1}{2}$" (81 x 105.5 cm)
Inscribed "F. M." (top right)
Bernhard Koehler Donation, 1965
G 13 322

In terms of both form and content *In the Rain* stands out from the rest of Marc's mature work. Through the diagonal grid of falling raindrops one sees the broken outlines of a human couple, dressed in the style of the period, with a large white dog running ahead of them. From 1910 onward, Marc had devoted himself almost entirely to painting animals; in this work, however, he depicts himself and his wife Maria, caught in a heavy rainstorm with their dog Russi. The picture, which powerfully conveys the experience of battling against the elements, betrays particularly strong Futurist influence. The clearly recognizable clothes and faces of the couple strike an unusually "modern" note. Marc's first exposure to Futurist painting was through the catalogue of an exhibition at Herwarth Walden's Galerie Der Sturm in Berlin; he later saw the pictures themselves at the Gereons-Club in Cologne, where he helped Macke to hang them, and at the Thannhauser gallery in Munich in November 1912. After seeing the reproductions in the Berlin catalogue, he wrote to Kandinsky: "I cannot get over the strange conflict between my estimation of their ideas, most of which I find brilliant and *fruitful,* and my view of their pictures, which strike me as, without a doubt, utterly mediocre." Yet when he had seen the originals, he also waxed enthusiastic about the formal qualities of the pictures. When they were shown in Munich, he wrote to Macke: "The effect is magnificent, far, far more impressive than in Cologne." Though his animal pictures, painted in the rural isolation of Sindelsdorf in southern Bavaria, may seem highly idiosyncratic, even quirky, Marc was in fact very receptive to the latest developments in modern art, as his essays in The Blue Rider almanac clearly demonstrate. He also possessed considerable organizational skills, helping to arrange the Blue Rider exhibitions, the Sonderbund exhibition in Cologne, and the Erster Deutscher Herbstsalon (First German Salon d'Automne) in Berlin in 1913. In addition, he was a member of the Sonderbund and the Berlin Secession. Such were the contradictions of Marc's artistic personality, which expressed themselves in the conflict between modern forms and Romantic ideas that runs through his entire work.

Franz Marc

53 **THE BIRDS (Die Vögel)** 1914

Oil on canvas, 42 7/8 x 39 3/8" (109 x 100 cm)
Inscribed "M" (lower right)
G 17 489

The Birds is one of the most important pictures which Marc painted in the period immediately before the outbreak of World War I. The brightly colored, angular forms of the picture evoke the fluttering, whirring movement of the three birds and, at the same time, convey a magical sense of stillness and calm, suggesting the presence of a larger bird slowly spreading its wings. Both forms and colors testify to Marc's interest in Futurism and the art of Robert Delaunay.

In the pictures which he painted toward the end of his career, Marc increasingly tended to use abstract forms. This was a logical consequence of the striving for artistic purity which had led him to concentrate exclusively on animals, the incarnation of natural innocence. Eventually, however, he came to see even animals as unsuitable subjects for a genuinely "pure" art. He explained this shift of attitude in a wartime letter, written from the Western Front to his wife in 1915: "Very early on I saw human beings as 'ugly'; animals seemed to me purer, more beautiful, but even in them I found so much that was ugly and contrary to feeling that, following an inner compulsion, my pictures instinctively grew more schematic and abstract, until I suddenly became aware of the ugliness, the *impurity* of nature. Perhaps our European eyes have poisoned and distorted the world; that is why I dream of a new Europe." Marc's last pictures are indeed entirely abstract; in *The Birds,* he makes a final attempt to reconcile animal forms with the urge for purity. As the reception subsequently accorded his work shows, his mature pictures have a specifically modern formal quality which has outlasted their content. Marc himself implicitly recognized this in his essay "Zur Kritik der Vergangenheit" ("Notes for a Critique of the Past"). "How is it possible," he asked, "that people who do not seem to be surprised by Dürer's arabesques or the folds of a Gothic garment are enraged by the triangles, disks, and tubular forms of our pictures? Surely they must be full of wires and tensions, of the wonderful effects of modern light, of the spirit of chemical analysis which decomposes energy and reassembles it in its own way. All this is the outer sensuous form of our pictures."

Franz Marc

54   **FOUR FOXES (Vier Füchse)**   1913

Watercolor on paper, 5½ x 3½" (14 x 9 cm)
Postcard to Kandinsky, February 4, 1913
GMS 746

Among the manuscript sources relating to the work of Marc is his extensive correspondence with a wide variety of artists, writers, collectors, and art dealers, among them, Macke, Kandinsky, Münter, Klee, Alfred Kubin, Robert Delaunay, Lyonel Feininger, Else Lasker-Schüler, Bernhard Koehler, and Reinhard Piper (archive of the Germanisches Nationalmuseum, Nürnberg). While the letters he wrote to these and other individuals are invaluable historical documents, the postcards which he began to send to his friends in 1912 contain in miniature the very essence of his art. The majority of the cards date from 1913,

Marc sometimes sending as many as two or three in a single day. With their singular poetic charm, these small pictures are veritable jewels of early modern art. The illustrations on the cards, apart from those sent to Lasker-Schüler, often bear no relation to the text, which is generally concerned with practical matters. The text on the reverse of *Four Foxes* reads as follows: "Dear Kandinsky, Your book is wonderful, the text in particular is closer to me than I had felt it to be when I heard it read aloud; I am absolutely thrilled. Once again, many thanks for the book and the watercolor, and kindest regards in the [here Marc drew a square, a circle, and a cross]. F. Marc." The book which Marc mentions may well be Kandinsky's poetry album *Klänge (Sounds)*. The front of the card shows for young foxes sitting at the entrance to their lair; the mixture of shyness and playfulness with which they sniff the air and inspect their surroundings is depicted with characteristic economy.

Franz Marc

55 **VERMILION GREETING (Zinnobergruss)** 1913

Tempera on paper, 5½ x 3½" (14 x 9 cm)
Postcard to Kandinsky, April 9, 1913
GMS 726

On the front of this postcard two red and blue animals can be seen grazing in the midst of a landscape whose colors – yellow and dark orange – are almost garish. In the dark sky above their heads the following message to Kandinsky is painted in vermilion letters: "Dear K., Hartley is coming on Monday; I have arranged to meet him at the Goltz Gallery, where he has some pictures. Why don't the two of you come along as well: maybe we can all go and eat somewhere. We are traveling back on Wednesday evening. Vermilion greeting. F. Marc." With the single word *Zinnobergruss* (vermilion greeting), which contains a multiplicity of sensual and mental associations, Marc establishes a relationship between the text and the magical world of the animals below, one of which is colored in the same brownish red as the salutation. The "vermilion greeting" testifies to the closeness of the relationship between Marc and Kandinsky, each of whom trusted the other to understand his work intuitively.

Franz Marc

56   LANDSCAPE WITH RED ANIMAL
(Landschaft mit rotem Tier) 1913

Tempera on paper, 3½ x 5½" (9 x 14 cm)
Postcard to Alfred Kubin, March 18, 1913
Kub. No. 1

This charming miniature landscape was sent to the artist Alfred Kubin, who regularly corresponded with Marc and numerous other artistic and literary figures. There is a singular lack of documentary material relating to Kubin's membership of the Blue Rider circle, although he is known to have enjoyed close contacts with Marc, and with Klee, Kandinsky, and Münter until well into the 1920s: he and the other members of the circle frequently exchanged pictures and opinions. Together with Marc and Münter, Kubin had been one of the first artists to side with Kandinsky at the time of the controversy which led to the founding of the Blue Rider, when the Russian painter's *Composition V* was rejected by the *Neue Künstler-Vereinigung München* in 1911.

The text of the card reads as follows: "Dear Mr. Kubin, I am extremely pleased that you are joining in. Kokoschka's acceptance is still outstanding. How right you are about him. It is all to the good if some of the people involved have 'tough' views – Kandinsky and I are somewhat pathologically inclined.

We can talk about the further details when we meet. Of course, there's no question of rushing anybody. Kind regards, F. Marc." The message refers to the illustrated edition of the Bible which Marc planned to publish. The previous week he had written to Kubin to ask him whether he would be interested in participating in the project: "How would you like to illustrate the Bible, a large-format edition in separate volumes? Kandinsky is doing the Apocalypse, I am going to do Genesis." The other contributors were to be Erich Heckel, Klee, who chose to illustrate the Psalms, and Oskar Kokoschka, who opted for the Book of Job. Kubin took on the Book of Daniel and, in fact, was the only one of the six artists to produce a finished set of illustrations, in the spring of 1914. These pictures were published as a separate volume in 1918.

In the last two years of his artistic career Marc turned to the subject of the Creation, which forms the theme of a number of his later woodcuts and drawings. In his *Skizzenbuch aus dem Felde* (*Sketchbook from the Field*) he noted several "inspirations" for the Bible illustrations. *Landscape with Red Animal* hints at the magic of this new beginning. In the background, standing out against the "spiritual" blue of the sky, a solitary red deer grazes on the brow of a hill. The foreground is dominated by three black trees whose stylized trunks are twisted and bent. The depiction of the surrounding countryside, reminds one of a miniature in a medieval manuscript.

Franz Marc

57 **ALTAR LAMB FROM LANA**
(Altarschaf aus Lana)   1913

Watercolor, ink, 3½ x 5½" (9 x 14 cm)
Postcard to Gabriele Münter, 12.4.1913
GMS 741

The motif on this postcard is another that was inspired by Franz Marc's trip to South Tyrol in April 1913 (see plate 59), in this case by medieval art in the church of the small town of Lana. Some years earlier, in the spring of 1908, Kandinsky and Münter had also stayed there. Marc expressly refers to the fact in the first sentence of his postcard, which is written in the intimate language of artist friends and addressed to Gabriele Münter: "Dear friends, this is an altar lamb from Lanna [sic]." Above the text written along the bottom edge of the picture lies a ruby red lamb, stretched out and lost in thought on a slightly undulating,

deep blue strip of landscape. The ground's structure and color suggest it should be interpreted as a 'landscape of the world.' The sacred atmosphere is further underscored by the broad yellow rays forming a mandorla-like backdrop behind the animal, against a semicircle of black ink. Its poetic spell makes Marc's *Altar Lamb from Lana* less a traditional Christian symbol of the Lamb of God, than an icon of innocent animal existence. Writing about Marc's postcards, Klaus Lankheit quotes a text by Georg Schmidt of 1954 and refers to the memorable situation "that the much disapproved century of technology and rational mastery of life was actually what brought forth an artistic idiom that is extraordinarily poetic in essence." The poetic element in the art of Marc, as well as of Klee and Chagall, "is, however, not to be sought in the subject matter – that is indeed as poetic as can be – but, much more originally and lastingly, in the form and color, that is, in the particular structure of the artistic idiom in which Franz Marc speaks of these poetic subjects."

Franz Marc

58 TWO BLUE HORSES IN FRONT OF A RED ROCK
(Zwei blaue Pferde vor rotem Felsen) 1913

Tempera on paper, varnished, 5½ x 3½" (14 x 9 cm)
Postcard to Kandinsky, May 21, 1913
GMS 742

Two Blue Horses in front of a Red Rock is a singularly pure evocation of the imaginative world of Franz Marc. Two blue foals are depicted lying on a patch of grass in front of a red rock which has a semitransparent, crystalline appearance. Their pose and expression connote a mixture of happiness in the here and now and soulful longing for a paradise which lies beyond the confines of earthly existence – a longing for what Marc called the "indivisibility of being."

The text refers to more prosaic matters: "Dear K. Why don't the two of you come with us to see Sakharov? There is no question of us attending the theatrical supper afterward, so the four of us can go off and have dinner somewhere. If you decide to go, then get tickets for us and send us a note: we can meet at the box office. If you don't go then we shall get tickets for the Friday and come round to see you on Saturday afternoon at about 4 o'clock. Is this all right with you? We have a prior engagement in the evening. Kind regards 2 × 2, Fz. Marc."

Franz Marc

59 RED AND BLUE HORSE
(Rotes und blaues Pferd) 1913

Watercolor on paper, 3½ x 5½" (9 x 14 cm)
Postcard to Kandinsky, April 5, 1913
GMS 743

With their sinuous pale red and blue outlines, the two leaping horses on this postcard convey a sense of dynamic movement which is unusual in Marc's animal pictures. In 1913 Marc was inspired by the example of Delacroix' pictures of horses and beasts of prey to make a number of studies of animals in motion, including the woodcut *Löwenjagd nach Delacroix* (*Lion Hunt After Delacroix*). The elongated horse on the left of *Red and Blue Horse* is based on a fresco which Marc discovered in a medieval church in South Tyrol and this same motif recurs several times in his work.

The text of the postcard begins on the front: "Dear K., I am ill, have strained a muscle in my back. I shall send a telegram to Walden; perhaps he will come out here. Otherwise Campendonk will come in my stead," and continues on the back: "into town, so that you will not be left with all the work. At least Campendonk will bring me the news, etc. The Sonderbund: I have handed in my resignation, without giving a reason; they can work it out for themselves. As far as the Bible business is concerned, we should stick to six people. Kindest regards 2 × 2 Fz. Marc." Marc had joined the Sonderbund, an association of Rhineland artists, in 1912, but left the group a year later on the grounds that its members failed to take sufficient account of the interests of the Blue Rider artists. The "Bible business" refers to the projected publication of an edition of the Bible with illustrations by Marc himself, Kandinsky, Klee, Erich Heckel, Oskar Kokoschka, and Alfred Kubin.

Gabriele Münter
b. 1877 in Berlin – d. 1962 in Murnau

Münter moved to Munich in 1901; a year later she began attending Kandinsky's newly founded *Phalanx* school of art. From
1903 until the beginning of World War I she and Kandinsky
lived and worked together. From 1904 on, the couple traveled
extensively; in 1906 they moved to Sèvres, near Paris, and
stayed there for nearly a year. After their return to Germany in
1908, they discovered the small town of Murnau in southern
Bavaria, where Münter bought a house; during the following
years she and Kandinsky spent much of their time in Murnau,
often inviting other members of the Blue Rider circle to come
and stay with them. In 1909 Münter and Kandinsky joined the
Neue Künstler-Vereinigung München (New Artists' Association,
Munich), whose other members included Jawlensky, Marianne
von Werefkin, Adolf Erbslöh, Alexander Kanoldt, and Albert
Bloch; Marc joined the group in 1910. Münter painted in a
free, original style, using simple but bold structures; her work is
quite distinct from that of the other Blue Rider artists. In 1911
she followed Kandinsky's lead in breaking with the *Neue
Künstler-Vereinigung*. She took part in the first Blue Rider exhibition in the winter of 1911/12 and in all the further exhibitions of the group. Münter's last meeting with Kandinsky was
in Stockholm in 1916. She then abandoned painting for nearly
twenty years, not taking it up again until the 1930s, when she
settled in Murnau.

Gabriele Münter

60 AVENUE IN THE PARK OF SAINT-CLOUD
(Allee in Park von Saint-Cloud) 1906

Oil on canvas, 16 x 19⅞" (40.5 x 50.5 cm)
Inscribed "G. Münter 1906" (lower left)
GMS 651

After training in drawing during her early art studies, Gabriele Münter first tried painting in oils in Kandinsky's art class at the *Phalanx* art school in the winter of 1901–02. This is where she learned the palette knife technique that she and Kandinsky used over the next few years while under the influence of late Impressionism. In the following years, on their travels from 1904 until their stay in Paris in 1906–07, the young artist essentially retained this style.

Avenue in the Park of Saint-Cloud, painted on canvas in the palette knife technique, is one of Münter's largest plein air paintings dating from the year in Paris. It also stands out in quality amongst her early oil-studies, usually executed on smaller pieces of cardboard. Münter employs an Impressionist technique and a subtly graded palette of violet, green, brown and white-yellow shades with remarkable assurance. The visual effect of the picture is carefully composed. The gaze is led along an avenue through the park towards the background. Sunlight shines through the foliage overhead, creating numerous lights – or colorfully subdued – reflections. The pastose dabs of paint applied with the palette knife are shorter and more regular than in many of Münter's earlier studies of this kind. They blend to create a lively, vibrating impression comparable to that in French painting. Strikingly different, however, is the bold placement of a darkly glowing blue between the tree trunks and leaves. The same is true for the powerful relief of the palette knife's strokes. It stands out even more forcefully in the painting of the same subject by her partner Wassily Kandinsky, *In the Park of Saint-Cloud* (see plate 2).

Gabriele Münter

61   **MURNAU LANDSCAPE**
(Blick aufs Murnauer Moos) 1908

Oil on cardboard, 12⅞ x 16" (32.7 x 40.5 cm)
Inscribed "M 08" (lower right), "Münter 1908 Blick aufs Moos"
(reverse, in the artist's hand)
GMS 654

Murnau Landscape, a view of meadows and mountains near the
Staffelsee, is one of the first of a series of landscapes which
Münter painted in the Murnau area. The distinction between
foreground and background is blurred by the additive technique;
the colors of the landscape are sketched in with quick, confident
brushstrokes which leave patches of the cardboard bare. With its
economical but bold mixture of blues and greens, this evening
scene realizes, in an exemplary fashion, the programmatic aims
of Münter, Kandinsky, and Jawlensky: the reduction of form,
the liberation of color from representational functions, the
abandonment of perspective, and the simplification of objects
in order to heighten their expressive value. The importance of
this program of formal renewal in the development of modern
German art cannot be emphasized too strongly: the only parallel
to it is to be found in the landscapes of the North German
Expressionists Ernst Ludwig Kirchner, Erich Heckel, and Karl
Schmidt-Rottluff.

The experience of being exposed to the Alpine landscape
and its intriguing light effects almost certainly contributed to
the liberation of Münter's visual imagination: in the foothills
of the Alps, the colors of the landscape often take on an
unreal quality, and the viewer's sense of perspective becomes
distorted. Hence it seems likely that the coloring of the picture,
its seemingly arbitrary combination of violet, blue, and green,
corresponds to an actual impression of nature, from which
Münter extracted the basic essence. In Murnau, her main artistic
strengths – her intensity of vision and her ability to simplify the
physical appearance of reality – came into their own. Her friends
greatly admired her pictures and regarded her technique as having
exemplary significance for their own work.

Gabriele Münter

62 JAWLENSKY AND WEREFKIN
(Jawlensky und Werefkin) 1909

Oil on cardboard, 12⅞ x 17½" (32.7 x 44.5 cm)
Inscribed in Johannes Eichner's (?) hand "Marianne v. Werefkin und Jawlens.
um 1908/09 (unverkäuflich)" (reverse)
GMS 655

For Münter, as for her friend and colleague Kandinsky, the
discovery of the area around Murnau in southern Bavaria was
a major event which marked the beginning of a new departure
in the development of her artistic approach. In the fall of 1908
the couple had returned to Munich after spending several years
abroad and moved into a shared apartment on Ainmillerstrasse
in Schwabing. The previous spring they had visited Murnau
for the first time and were so taken with the small country
town that they returned there in the summer to spend an
extended painting holiday with Jawlensky and Marianne von
Werefkin. In her diary Münter enthusiastically described the
sense of liberation which she felt in Murnau: "We had seen the
town in the course of an excursion into the countryside and
recommended it to Jawlensky and Werefkin, who told us to
come and join them there. We stayed at the Griesbräu, and the
place appealed to us. After a short period of agony I took a
great leap forward, from copying nature – in a more or less
Impressionist style – to abstraction, feeling the content, the
essence of things."

The picture of Jawlensky and Werefkin, which shows the
couple reclining in a meadow, documents Münter's abrupt
abandonment of Impressionism in favor of an uncompromi-
singly modern style of her own making. Radically simplifying
the forms of nature and the human figure, she uses boldly
contrasting, luminous colors. The almost faceless figures of her
two friends are seen in outline only, standing out against the
homogeneous green of the meadow and the blue of the sky and
the mountains. Münter uses the *cloisonniste* technique which
Jawlensky had copied from Gauguin, outlining all the important elements of the picture in black. Her work, with its direct,
uncluttered view of reality, was particularly influenced at this
point by Jawlensky's notion of "synthesis," that is, the reduction of the picture to a small number of characteristic forms.
During her stay in Murnau in 1908 she painted a considerable
number of major pictures which formed the basis for her
contribution to the subsequent Blue Rider exhibitions. In her
diary she wrote: "It was an interesting, cheerful time. We had
lots of conversations about art with the enthusiastic 'Giselists'
[Jawlensky and Werefkin, who lived on Munich's Giselastrasse].
I particularly enjoyed showing my work to Jawlensky, who
praised it lavishly and also explained a number of things to me:
he gave me the benefit of his wide experience and talked
about 'synthesis.' He is a good colleague. All four of us were
keenly ambitious, and each of us made progress. There were
days when I painted as many as five studies; often it was three,
and the days were rare when I didn't paint at all. We all worked
very hard."

Gabriele Münter

63 PORTRAIT OF MARIANNE VON WEREFKIN
(Bildnis Marianne von Werefkin)   1909

Oil on cardboard, 31 ⅞ x 21 ⅝" (81 x 55 cm)
Inscribed "Münter" (lower right), "Gabriele Münter. Bildnis Marianne von
Werefkin. Wahrscheinlich 1909" (reverse, in the artist's hand)
GMS 656

In 1909, at the height of their creative work together, Gabriele Münter painted this portrait of her artist friend Marianne von Werefkin. An unusually lively, positive feeling portrait for Münter's oeuvre, it confronts the viewer with the fascinating personality of this woman. Against a maize yellow, rippling, textured background, she looks out from under a huge hat covered with flowers over her right shoulder at the viewer. The solid base of her broad upper body is seen in profile rising upwards, vibrating with the same energetic brushstrokes as the background, framed by the purple band of her scarf. Violet shadows play under her hat, around her eyes, in her hair and on the slightly opened lips that, along with her keen expression hint at a lively intellect and energy. Only rarely, and surely only under the momentary influence of Jawlensky, did Gabriele Münter come as close to the vital painting style of the Fauves as in this picture.

In an undated note, Münter reveals how this portrait was painted, saying that she painted her artist friend out of doors in front of the wall of her house in Murnau: "I painted Werefkina [sic] in 1909 in front of the yellow base course of my house. She was a woman of grand appearance, self-confident, commanding, extravagantly dressed, with a hat as big as a wagon wheel, on which there was room for all sorts of things."

The *Portrait of Marianne von Werefkin* is one of the most important portraits to come from the Blue Rider group. These artists generally made less of an effort at realistic portrayals of people, or rather, in the case of Macke and Jawlensky, moved away from portraiture. According to Münter, however, a person's face in a portrait could not be dissolved or replaced by anything symbolic. There is no need, as she once wrote, clearly referring to Kandinsky's divergent view, for a "spiritual metaphor" for the human face: "For the personality is rooted in the spiritual and operates from an invisible source. The natural symbol of this invisible element, which is all that matters, is the visible physical appearance."

Gabriele Münter

64 TOMBSTONES IN KOCHEL
(Grabkreuze in Kochel) 1909

Oil on cardboard, 16 x 12⅞" (40.5 x 32.8 cm)
Inscribed "Mü" (lower left), "Grabkreuze in Kochel 1909" (reverse, in the
artist's hand)
GMS 658

Tombstones in Kochel was painted while Münter and Kandinsky
were staying with the composer Thomas von Hartmann in
February 1909, at the same time as Kandinsky painted *Kochel
– Graveyard and Rectory* (plate 6) and a number of other winter
pictures. The similarities between the landscape studies of
Münter and Kandinsky at this point are greater than at any
other time in their respective careers. Many critics have emphasized the importance of the pupil-teacher relationship between the two artists and have noted that, for a time at least,
it was far from easy to tell their pictures apart. Up to 1911,
and especially during the Murnau years, they did indeed work
closely together, exchanging ideas on form and technique, and
it seems certain that Kandinsky exerted a considerable influence
on Münter's artistic approach. As she later wrote, "he loved,
understood, protected, and nurtured my talent."

Kandinsky took a photograph of Münter in a winter coat
working on this picture in the graveyard at Kochel. At the time
when he was teaching at the *Phalanx* school of art, Kandinsky
had placed great emphasis on the importance of plein air painting as a means of liberating art from academic restrictions, and
he and Münter continued to paint outdoors when they were
working together in Murnau. However, despite the similarities
between the Kochel pictures, they also exhibit certain differences. Münter's choice of motif betokens her interest in the
visual play of objects themselves, which is clearly apparent in
her later still lifes. She stylizes the crosses in a way that lends
them added drama, which is enhanced by those blue shadows
in the snow that so fascinated Kandinsky. Münter's colors do
not have the separated, glowing quality of those used by
Kandinsky: the wintry yellow is mixed into the white, thereby
binding the picture together into a unified whole. Looking at
Kandinsky's Kochel pictures, it seems possible that he to some
extent copied Münter's natural, flowing brushstroke.

Gabriele Münter

65 LISTENING (PORTRAIT OF JAWLENSKY)
(Zuhören [Bildnis Jawlensky]) 1909

Oil on cardboard, 19⅝ x 26" (49.7 x 66.2 cm)
Inscribed "Münter" (upper left), "G. Münter Zuhören 1909" (reverse, in the
artist's hand)
GMS 657

Münter gives the following account of the genesis of this
painting: "All three of them [Kandinsky, Klee, and Jawlensky]
talked incessantly about art, and initially each of them had his
own views and his own style. Jawlensky was less intellectual,
or less intelligent, than Kandinsky and Klee, and he often found
their theories confusing. On one occasion I painted a portrait
which I called *Listening* and which showed Jawlensky with an
expression of surprise on his chubby face, listening to Kandinsky explaining his latest theories of art." In portraying her
friends, Münter often took a characteristic situation as her
point of departure, rather than the physiognomic peculiarities
of the individual subject. Here she employs a deliberately naive
technique to capture Jawlensky's expression of bewilderment.
The Russian artist sits on the right at a table indicated by a
horizontal black line. The curving line of his pink shirtfront
runs up his broad, two-dimensional body to his round, reddish
head with its blue eyes and raised eyebrows; the slightly cocked
position of the head lends his entire body the appearance of a
question mark. The angle of his body is picked up and further
emphasized by the two curved sausages on the plate and the
base of the petroleum lamp. Despite their simplicity, the elements in the center attract the viewer's attention by virtue of
their pure complementary colors and banish the figure of
Jawlensky into a peripheral position behind the table. With
its deliberately simple, avowedly representational technique,
Münter's picture seems to comment ironically on Jawlensky's
inability to grasp Kandinsky's complicated theories and, in
addition, on Kandinsky's pictorial practice, which Münter herself found far from easy to understand.

Gabriele Münter

66 STILL LIFE WITH CHAIR
(Stillleben mit Sessel) 1909

Oil on cardboard, 28½ x 19¼" (72.5 x 49 cm)
Inscribed "Münter 09" (lower left)
Gabriele Münter and Johannes Eichner Foundation
FH 294

Still Life with Chair offers a further demonstration of Münter's exceptional talent for painting fascinating, highly individual pictures of simple, everyday objects. Three small vases of flowers and a pot plant stand on a small red table next to a dark wine-red chairback. Their blues and yellows form a garland of color around the large pot behind them, which contains a shrub with a profusion of dark pink flowers. Together with the intriguingly strange arrangement of the objects, the boldly masterful combination of the various reds with the dark yellow background and its brightly colored plate allows this little-known still life to be ranked among Münter's major early works. The picture was shown, alongside six other works by Münter, at the second exhibition of the *Neue Künstler-Vereinigung München* in 1910.

Gabriele Münter

67   STILL LIFE IN GRAY (Stillleben grau) 1910

Oil on cardboard, 13½ x 19¾" (34.2 x 50.2 cm)
Inscribed "Münter" (lower left)
GMS 662

Still Life in Gray owes a particular debt to Jawlensky and the French tradition. In a manner similar to Jawlensky's *Still Life with Fruit* (plate 83), the picture is divided by a central line into two differently colored but corresponding zones; the upper zone is gray-blue and the bottom half of the picture light gray. The vase, the apples, and the leaves in the lower zone are thinly edged in black; they seem to derive their substance solely from the paint itself. The perspective of the picture and the deliberate symmetry of the arrangement on the table create a sense of order and harmony. In an undated note, Münter declared on one occasion: "If I had a formal model – and from 1903 to 1913 this was to some extent the case – then it was probably Van

Gogh, via Jawlensky and his theories (the notion of synthesis)." However, she went on to emphasize that the main influence on her work was Kandinsky. In order to grasp the formal antecedents of a picture such as *Still Life in Gray*, it is necessary to bear in mind not only Van Gogh but also Matisse and Cézanne, to whose work Münter was introduced by Jawlensky. These artists' manner of experimenting with the laws of form and color led, in its own way, to a "spiritualization" and dematerialization of the object. Marc pointed this out in his discussion of the second exhibition of the *Neue Künstler-Vereinigung München* in 1910: "This bold attempt to spiritualize the material reality to which Impressionism clings with such dogged obstinacy is a necessary reaction which began with Gauguin in Pont-Aven and has already given rise to innumerable experiments. The reason why this latest experiment by the Neue Künstler-Vereinigung seems to us so promising is that, in addition to their highly spiritualized meaning, the pictures of the group offer highly valuable examples of rhythm, composition, and color theory."

Gabriele Münter

68 MAN AT THE TABLE (KANDINSKY)
(Mann am Tisch [Kandinsky]) 1911

Oil on cardboard, 20¼ x 27" (51.6 x 68.5 cm)
Inscribed "Münter" (lower right), "Münter Skizze Mann am Tisch"
(reverse, in the artist's hand)
GMS 665

Man at the Table shows Kandinsky sitting at a table with his arms folded, facing the artist as if in a sudden moment of keen attention. In contrast to conventional portraiture, where the prime focus is on the human subject, the slender, huddled figure of Kandinsky is juxtaposed with the objects on the table in a manner reminiscent of still-life painting. The muted colors of the cup, the plate, the cake, and the flowerpot – ocher, brown, and olive green – are complemented by the dull white of the tablecloth. With its aggressively stiff, stylized leaves, the tall green pot plant extends into the left-hand section of the picture and appears almost to threaten the man at the table. The somber, dully economical colors, whose monotony is scarcely relieved by the orange of the fruit on the table, also convey an impression of dissonance. Münter's manner of abstract seeing often reveals a hidden layer of meaning behind the physical appearance of reality: here, it seems to disclose an underlying psychological tension between the artist and her subject, who appears to be watching her from within the picture. Technically, the most striking feature of the work is its graphic reduction of the figure and the objects: it is interesting to note that Münter herself referred to the picture as a "sketch." Kandinsky was greatly impressed by *Man at the Table*: he commended the "modesty" and simplicity of Münter's painting, which displayed "no trace of feminine or masculine coquetry," and he included a reproduction of the picture in The Blue Rider almanac.

Gabriele Münter

69   DARK STILL LIFE (SECRET)
(Dunkles Stillleben [Geheimnis])   1911

Oil on canvas, 30⅞ x 39⅝" (78.5 x 100.5 cm)
Inscribed "13. IV. 11" (upper right)
On permanent loan from the Gabriele Münter and Johannes Eichner Foundation
FH 294

In the eventful years between 1910 and 1912, when Kandinsky
and Marc were putting their ambitious plans for a new art into
practice, Münter was developing and refining her narrow
repertoire of themes, painting mainly landscapes, still lifes,
and flowers. Her still lifes in particular bear the mark of her
distinctive talent. In the pictures from this period, small statuettes and carved wooden figures, taken from Münter and
Kandinsky's collection of folk art, are often used to lend an
added sense of animation to the selection of objects. Although
the initial stimulus for the pictures came from the chance
arrangement of these artifacts on a shelf or table, the figures
in Münter's still lifes are caught up in a network of secret
relationships.

A photograph of Münter and Kandinsky's Munich apart-
ment enables us to identify the source of *Dark Still Life (Secret)*.
In a corner of the apartment several figures stood on a small
table; a number of paintings on glass can be seen hanging on
the adjacent wall. With the help of the photograph it is possible
to ascertain that the pair of figures at the far left-hand side of
the picture was taken from a painting on glass depicting the
King of Bohemia confessing his sins to St. Nepomuk. The
objects on the table include an earthenware hen, an Easter egg,
a handpainted drinking goblet (now in the collection of the
Lenbachhaus), and a statuette of the seated Madonna. It seems
likely that the picture was inspired by the experience of suddenly catching sight of these familiar objects in the evening light.
However, Münter's choice of them was also motivated by their
specifically religious aura. As in *Still Life in Gray* (plate 67), one
is struck by the extent to which the still lifes from this period
mirror the expressive power of the objects themselves, as well
as the subjectivity of the artist. In a letter to Marc written in
the fall of 1911, August Macke commented: "I have the feeling
that she [Münter] has a penchant for the mysterious (as in the
still lifes, the saints, the lilies in a corner of the garden, the
sharply lit storm clouds, the lamps, and the venerable old
chairs). There is something very 'German' about it all, a touch
of religious and family Romanticism. I like her immensely."

Gabriele Münter

70 STILL LIFE WITH ST. GEORGE
(Stillleben mit Heiligem Georg) 1911

Oil on cardboard, 20⅛ x 26¾" (51.1 x 68 cm)
Inscribed "Münter" (lower left), "G. Münter Stilleben mit St. Georg 1911"
(reverse, in the artist's hand)
GMS 666

Still Life with St. George anticipates the figure of the "Blue Rider."
Standing out against the soft violet and blue-green background,
the various figures in the picture appear mysteriously bound
up with the two-dimensional space surrounding them. In the
top left-hand corner one sees the figure of St. George mounted on a white horse and holding his lance triumphantly aloft,
echoing the idea of quasi-religious revival connected with
Kandinsky's Blue Rider (see plates 24, 41). The knight, surrounded by a reddish aureole, appears to float in space, thereby
obscuring the fact that this section of the picture was modeled
on a painting on glass which hung on the wall of Münter's apartment. The other objects in the picture include a statuette of
the Madonna; a large earthenware hen; a shimmering blue
vase, with a bunch of flowers painted in the same pinkish red
as the aureole surrounding the figure of St. George; two carved
wooden figures from a Christmas crib; and a further statuette of
the Madonna, seated on a throne and wearing a crown with a
double cross. These figures were part of a collection owned by
Münter and Kandinsky which is preserved in the Lenbachhaus as
part of the Gabriele Münter and Johannes Eichner Foundation.
The statuettes of the Madonna are copies of nineteenth-
century votive images, the carved wooden figures were bought
by Münter in Oberammergau, and the painting of St. George
is a copy of a picture by the Murnau artist Rambold.

With its glowing colors and soft, fluid lines, *Still Life with
St. George* has a quite exceptional atmospheric quality, which
makes it one of Münter's most important paintings. Hans
Konrad Roethel emphasizes the particular role of the colors in
creating the sense of magic which permeates the work, pointing
out that "the dominant color is blue, in the mysterious background, the cool patch of color which surrounds St. George,
the glowing tones of the vase and the two Madonnas." *Still Life
with St. George* was included in The Blue Rider almanac, where
Kandinsky wrote: "The still life by Münter demonstrates that
the different interpretation of objects to a different degree
within one and the same picture is not only not harmful, but
can, if correctly used, attain a powerful, complex inner sound.
That concordance of sounds which produces an externally
disharmonious impression is in this instance the source of the
inner harmonious effect."

Gabriele Münter

71   MURNAU FARMER'S WIFE WITH CHILDREN
(Murnauer Bäuerin mit Kindern)   *c.* 1909-10

Reverse glass painting, 8⅞ x 7⅝" (22.5 x 19.5 cm)
Inscribed (incised) "MÜ" (lower left)
GMS 733

Gabriele Münter was the first in the circle of the evolving Blue Rider group, probably in the spring of 1909, to begin copying works in the traditional religious folk art technique of painting in reverse on the underside of glass. Soon, she used this technique with her own designs. She learned it quickly in the studio of Heinrich Rambold, one of the last glass painters still active at the time, whose models she also copied. Besides the simple reduction of the forms, the clear, often schematized outline drawings and the brilliant planes of color without any shading, it was especially the naiveté, originality and deep feeling of these works that inspired Münter, Kandinsky, Jawlensky, and later also Marc, Macke and Campendonk (see plates 40–42, 97–98).

In this reverse glass painting, Münter abandoned the religious models she had copied at first, such as images of St. George or St. Florian, or traditional votive scenes. Instead, she depicts an elderly farmer's wife with a deep blue skirt, red kerchief and a small child on her arm dressed in pink. In the background is the Murnau castle on the hill, a motif Münter often chose to paint during this period. As the castle's basic contours are shown true to life, the people are probably also live models from her circle of acquaintances. The old farmer's wife, for instance, recalls the grandmother of the Echter family. The little girl in the dirndl looks like Münter's niece Friedel, who visited in the summer of 1909 and was painted by Münter in a very similar dress in front of the house in Murnau. In her depiction of the faces and in the nervous lines of the clouds and the tree on the right, Münter goes beyond the calm schematic drawing of her traditional sources and lends her own motif an expressive touch.

Gabriele Münter

72 **VILLAGE STREET IN WINTER**
(Dorfstrasse im Winter) 1911

Oil on cardboard mounted on wood, 20⅝ x 27¼" (52.4 x 69 cm)
Inscribed "Münter 1911" (lower left)
GMS 664

With its strong, bold colors, *Village Street in Winter* testifies once more to the simple, natural character of Münter's talent and, at the same time, documents her striving for radical innovation. The glowing patches of color have an unnatural appearance. Above the green, red, white, and dark blue houses which line the street, the blue-green of the sky is streaked with white and takes on a turquoise tinge. On the left, a line of violet washing hangs above a yellow background. The houses have a tilted, deliberately "deformed" appearance, which is accentuated by their dark outlines and lends the picture a sense of dynamic energy. Despite the unusual contrasts, the colors do not directly clash; the careful, clear juxtaposition of the parts welds the picture into a unified whole. As in the work of Kandinsky, the overall impression is of stylistic economy.

A Swedish critic, discussing Münter's approach to new ways of seeing in connection with her 1916 exhibition in Stockholm, commented: "Frau Münter is a highly radical artist, but her temperament is such that her radicalism remains unobtrusive."

Gabriele Münter

73 KANDINSKY AND ERMA BOSSI, AFTER DINNER
(Kandinsky und Erma Bossi am Tisch) 1912

Oil on canvas, 37⅝ x 49⅜" (95.5 x 125.5 cm)
Inscribed "G. Münter, Nach Tisch" (on the stretcher, in the artist's hand)
GMS 780

This picture was painted after a spontaneous pencil sketch which Münter made of Kandinsky and the painter Erma Bossi engaged in after-dinner conversation. The two artists are seated at a table in a corner of the living room of their house in Murnau; the dark wall behind them evokes a particular sense of intimacy. Kandinsky is holding forth, raising his hand to emphasize a point; on the other side of the table Erma Bossi, who had known Kandinsky for several years, since the days of the *Neue Künstler-Vereinigung München*, is listening intently to his pronouncements. The viewer's eye is drawn to the speaker, with his bright blue jacket and light-blue spectacle lenses, rather than to the less obtrusive figure of the listener, whose black skirt and white blouse merge into the background. The blues of Kandinsky's jacket and spectacles are picked up by other elements in the picture, especially by the simple blue-and-white crockery on the table and the deep blue of the artifacts on the shelf above the artist's head.

Here, as in *Listening (Portrait of Jawlensky)*, Münter was less concerned with graphic accuracy than with the attempt to convey the essence of a particular situation. The formal relationships in *Kandinsky and Erma Bossi, After Dinner* are simple but charged with tension: this is particularly apparent in the open and closed rectangles which surround the couple in the center. Münter demonstrates a fine sense of economy in her depiction of the living room, with its collection of *objects d'art,* and of the figure of Kandinsky, dressed in traditional Bavarian costume with green calf-protectors and rough sandals. The painting accurately captures the atmosphere of the often heated discussions in the Blue Rider circle and also strikes a humorous note, gently ironizing Kandinsky's role as the intellectual leader of the group.

Gabriele Münter

74   PENSIVE WOMAN (Sinnende)   1917

Oil in canvas, 26 x 39¼" (66 x 99.5 cm)
Inscribed "Münter 31.III.1917" (upper left)
GMS 646

Gabriele Münter's works during the years she spent in Scandinavia, from 1915 to 1929, show a definite stylistic change compared to her Blue Rider period. After her arrival in Stockholm, Münter soon came into contact with Swedish avant-garde artists, including the couple Isaac Grünewald and Sigrid Hjertén as well as Einar Jolin and Leander Engström. The influence of these pupils of Henri Matisse, with their Fauvist design principles, decorative pictorial structure composed of planes, and subtly mixed colors, soon became unmistakable in Münter's work. Sabine Windecker writes about the transformation in Münter's style and choice of subject matter due to her interaction with the Swedish artists: "The choice of subject matter alone shows definite common features. Not only for Grünewald, Hjertén and Jolin does the subject matter of choice consist of arrangements of figures, portraits, interior and urban landscapes. . . . Moreover, Münter also orients herself on the style of these painters in color and form, for her paintings now suggest the decorative expressionism of Matisse, particularly his rhythmic lines. Above all, this means that in the portraits and figural compositions the shape of the body is subordinated – often in favor of an idealized representation of people – to the curving line."

Female portraits in particular are Münter's theme of choice throughout these years and far into the next decade. In the spring of 1917 Münter painted a series of large, symbolic portraits with titles such as, *Future*, *Pensive Woman* and *Sick*, in which the figure of the woman is also the carrier of a psychological message about waiting, hoping, thinking or suffering. The model for all of these paintings, as well as other portraits of this period, was a young Swedish woman of Jewish descent, Gertrude Holz. The painting of the *Pensive Woman* shows her in a hermetically sealed room, its outer edges cut off on all sides by the wide oblong shape of the picture. Portrayed as a half figure, lost in thought and gazing past the viewer, she sits in the lower left foreground in front of a table with a still life-like arrangement of flowers, apples and a lamp. The table cuts off the pictorial space as abruptly as the dark green upholstery and the opaque window, partly covered by curtains, right behind it. The face of the *Pensive Woman*, which is particularly detailed as opposed to her remarkably abstract body, is further emphasized by the matte blue flowers behind her. The broken rhythm of the black lines in the flat planes of the overall composition and the cool colors mixed with black: dark red, green and matte grey, underscore the portrait's melancholy atmosphere. They make the connection to Münter's own emotional state during this period movingly apparent.

Gabriele Münter

75 THE RUSSIANS' HOUSE
(Das Russen-Haus) 1931

Oil on canvas, 16¾ x 22½" (42.5 x 57 cm)
Inscribed "Münter 1931" (lower right)
GMS 773

Following her last meeting with Kandinsky, in Stockholm in
1916, Münter lived an unsettled, nomadic life in numerous
cities throughout Germany and northern Europe. Her creativity
dried up: it was not until 1931, when she finally returned to
Murnau, that she took up painting again. *The Russians' House*
shows the house which she had shared with Kandinsky in
Murnau; Münter had used the same view from the garden in a
number of other paintings, such as *Country House* (1910; private
collection). The nickname *Russen-Haus,* conferred on the house
by the local people, reflected their attitude of amused puzzle-
ment at the comings and goings of the foreigner Kandinsky
and his Russian friends Jawlensky and Marianne von Werefkin.
Münter's account of the purchase of the house conveys something of the elan of the Murnau years: "Kandinsky had fallen
in love with the house at first sight, and his love remained
constant. We debated the matter, he applied a certain amount
of pressure, and in the late summer the villa was bought by
Fräulein G. Münter."

The picture depicts the attractively proportioned house,
with its friendly colors, as a place of refuge. Münter lived there
until her death in 1962.

Gabriele Münter

76   **MOUNTAIN VIEW (Blick aufs Gebirge)**   1934

Oil on canvas, 18¼ x 21⅝" (46.5 x 55 cm)
Inscribed "Münter 1934" (lower right)
G 12 944

After World War I, and especially after her return to Murnau
in 1931, Münter did not embark on any new experiments
but stuck to the style of her earlier pictures, reducing and
simplifying natural forms. In *Mountain View* the eye is drawn
from the two large barns and the meadow in the foreground
toward the schematic blue and brown hills in the middle
distance, and is finally arrested by the tall blue mountain at the
top of the picture. The dark colors convey a certain sense of
melancholy, but at the same time the landscape has an air of
comfortable familiarity, despite the close layering of the surfaces. Once again, Kandinsky springs to mind, with his comment that Münter's art embodied "a simple harmony, made
up of a number of wholly *serious colors,* which, through their
deep tones, form a quiet chord with the drawing." Münter
was the only member of the Blue Rider circle who remained
faithful to the Murnau landscape, where her style had first
evolved and which had been the scene of so many revolutionary new developments that changed the face of modern art.

Alexei Jawlensky

b. 1864 in Torzhok, Russia - d. 1941 in Wiesbaden

The son of a Russian colonel, Jawlensky initially embarked on a military career. In 1889 he applied for a transfer to Moscow in order to study painting at the Academy; there he met the artist Marianne von Werefkin, who for many years was his mistress and companion. Seven years later the couple moved to Munich in order to continue their studies, and soon afterward Jawlensky made the acquaintance of Kandinsky at Anton Až-be's private art school. Between 1903 and 1907 Jawlensky spent much of his time in France, where he came under the influence of Vincent Van Gogh, Neo-Impressionism, and Fauvism; he was particularly impressed by the work of Henri Matisse. In 1908 and 1909 he lived and worked with Kandinsky, Münter, and Werefkin in Murnau in southern Bavaria, developing and refining his style in a series of landscape paintings. Subsequently, however, Jawlensky's main field of interest became the human figure and the portrait, in which the eyes are the dominant motif. Following the outbreak of World War I, Jawlensky moved to St. Prex on Lake Geneva and later to Wiesbaden, where he lived for the rest of his life, working on the representation of the human face. The formal austerity of his later, abstract pictures echoes the spiritualized, meditative character of Russian icons.

Alexei Jawlensky

77 THE HUNCHBACK (Der Bucklige) 1905

Oil on cardboard, 20⅝ x 19½" (52.5 x 49.5 cm)
Inscribed "A. Jawlensky" (lower left)
Purchased in 1963 with a grant from the estate of Gabriele Münter
G 13 107

The Hunchback was painted some ten years after Jawlensky's
arrival in Munich in 1896. In the intervening period he had
devoted a great deal of energy to studying the various styles
of modern art, with particular emphasis on French painting.
In 1903 he had traveled to Normandy and Paris; two years
later he paid an extended visit to Brittany, where he painted a
number of landscapes and character studies, sensing for the first
time that his style was developing in a new direction, away from
the late Impressionist manner of his early landscapes and still
lifes. Most importantly, the works which he painted in Brittany
exhibited a new vitality in their use of color: "the colors
glowed," he later wrote, "and my inner self was satisfied."
The Hunchback is painted with vigorous, impulsive brushstrokes whose impasto quality reminds one of Van Gogh,
whom Jawlensky greatly admired at that time: in 1908 he
made a considerable financial sacrifice to buy a landscape by
the great Dutch master. Jawlensky used the motif of the hunchback in several other pictures, notably in *Humpback* (1911),
which shows the distorted figure of a peasant woman painted
in a glaring red. Together with a number of other works, the
picture of the young Breton was exhibited at the Paris Salon
d'Automne in 1905 and earned Jawlensky a measure of international recognition. It was on this occasion that he first made
the acquaintance of Matisse.

Alexei Jawlensky

78 **PORTRAIT OF HEDWIG KUBIN**
(Porträt Hedwig Kubin) 1906

Oil on cardboard, 29½ x 22½" (75 x 57 cm)
G 15 670

This portrait of Alfred Kubin's wife, Hedwig, was probably
painted in Jawlensky's Munich apartment at the beginning of
1906. The visionary drawings of the young, eccentric Alfred
Kubin had caused a considerable stir in the Munich art world,
and he had recently made the acquaintance of Jawlensky. He
was a frequent guest at the salon presided over by Jawlensky
and Marianne von Werefkin. In 1904, following a severe nervous
breakdown, Kubin had married Hedwig Gründler, a widow
considerably older than himself. Jawlensky uses broad, colored
brushstrokes to portray the mature features, already marked by
suffering, of the woman who, although herself chronically ill,
provided Kubin with the security he so badly needed. Although
the treatment of the folds of her dress and the modeling of the
face betray the lingering influence of late Impressionism, the
free choice of colors points in the direction of Fauvism. In
May 1906 Kubin and his wife moved to the isolated village of
Zwickledt in northern Austria, where Hedwig Kubin died in
1948, eleven years before her husband.

Alexei Jawlensky

79   PORTRAIT OF THE DANCER
ALEKSANDR SAKHAROV
(Bildnis des Tänzers Alexander Sacharoff) 1909

Oil on cardboard, 27⅜ x 26⅛" (69.5 x 66.5 cm)
G 13 388

In this picture one encounters for the first time the motif of
the wide-open, piercing eyes which plays such an important
part in Jawlensky's work. The sitter faces the viewer head on,
staring out of the picture with a disarming directness that is
emphasized by the heavy stage makeup around his eyes; together with his seductive pose and the bright red of his costume,
which is echoed in his mouth, his gaze exercises a fascination
which is hard to resist. Jawlensky painted several portraits of
Sakharov, a close friend who sat for him at least three times in
1909 alone. According to Clotilde von Derp-Sakharov, this
picture was painted one evening on the spur of the moment,
when the dancer visited Jawlensky in his studio, in full costume
and makeup before a performance. Although the colors were
still wet, Sakharov took the picture with him, fearing that if
he left it behind, Jawlensky would paint it over, as he had
frequently done in the past. The speed with which the work
was painted would explain why its bold sweeping lines and
the impression it conveys of an immediate personal presence
have retained their freshness. Jawlensky was particularly intrigued by the dancer's androgynous appearance: in his later
pictures of the human face, he eliminated all personal attributes,
including those of gender.

Alexei Jawlensky

80 **MURNAU SKETCH**
(Skizze aus Murnau) 1908-09

Oil on cardboard, 13⅛ x 16¼" (33.3 x 41.3 cm)
GMS 677

In the spring of 1908 Kandinsky and Münter had discovered the town of Murnau in the foothills of the Alps and they recommended it to Jawlensky and Werefkin, who visited Murnau that summer and wrote to Kandinsky and Münter, suggesting that they should come and join them. This was the beginning

of the cooperation between the four artists who formed the nucleus of the Blue Rider circle. A particularly close friendship grew up between Jawlensky and Münter. Jawlensky, who had already gained a measure of international recognition, initially saw himself as the "teacher" of the group and supplied his friends with a fund of new ideas based on his experiences in France. The small, plain *Murnau Sketch* is clearly influenced by French street scenes, although its vivid colors also strike a distinctly Russian note. In the facades of the houses the ocher ground of the cardboard, which Kandinsky and Münter also used for their landscapes, shows through the surface of the picture.

Alexei Jawlensky

81 SUMMER EVENING IN MURNAU
(Sommerabend in Murnau) 1908–09

Oil on cardboard, 13 x 17¾" (33.2 x 45.1 cm)
Donated by Gabriele Münter, 1960
G 13 109

With its graphic economy, its intense colors, and its use of dark contours, *Summer Evening in Murnau* is remarkably similar to Münter's landscapes from the same period (for example, plate 61). In accordance with his concept of "synthesis," Jawlensky reduces the landscape to a set of broad outlines, with only a few sparse details in the center. In 1907 he had met and befriended the Benedictine friar and painter Willibrord Verkade, who introduced him to the work of the Nabis circle, a group of French artists who were followers of Gauguin. The technique of *cloisonnisme,* that is, the rhythmic organization of the picture in flat areas often bounded by black contours, was one of the distinguishing features of the art of Gauguin, who strove to interpret reality in a new, subjective manner. "Art is above all a means of expression" – this was the message propagated by Paul Sérusier, the leader of the Nabis group, who visited Verkade in Munich in 1907 and also met Jawlensky. In this way the concept of synthesis, which features prominently in discussions of the theory of art at the turn of the century, was adopted by Jawlensky, who in turn passed the idea on to Kandinsky and his other Munich friends. Within the fledgling Blue Rider circle the notion of synthesis took on a new meaning, colored by Kandinsky's idea of "inner necessity." Kandinsky, who was particularly inspired by the dynamic structure and the "wild" colors of a number of Jawlensky's Murnau pictures, later looked back with gratitude "to the time when you [Jawlensky] were my teacher."

Alexei Jawlensky

82   **MURNAU LANDSCAPE**
(Murnauer Landschaft) 1909

Oil on cardboard, 19$^7/_8$ x 21$^1/_2$" (50.5 x 54.5 cm)
Inscribed "A. Jawlensky/09" (lower right)
GMS 678

For a time at least, Jawlensky was the most "progressive" of the quartet of artists who worked together in Murnau. This is borne out by *Murnau Landscape*. Jawlensky achieves a high degree of stylization, reducing the landscape to a series of jagged geometrical forms and using deliberately unnatural colors. The distinction between objects and their shadows, between the sky and the landscape itself, has been eliminated, and the harsh contrasts between the artificially bright violet, yellow, green, and orange are heightened by the red of the tree in the background and the turquoise of the range of hills on the left. The color samples in the bottom right-hand corner emphasize the autonomous character of the picture, whose reality is located outside the world of sense-impressions.

It has been shown that the jagged, distorted forms of the picture were influenced by French Cubism, in particular by the work of Henri Le Fauconnier, whose approach to painting was in turn influenced by Gauguin and Emile Bernard. Together with Picasso, Georges Braque, André Derain, Maurice Vlaminck, Kees van Dongen, and a number of other artists, Le Fauconnier was invited to contribute to the second exhibition of the *Neue Künstler-Vereinigung München*.

Alexei Jawlensky

83 STILL LIFE WITH FRUIT
(Stillleben mit Früchten) *c.* 1910

Oil on cardboard, 18⅞ x 26⅝" (48 x 67.7 cm)
Inscribed "A. Jawlensky" (lower left)
GMS 680

In 1910 Jawlensky painted a series of still lifes which rank
among his finest works from the period before World War I.
From 1911 onward, he devoted himself almost exclusively to
the theme of the human face; his later, obsessive concern with
this subject is anticipated by these early portraits. Hence the
blue still life of 1911 in the Hamburg Kunsthalle can be seen
as his last major work in a genre to which he did not return
until the end of his life, when he was chronically ill. All his
still lifes from 1910/11 testify to the influence of Henri Matisse,
whom Jawlensky unreservedly admired. After his first encounter with Matisse in 1905, he had returned to Paris in 1907 and
paid several visits to the French master's studio, which at that
time was a meeting place for young artists from all over
Europe. In *Still Life with Fruit,* a cluster of apples, two jugs, a
drinking vessel, and the heads of three dark blue stylized flowers are arranged on a blue-gray surface; these miscellaneous
objects are separated from the intense bluish-green background
by a thin line running across the center of the picture. The
difference between Jawlensky's approach to painting and that
of Matisse lies in the heaviness of the brushstrokes, which
indicates a considerable expenditure of physical effort, and in
the somewhat leaden seriousness of the picture. "In the still
lifes," Jawlensky declared, "I was not searching for the material
object; instead, I wanted to express an inner vibration by means
of form and color." This comment points to a considerable
disparity between the aims of Jawlensky and those of Matisse.
Comparing *Still Life with Fruit* with Münter's *Still Life in Gray*
(plate 67), it is possible to see how Münter used Jawlensky's
work as a point of departure for her own painting.

Alexei Jawlensky

84   **MATURITY (Reife)** *c.* 1912

Oil on cardboard, 21 x 19½" (53.5 x 49.5 cm)
Inscribed "A. Jawlensky" (lower right)
G 13 300

Maturity marks a considerable change in Jawlensky's approach
to the representation of the human face. Toward the end of his
life the artist wrote to Willibrord Verkade: "In 1911 I arrived
at a form and color of my own and made a name for myself
by painting massive figurative heads." The figure in *Maturity*
faces the viewer head on, with an imploring expression and
staring eyes edged in black. The garish, unreal colors, whose
"wildness" exceeds even that of the Fauves, are held in check
by a solid structure of black lines. The face, from which all
trace of individuality has been expunged, has the appearance
of a mask. In the almost square format of the picture the
figure's body is cut off below the neck; the viewer's attention
is focused on the round, rudimentary form of the head and, in
particular, on the green eyes, which resemble those of a pagan
idol. The title *Maturity* also indicates a degree of abstraction
from the reality of the sitter's face: Jawlensky uses the glowing
colors of summer to create an archetypal form. The stylized,
schematic appearance of the face anticipates the "mystical"
portraits which Jawlensky began to paint in 1917. Jawlensky
spent the summer of 1911 in the small seaside town of Prerow
on the Baltic coast: it was some time after this, probably in
1912, that he painted *Maturity*. He later wrote: "That summer
saw a major development in my art. In Prerow I painted my
best landscapes and large studies of the human figure in very
strong, glowing colors, which were absolutely non-naturalistic. I used a great deal of red, together with blue, orange,
cadmium yellow, and chrome green. The bold contours of the
forms were painted in Prussian blue, and the pictures were the
product of an overwhelming inner ecstasy."

Alexei Jawlensky

85 SPANISH WOMAN (Spanierin) 1913

Oil on cardboard, 26⅜ x 19" (67 x 48.5 cm)
Inscribed "A. Jawlensky 13" (top left)
G 12 556

In the years immediately preceding the outbreak of World
War I Jawlensky devoted nearly all his energies to painting
women's faces with sharp black contours and dark, staring
eyes. The formal problems remain the same throughout this
series of over one hundred pictures; the eyes alone convey, in
each case, something of the individual character of the figure,
taking on the status of a highly suggestive sign, whose meaning
can only be ascertained in relation to the series as a whole. In
these pictures Jawlensky was evidently struggling to achieve a
deeper understanding of the principles underlying his own
approach to painting. In 1913 he painted a total of five pictures
entitled *Spanish Woman.* In the present work, with its tall
format, the olive-skinned face of the woman is slightly off-
center. Together with the black mantilla which falls around
her shoulders, the roses in her hair and around the neckline of
her dress form a decorative framework which, rather than distracting the viewer's attention from her face, serves to heighten
the effect of her atavistic gaze. According to Elisabeth Macke-
Erdmann, Jawlensky used the dancer Aleksandr Sakharov (see
plate 76) as his model for the *Spanish Woman* pictures, but the
degree of formalization in the faces makes it impossible to determine whether this was in fact the case. Pictures such as
Byzantinerin (Byzantine Woman), *Kreolin (Creole Woman)*, and
Sizilianerin (Sicilian Woman), all painted in the same year and
now in private collections, offer further evidence of Jawlensky's
attempt to abstract the general from the particular.

Alexei Jawlensky

86   NIGHT IN ST. PREX (Nacht in St. Prex) 1916

Oil on cardboard, 14 x 10⅝" (35.7 x 27 cm)
Inscribed (barely legible) "A. Jawlensky" (lower left)
Bernhard Koehler Donationn, 1965
G 14 669

At the beginning of World War I Jawlensky, as a former officer in the Russian army, was immediately expelled from Germany and fled to Switzerland with Marianne von Werefkin and their maid-companion Helene Nesnakomoff. Until 1917 the trio lived together in a house in St. Prex on Lake Geneva. In his reminiscences Jawlensky wrote: "In our small house I had only a tiny studio with a single window. I wanted to paint huge pictures with strong colors, but I sensed that this was impossible. My soul would not allow me to do this kind of sensual painting, although there is much beauty in my pictures. . . . I sat at my window. In front of me I saw a path and a few trees, and from time to time it was possible to see a mountain in the distance. I began to seek a new artistic approach. It was hard work. . . . My formats grew smaller: 30 × 40 centimeters. I painted a large number of pictures which I called *Variations on a Landscape Theme.* They are songs without words."

The landscapes which Jawlensky painted of the view from his room in St. Prex do indeed constitute a new departure in his work. His exclusive concentration on a single theme points to a desire for contemplative isolation, a retreat from wordly distractions. This tendency is clearly apparent in *Night in St. Prex,* in which the visible motifs – the trees and the shrub-lined path leading down to the lake – allude only superficially to reality. Jawlensky varied the theme of the view from his window in over one hundred pictures, some of which were painted as late as 1921, long after he had left St. Prex: "Working very hard and with great concentration, I gradually found the right forms and colors to express what my spiritual self demanded. Every day I painted these colored variations, taking my inspiration from the mood of nature and from my own spirit. It was here that I produced a whole series of my most beautiful variations, which to this day are unknown to all but a few people." Jawlensky's fellow members of the Blue Rider circle were initially taken aback by this radical shift in his painting style. The degree of abstraction in works such as this is determined by the function of nature as a key to the inner life of the artist.

Alexei Jawlensky

87 MEDITATION 1918

Oil on cardboard, 15¾ x 12¼" (40 x 31 cm)
Inscribed "A. Jawlensky" (lower left)
Bernhard Koehler Donation, 1965
G 13 340

In 1917 Jawlensky moved from St. Prex on Lake Geneva to Zurich. It was at this point that he turned his full attention to the depiction of the human face, which was to occupy him – with a degree of obsessiveness unparalleled in modern art – for the rest of his life. In the first group of works, painted between 1917 and 1921, Jawlensky used portraits of women and girls as the basis for a series of so called "mystical heads" and "saints, heads." One of these portraits was of Emmy Scheyer, herself an artist, who had seen a selection of Jawlensky's pictures at an exhibition in Lausanne in 1915 and promptly decided to devote herself to the task of promoting his work. Her features are alluded to in the narrow oval face and the stylized curls of the woman in *Meditation*. The face, with its fine structure of colored lines, seems to hover over the ocher ground; all further details of the hair and the neck have been eliminated. The closed eyelids and the three lopsided lines of the mouth contribute to the expression of a general, rather than individual, experience of human life and suffering.

In the basic geometrical figure of *Meditation*, and especially in the center of the face, with its closed eyes and the colored flecks of the "mark of wisdom" at the root of the nose, the elements are assembled which were to form the basis of all the subsequent "saints, heads," "abstract heads," and "meditations." Jawlensky painted literally hundreds of these faces, which for him were far more than merely formal studies. In his work, the human face became a medium for the experience of transcendence; the continuous variation of the same basic form was "a pathway to God." In a letter to his friend Father Willibrord Verkade, written in 1938, Jawlensky spoke of the reasons for this radical reduction of the function of art to a means of religious self-expression, which alone explains the limitation of his work to a single motif over a period of some twenty years:"For a number of years I painted these variations, and then it became necessary to find a form for the face, since I had understood that great art can only be painted with religious feeling. And for that, the human face was the only vehicle. I understood that the duty of the artist is to express, through forms and colors, that which is divine in himself. Hence the work of art is a visible god, and art itself is 'a longing for God'."

Alexei Jawlensky

88 MEDITATION "THE PRAYER"
(Meditation "Das Gebet") 1922

Oil on cardboard, 15¾ x 11¾" (40 x 30 cm)
Inscribed "A. J." (lower left)
Bernhard Koehler Donation, 1965
G 13 341

In 1921 Jawlensky put an end to his previous nomadic existence
by settling in Wiesbaden, where a highly successful exhibition
of his work had recently been held. It was there, in the 1920s
and 1930s, that he painted his extensive series of "abstract
heads," which are a logical continuation of the earlier "mystical
heads" and "saints' heads." Like many of the early picures in
the series, *Meditation "The Prayer"* features the light, almost
transparent colors found in the works from the first phase of
Jawlensky's interest in the human face. The artist reduces the
shape of the face to a schematic outline and twists it slightly to
one side, using subtle effects of line and color to lend it an air
of meditative rapture.

Armin Zweite has described this phase of Jawlensky's development thus: "Especially in the early 1920s, the forms of
Jawlensky's work take on a steadily increasing precision. The
formerly shapeless patches of color metamorphose into clearly
defined circles, which contrast with the orthogonal structure or
lines; the color itself also becomes more homogeneous. Step
by step, Jawlensky reduces the expressive content of the pictures, using a restricted vocabulary of stereotyped forms. The
cheeks and the chin are indicated by a large U-shape; the thin
lines of the nose and eyebrows generally meet at right angles,
vaguely hinting at the form of a cross. A horizontal line marks
the mouth, beneath which a semicircular colored shadow
paraphrases the curve of the chin. Over the forehead there is a
triangle, the tip of which points toward the crown of the head.
All that remains of the eyes, the most expressive feature of the
human face, is a horizontal or downward-curving line, which
in some of the pictures is accentuated by blurred bands of color.
The only reminder of Jawlensky's earlier work is to be found
in the curling strands of hair hanging down each side of the
face." Drawing on this limited repertoire of forms, Jawlensky's
"abstract heads" achieve a maximum degree of spiritual concentration. Despite the deliberate elimination of individual
features, the faces are by no means devoid of expression: on the
contrary, they have a specifically human, animated quality, and
convey the impression of, as the artist himself put it, "great
spirituality."

Alexei Jawlensky

89 **LOVE (Liebe)** 1925

Oil on cardboard, 23¼ x 19¼" (59 x 49.5 cm)
Inscribed "A. J." (lower left), "X.25" (lower right)
G 15 678

The large-format painting *Love* is one of the main works in
the series of pictures of the human face which Jawlensky created
in the 1920s. Its pure forms have a geometrical clarity and
precision which call to mind the work of other contemporary
artists. The austere horizontal and vertical lines, the circles and
semicircles, and the even application of the paint, from which
all irregularity has been banished, place the picture in a general
context of experimentation with the constructive laws of form.
In the mid-1920s Jawlensky temporarily emerged from his
self-imposed isolation and joined forces with Kandinsky, Klee,
and Lyonel Feininger – who at that time were teaching at the
Bauhaus – to form the group known as *Die Blauen Vier* (The
Blue Four). Although the name of the group echoes the program
of the Blue Rider, The Blue Four was primarily concerned with
the practical issues of exhibiting and marketing the pictures of
its members, especially in the USA, where its cause was energetically promoted by Emmy Scheyer. Jawlensky's contacts
with his three colleagues had little or no influence on his artistic
goals. Whereas in the work of Kandinsky, Klee, and Oskar
Schlemmer the use of elementary, schematic forms was bound
up with an attempt to uncover the spiritual foundations of the
world of appearances, Jawlensky was principally interested in
constructive form as a means of extending the possibilities of
personal religious experience. In his finest pictures from this
period he comes very close to capturing the essence of a mysterious original form which embodies an archetypal image of
human spirituality.

Alexei Jawlensky

90 **MEDITATION ON GOLD GROUND**
(Meditation auf Goldgrund) 1936

Oil on paper mounted on cardboard, 5½ x 4⅜" (14 x 11 cm)
Inscribed "A. J." (lower left), "36" (lower right)
Bernhard Koehler Donation, 1965
G 13 339

From 1929 on, Jawlensky suffered from arthritis, which made it increasingly difficult for him to paint at an easel. In the confessional letter which he wrote in 1938 to Father Willibrord Verkade, he described how the condition finally forced him to give up painting: "Years of toil passed. And then I fell ill; although my hands got stiffer and stiffer, I was still able to work. I could no longer hold the brush in one hand; I had to use both hands, and it was always very painful. I used a very small format, and I had to find a new technique. For three years, like one possessed, I painted these small abstract heads. I sensed that I would soon have to give up work altogether. And that indeed turned out to be the case."

In the series of "meditations" painted between 1934 and 1937 a further decisive change takes place in Jawlensky's treatment of the human face: the pictures attain an extreme degree of stylization. Armin Zweite offers the following comments on these works from the final stage of Jawlensky's career: "In one picture after another thick black lines are used to create a series of variations on the form of the Greek Orthodox cross, which rests on the horizontal line of the mouth and extends up to the eyebrows at the top. The parallel brushstrokes confer an independent structure on the zones of color between the lines. The transparent lines of the brushwork overlap at the edges and frequently form narrow opaque zones of thickened color, with the result that the dark and light areas merge into a unified whole. At the root of the nose the light-colored 'mark of wisdom,' which is added as a finishing touch, emphasizes the religious, meditative character of the pictures." This character is especially apparent in the present work, which is painted on a gold ground. Jawlensky's friend, the painter Alo Altripp, had suggested the use of this traditional medieval and Greek Orthodox technique in order to underline the symbolic quality of his depiction of the human face. The experiment was rarely repeated: Jawlensky, who always worked on several pictures at once, covering them with laborious brushstrokes, painted a mere five "meditations" on a gold ground.

Alexei Jawlensky

91 **MEDITATION** 1937

Oil on canvas mounted on cardboard, 9⅞ x 6⅞" (25 x 17.5 cm)
Inscribed "A. J." (lower left), "37" (lower right)
FH 234

This "meditation" is one of a large number of similar pictures
which Jawlensky painted in 1937. It is one of the last works he
created before his arthritis forced him to give up painting
altogether. He presented it to Willibrord Verkade, who was at
that time living in the Monastery of St. Martin in Beuron. On
the back he wrote the following dedication: "To my dear
friend Father Willibrord Verkade I send a splinter of my soul
A. Jawlensky." The late "meditations" are indeed a personal
confession which Jawlensky struggled obsessively to formulate
while battling with the pain that ultimately put an end to his
work. In this picture, only a vague trace remains of the human
face, indicated by the heavy lines of the Greek Orthodox cross.
From 1934, one notices a continuous darkening of the colors
in the "meditations." Jawlensky himself explained: "In my last
pictures I took away the magic of color in order to concentrate
still further the spiritual depth." The coarse brushwork bears
witness to the crippling pain suffered by the artist, who at the
end of his life could only paint by holding the brush in both
hands and moving the whole of his upper body. The extent to
which Jawlensky was prepared to suffer for his art testifies in
turn to the intense spiritual obsession that lies behind a large
part of his work.

Marianne von Werefkin

b. 1860 in Tula – d. 1938 in Ascona

Marianne von Werefkin, the daughter of a general, was born in Tula, south of Moscow. In 1886 her family moved to St. Petersburg, where her father was appointed the commandant of the fortress of SS Peter and Paul. Werefkin was the pupil of the famous realist painter Ilja Repin for the next ten years. In 1891 she met Alexei Jawlensky through her teacher. They worked together from then on, moving to Munich with Alexei Jawlensky that same year, where they occupied two grand adjoining flats in Giselastrasse in the Schwabing district. At first Jawlensky attended Anton Ažbe's private art school with his compatriots Igor Grabar and Dmitry Kardovsky, while Werefkin gave up painting for the next ten years in order to devote herself entirely to furthering Jawlensky's talent. After a summer holiday in Normandy in 1903, she and Jawlensky traveled to Paris and the south of France in 1905, which provided a decisive impetus for Werefkin to take up painting again. At the end of 1911, Werefkin and Jawlensky did not join the others in quitting the NKVM and founding the Blue Rider group. They did, however, take part in the group's exhibitions in the years to follow. At the outbreak of World War I in August 1914, Werefkin and Jawlensky, with Nesnakomoff and Andreas, being enemy aliens, had to leave the country. At first they rented a place to live in St. Prex, then in 1917 in Zurich and from 1918 on in Ascona. Their personal and financial situation deteriorated increasingly during this time. 1921 saw Werefkin and Jawlensky's final separation. Jawlensky moved to Wiesbaden with his family, while Werefkin stayed and worked in Ascona for the rest of her life.

Marianne von Werefkin

92 WASHERWOMEN (Wäscherinnen) *c.* 1909

Tempera on paper mounted on cardboard,
19⅞ x 25¼" (50.5 x 64 cm)
GMS 711

Unlike her artist friends Jawlensky, Kandinsky and Münter,
Werefkin continued with figurative painting during their intensely creative period together. In a very personal style, related
in form and palette to Symbolism, but developed by her from
1906/07 on, she incorporates inspirations from Van Gogh,
Gauguin and the Nabis, Japanese woodcuts and both European
and Russian Symbolism. The special characteristic of her
painting has often been described as 'painting of the soul.'
She succeeds in the metaphorical expression of psychological
states or hidden strengths. Combining the influence of her
much-esteemed Edvard Munch's 'painting of the soul' with
a dark palette fully oriented to its expressive powers, she rep-
resents a decidedly symbolic kind of painting within the *Neue
Künstlervereinigung München* (New Artists' Association of Munich).
She thus occupies the position of an artist depicting "inner experience" as called for by Kandinsky in the group's founding
circular.

The *Washerwomen*, painted in the liquid opaque tempera
Werefkin almost always used, stylistically reflects the influence
of the school of the Nabis succeeding Paul Gauguin. They had
attained a pictorial 'synthesis' through compositions of simple
planes of color with dark outlines. The central focus of Werefkin's
painting is the intense blue of the washtubs leaning against a
colorful flowerbed in the foreground and being held by the two
women in the front. Blue reappears in subtly varied nuances in
the aprons of the laundresses, the dress of the little girl on the
right, and the blue-gray zone of the sky, lending these elements
a particular emphasis. Werefkin applies a principle of organization
that further underscores the symbolism of the depiction: the
regular repetition of motifs showing movement. In this case
the laundresses in the front and the back both turn their backs to
the viewer in the same position. Additive rows, often of women
in black or of symbolically shaped architectural or landscape
elements, are a feature Werefkin will continue to develop in her
work. It often casts an aura that is not only visionary but also
uncannily mysterious. In the *Washerwomen* it acquires a special
touch through the contrast between scarlet, carmine, and blue-
gray flashing up on the right.

Marianne von Werefkin

93   **SELF-PORTRAIT (Selbstbildnis)**   *c.* 1910

Tempera on paper mounted on cardboard,
20⅛ x 13⅜" (51 x 34 cm)
Purchased with funds from the Gabriele Münter bequest in 1963
G 13 144

Her contemporaries described Marianne von Werefkin un-animously as a commanding personality with an extraordinary temperament and intellectual charisma. In the salon she and Jawlensky hosted in Giselastrasse in the district of Schwabing in Munich, which attracted large numbers of artists, writers, dancers and Russian aristocracy passing through town, she was the predominant center of attention, "the broadcasting station, as it were, of almost physically palpable waves of energy" (Gustav Pauli). Even in the years when she herself did not paint, she played a decisive role in the discussions on art theory in her salon, especially as she was thoroughly occupied with the trends of the French and Russian avant-garde.

Her *Self-Portrait* was painted around 1910 and shows her at her creative prime. With its outstanding boldness in color and expression, it is to this day one of the most unusual female self-portraits in the history of art. As if with a spontaneous movement, Werefkin turns around from a three-quarter profile to face the viewer. Most striking are the vermilion eyes, their point-shaped pupils on a steel-blue background, with which she stares at her opposite. Along with the open mouth in a warmer red, which has a touch of aggressiveness – yet also a slight bitterness – they testify to her overwhelming energy as well as her contradictory personality. The red of her lips and their curving shape are accented by the soft curve of her hat. Above her dark hair, it surrounds the elongated form of her face like a cap. The complementary blue-green and yellow shades of the background, its expressive brushstrokes showing the influence of Van Gogh, are repeated in refracted form in the face and throat of the sitter. They thus heighten the por-trait's 'wild' impression, something achieved in a similar fashion only by the Fauve painters and, later the *Brücke* artists.

August Macke

b. 1887 in Meschede – d. 1914 near Perthes-les-Hurlus, France

Macke studied painting from 1904 to 1906 at the Düsseldorf Academy. In 1907 he traveled for the first time to Paris, where he encountered the work of the Impressionists, whose use of color and emphasis on the sensual immediacy of experience exercised a fruitful influence on his artistic development. In 1907–08 he studied for six months with Lovis Corinth in Berlin. After a further stay in Paris he lived for a year by the Tegernsee lake in southern Bavaria. In 1910 he met and befriended Marc. Although Macke moved to Bonn the following year, he was one of the founding members of the Blue Rider group; he contributed to the almanac and took part in the group's exhibitions. In Bonn he became an important mediator between the Blue Rider and the Rhineland Expressionists. However, he rejected the mystical, "spiritual" emphasis of Marc and Kandinsky: for him, painting was a joyful recreation of nature by means of blocks of glowing color. This view of painting was confirmed by a visit with Marc to Robert Delaunay's Paris studio in 1912. The following year Macke spent eight months living on Lake Thun near Bern. Together with Klee and Louis Moilliet, he traveled to Tunis in the spring of 1914 and returned to Germany with a fund of new material. In August he was drafted into the army and, only a few weeks later, was killed in action in the Champagne region.

August Macke

94   PORTRAIT WITH APPLES
(Porträt mit Äpfeln) 1909

Oil on canvas, 26 x 23³/₈" (66 x 59.5 cm)
Inscribed "AMacke 1909" (center right), "(7) Porträt mit Äpfeln, Macke" (reverse)
Bernhard Koehler Donation, 1965
G 13 326

Macke painted *Portrait with Apples* shortly after moving with his young bride to Tegernsee, where he lived for over a year from the end of October 1909. The year in Tegernsee saw a decisive advance in Macke's artistic development. It was here that the basic direction of his early work emerged and that he found the leisure to digest in full the wide variety of influences to which he had been exposed in the course of his brief career: he had only begun to study art in 1905. During his stay in Tegernsee he created over 150 paintings, plus a large number of watercolors and drawings.

Macke's attractive young wife was one of his main sources of artistic inspiration. She had always been his favorite model, and in many of his pictures she is seen as a kind of female prototype, the very incarnation of womanhood. With its gently undulating contours, its sensitive use of color, and its careful composition, *Portrait with Apples* is patently the work of early masterhood. Facing the viewer head on, the pregnant woman stands in front of a dark brown background; in her hands she holds a bowl containing three apples. The yellow curtain on the right, the woman's calm face, with its downcast eyes, the dull white shawl around her shoulders, and the curve of her breasts are gently and evenly modeled in the soft light that falls from the front. One is reminded of the late pictures of Paul Cézanne, to which Carl Hofer had drawn Macke's attention on his recent trip to Paris. The bowl, in particular, with the red and yellow apples depicted in the manner of a still life, is clearly influenced by the work of the Frenchman. One of the most prominent features of Macke's art is the balanced arrangement of individual elements to create what the artist called "total harmony," an integration of color and form, of the figure and its surroundings. In this picture, the sense of harmony derives to a considerable extent from the air of contemplative calm which surrounds the central figure. In the early years of their marriage Macke painted numerous portraits of Elisabeth reading, sewing, or holding their child; her head is invariably lowered, which heightens the effect of quiet concentration. Macke was particularly proud of *Portrait with Apples,* which was shown at the 1912 Sonderbund exhibition in Cologne and subsequently bought by his wife's uncle, Bernhard Koehler (see plate 95).

August Macke

95 PORTRAIT OF BERNHARD KOEHLER
(Bildnis Bernhard Koehler) 1910

Oil on canvas, 25 x 16⅛" (63.5 x 41 cm)
Bernhard Koehler Donation, 1965
G 13 335

From the beginning of Macke's career, his wife's uncle, Bernhard Koehler, a wealthy Berlin industrialist, was a generous friend and patron. He helped to finance Macke's first trip to Paris in 1905, and later that year, when the aspiring young artist spent several months studying with Lovis Corinth in Berlin, he was warmly welcomed as a temporary member of the Koehler household: Koehler even gave him the money to buy paints and other materials. The following year Macke, his wife and her uncle traveled again to Paris, where they visited numerous galleries and Koehler, under Macke's guidance, bought a number of contemporary French paintings for his collection. Koehler was subsequently to become the major patron of the Blue Rider. He not only donated a substantial sum of money to finance the publication of the almanac in 1912 and the organization of the Erster Deutscher Herbstsalon (First German Salon d'Automne) in 1913; he also frequently helped Macke and his colleagues by buying their pictures.

With its simple, elegant forms, the present portrait, one of several that Macke painted of Koehler, conveys a sense of the artist's respect for his sitter's distinguished personality. The restraint in the use of color and the absence of detail in the neutral background point to the influence of modern French portraiture, and especially to the work of Edouard Manet, which Macke greatly admired. Koehler's face, with its blue eyes and even-tempered expression, is framed by the beard and the quiff of gray hair; his high forehead has a faintly rosy glow, suggesting a lively temperament. This picture, like *Portrait with Apples* (plate 94), comes from Koehler's private collection. Unfortunately, a large part of this valuable collection, which included works by Paul Cézanne, Claude Monet, Edgar Degas, Charles Camoin, and Robert Delaunay, as well as by the Blue Rider artists, was destroyed in Berlin in 1945.

August Macke

96 FARMBOY FROM TEGERNSEE
(Tegernseer Bauernbub) 1910

Oil on canvas, 34⅝ x 26⅛" (88 x 66.5 cm)
G 12 195

During the year he spent in Tegernsee Macke worked extremely hard, experimenting with the motifs which were to form
the basis of his relatively limited repertoire of subjects: landscape, still life, the human figure, and details from his house
and garden. He frequently used his neighbors' children as
models: in addition to the boy depicted here, he painted a
Farmgirl with Straw Hat (also in the Lenbachhaus) and a picture
of the village blacksmith's daughter clutching a doll. The new
stylistic approach apparent in these portraits owes a considerable debt to the work of Henri Matisse, in which Macke had
begun to take a keen interest. At the end of January 1910, he
had traveled to Munich to see an exhibition of pictures by
Matisse at the Thannhauser gallery. Macke was one of the first
German artists to recognize the exceptional importance of the
French painter, whom he rated higher than the Impressionists
and Post-Impressionists and in whom he perceived something
of a kindred spirit. He was particularly attracted by Matisse's
vividly glowing colors, by the simplicity of his themes, and
the ease with which he allowed his subjects to unfold on the
canvas. In this picture, however, rather than directly imitating
Matisse's highly expressive Fauvist style, Macke depicts the
boy in a subdued manner reminiscent of still-life painting.
Dressed in traditional Bavarian costume, with a high-necked
jacket, the generously proportioned figure of the boy sits in a
position which lacks a clear sense of spatial definition. The
rather sullen expression on his fresh face probably reflects his
resentment at having to sit still for the portrait. The face in
particular, with its lively brown eyes, stands out clearly against
the pale blue background. Macke had not yet abandoned the
conventional shadow behind the figure, which in the work of
Matisse is dissolved in the play of colors. Yet it was Matisse
whom he regarded as a model for his own work. In a letter to
his mother-in-law in 1910 he wrote: "I instinctively find him
the most congenial of the whole bunch [the Fauves]. An altogether passionate painter, animated by a holy zeal. The fact
that he is alleged to be a very simple person doesn't surprise
me in the least. I never imagined him to be otherwise."

August Macke

97 AT THE CIRCUS (Im Zirkus) 1911

Painting on glass, 4⅝ x 3½" (11.8 x 8.9 cm)
Inscribed in Gabriele Münter's hand "August Macke Bonn, 1911"
(on the cardboard backing)
GMS 721

Like *Two Girls in a Landscape*, this small-format painting on glass is characterized by a highly skillful use of line and contains a hint of modern exoticism. In the circus ring, which is painted a dull white and bordered by coral red, the slender figure of a female acrobat, wearing a golden leotard, balances on a gold and black horse. A man in a green tailcoat holds up a hoop for her to jump through; in the background, one sees the finely drawn outline of a clown wielding a long whip. The picture, which was probably painted in Sindelsdorf, evokes in miniature the world of the stage and the circus. This world fascinated such modern French artists as Edgar Degas and Henri Toulouse-Lautrec, as well as the German Expressionists, and formed the subject of a number of Macke's most famous paintings, including *Russisches Ballet* (*Ballet Russe;* Kunsthalle, Bremen) and *Seiltänzer* (*Tightrope Walker;* Städtisches Kunstmuseum, Bonn). The dully gleaming frame, with its spots of violet and green, strikes an additional note of playfulness.

August Macke

98 THREE GIRLS IN A BARQUE
(Drei Mädchen in einer Barke) 1912

Painting on glass, 14½ x 22" (37 x 56 cm)
Inscribed "August Macke, Die Barke, 1912 Hinterglas"
(on the cardboard backing)
G 12 983

In a different way from *At the Circus* (plate 97) this picture transports the viewer into a strange, exotic world. Three naked girls are depicted sitting in an elegantly curved boat, which floats gently downstream in an indeterminate zone between the riverbank, with its luxuriant vegetation, and the shimmering waves of a river. An oarsman, wearing only a loincloth and a turban, stands at the stern with his back to the viewer. The style of this Oriental vision, which at first sight appears unique in Macke's œuvre, was influenced by an exhibition of Islamic art which Macke saw in Munich in May 1910 and which caused a con-

siderable stir in artistic circles: even Henri Matisse, accompanied by fellow painter Hans Purrmann, paid a special visit to the Bavarian capital in order to avail himself of this rare opportunity to see examples of Islamic art at first hand. The effect of this new stimulus can be seen in a number of Macke's drawings and paintings from the period. The motif of *Three Girls in a Barque* is not, in fact, as unique as it might seem: the theme of three naked women recurs several times in Macke's work, in such pictures as *Drei Akte mit blauem Grund* (*Three Nudes with Blue Background,* 1910; Lenbachhaus) and the later *Drei Mädchen mit Stadt im Hintergrund* (*Three Girls with Town in the Background,* 1913; Staatsgalerie moderner Kunst, Munich). Macke combines the classical ideal of harmonious physical proportion with the notion of an earthly Paradise, which played a significant part in his thinking throughout his career. His ideal of carefree existence, unencumbered by worry, determines the form and content of many of his later pictures, including *Zoological Garden I, Promenade,* and *A Stroll on the Bridge* (plates 102, 105).

August Macke

99   OUR STREET IN GRAY
(Unsere Strasse in Grau) 1911

Oil on canvas, 31 ½ x 22⅝" (80 x 57.5 cm)
Inscribed in an unknown hand "Unsere Straße in Grau, 1913" (reverse, on
the canvas foldover)
Bernhard Koehler Donation, 1965
G 13 333

At the end of 1910 Macke and his wife returned from Tegernsee
to Bonn, where the artist finally set up a studio in February of
the following year. In *Marienkirche im Schnee* (*St. Mary's in the
Snow;* Kunsthalle, Hamburg) and *Marienkirche mit Häusern und
Schornstein* (*St. Mary's with Houses and Chimney;* Städtisches
Kunstmuseum, Bonn), the first pictures which he produced in
Bonn, he depicted one of the city's characteristic architectural
features, as seen from his studio. Shortly afterward, he painted
Our Street in Gray, a view of Bornheimer Strasse directly
beneath his window. Macke's wife, Elisabeth, recalls that
Bornheimer Strasse was "a busy street which offered a constant
source of visual stimuli: children walking to school in long
rows, soldiers marching to the barracks, hussars on horseback,
wagons and carts piled high with baskets. It was close to the
industrial quarter of the city, whose life and bustle August
always loved. The railroad line to Cologne was also nearby;
it ran under the Victoria bridge, right in front of the house.
From the studio window one could see St. Mary's church,
which, surrounded by houses, showed itself in a different mood
every day."

Judging by the two tentatively blossoming trees, it would
seem that *Our Street in Gray* was painted in the first days of
spring, before winter had finally passed. The gray of the over-
cast sky resonates throughout the picture, mingling with the
yellow, orange, and violet in the facades of the houses and with
the greenish tint of the fence around the patch of waste ground
on the corner; the road surface and the sidewalk are also
painted a fine pearl gray. The deliberate foreshortening of the
perspective at the top edge of the picture recalls the street scenes
of the French Impressionists; one is reminded, for example, of
the work of Albert Marquet. A certain French influence is also
apparent in the black arabesques of the passersby, the delicate
lines of the street lamps on either side of the road, and the
graceful drawing of the trees. When he visited Paris in 1907
Macke sketched a number of street scenes similar to this one.
These impressions of Paris are echoed in *Our Street in Gray.*

August Macke

100   **FLOWERS IN THE GARDEN, CLIVIA AND
GERANIUMS (Blumen im Garten, Clivia und
Pelargonien)** 1911

Oil on canvas, 35⅜ x 28⅛" (90 x 71.5 cm)
Inscribed "Macke 1911" (lower right)
Bernhard Koehler Donation, 1965
G 14 665

In the course of 1911 Macke found himself confronted with a
wide variety of influences, including that of the other Blue
Rider artists. Hence his work from this period, which evinces
several quite different approaches to painting, betrays no overriding stylistic unity. *Flowers in the Garden, Clivia and Geraniums*
continues in the vein of the still lifes which Macke had painted
in Tegernsee and can be seen as the culmination of his Fauvist,
Matisse-inspired phase. The picture is dominated by the rich
greens of the stylized foliage, which soak up the light and form
a bold contrast with the reds of the flower pots and the flowers
themselves against the violet background. The sheer intensity
of the pure colors confers an almost threatening quality on the
essentially harmless motif of a corner of Macke's garden in
Bonn. Despite the decorative effects of the leaves and flowers,
the most fascinating aspect of this pictorial tribute to Matisse is
its use of color to create a sense of depth. Macke himself spoke
of his quest to release the "spatial energy" of colors. This played
a central part in his subsequent attempts to come to terms
with the challenge posed by Futurism and Cubism, which
eventually resulted in the original, prismatic solutions to the
problem of color seen in his mature work from 1913 onward.

August Macke

101 **INDIANS ON HORSEBACK**
(Indianer auf Pferden) 1911

Oil on wood, 17⅜ x 23⅝" (44 x 60 cm)
Bernhard Koehler Donation, 1965
G 13 327

Indians on Horseback is clearly influenced by the ideas and the
"spiritualized" style of the Blue Rider artists Kandinsky and
Marc. The choice of motif deviates from Macke's general
policy of concentrating on the depiction of the real, perceptible
world. Two delicately painted Indians with feathered head-
dresses are seen riding through a brightly colored imaginary
landscape; a third Indian carrying a spear walks ahead of them.
The transparent, stylized forms of the mountains and the slanting trees owe an obvious debt to the work of Marc. It is
possible that the picture was painted in the summer of 1911,
while Marc was staying with Macke in Bonn after his honeymoon in London. On this occasion the two artists worked
together in Macke's studio, as Macke had always dreamed of
doing. Since his return to Bonn from Tegernsee, Macke had
corresponded regularly with his friend: the artists' letters offer
a wealth of insights into their respective aesthetic theories. In
1910 Marc had tried to interest Macke in the ideas of the *Neue
Künstler-Vereinigung München*, which he himself had joined at
the instigation of Kandinsky. However, Macke, whose sense of
form was decidedly nontheoretical, was skeptical about the
group: "The association is a very serious affair," he wrote in
September 1910, shortly after visiting one of the association's
exhibitions, "and I prefer its art to anything else. But it doesn't
move me. . . . Kandinsky, Jawlensky, Bekhteyev, and Erbslöh
have tremendous artistic sensibility. But *their means of expression
are too big* for what they are trying to say. . . . It seems to me
that they are *struggling* too hard to find a form. There is a great
deal to be learned from this struggle. But to me, Kandinsky's
early pictures and a number of Jawlensky's things seem somewhat empty. And there is rather too much color in Jawlensky's
heads." Nevertheless, Macke subsequently allowed himself to
be drawn into the Blue Rider circle; in the fall of 1911 he
joined the committee which edited the almanac. He too became interested in "primitive" art, which formed the subject
of his essay "Die Masken" ("The Masks"), a poetic celebration
of the expressive power of primitive art forms which was
published in the almanac.

The interest in cultures untouched by civilization may have
determined his choice of Indian subject matter in this and two
further pictures. However, this taste for exotic narrative is only
one of the many facets of his art, in which form is invariably
seen as a means of exploring the essence of the material world,
rather than the realm of the spirit. In The Blue Rider almanac
he wrote: "Unfathomable ideas express themselves in comprehensible forms – comprehensible through our senses as stars,
thunder, flowers, as form. Our senses are the bridge between
the unfathomable and the comprehensible." The visible world
remained the focus of Macke's art, and he soon began to reject
what he saw as the excessive emphasis placed by the other Blue
Rider artists on abstract ideas. The year 1912 saw his first encounter with Futurism and Cubism, which gave a new formal
stimulus to his work.

August Macke

102 **ZOOLOGICAL GARDEN I**
(Zoologischer Garten I) 1912

Oil on canvas, 23 x 38⅝" (58.5 x 98 cm)
Bernhard Koehler Donation, 1965
G 13 329

Zoological Garden I is one of Macke's best-known pictures. The artist himself was extremely pleased with the work, whose underlying theme – the world of middle-class leisure – was to become one of his favorite subjects. He hit upon the motif of the zoo in the spring of 1912, while staying in Amsterdam, where he made a large number of preparatory sketches, including one of the parrot whose flamboyant plumage dominates the foreground of the present work. Subsequently, he set up his easel at Cologne Zoo and painted numerous studies there, which formed the basis not only of *Zoological Garden I,* but also of *Kleiner Zoologischer Garten in Gelb und Braun* (*Small Zoological Garden in Yellow and Brown;* private collection) and the triptych *Grosser Zoologischer Garten* (*Large Zoological Garden;* Museum am Ostwall, Dortmund).

The masterly composition of *Zoological Garden I* points to a new development in Macke's work. In January 1912 he had seen one of Robert Delaunay's paintings of the Eiffel Tower in an exhibition at the Gereons-Club in Cologne and had been greatly impressed by its transparent, fragmented forms. Delaunay's "Orphic" Cubism is echoed in the angular, broken forms which structure the rich colors of Macke's pictures from 1912 onward. A striking feature of *Zoological Garden I* is the even, rhythmical distribution of the stylized, bowler-hatted figures on the right, particularly noticeable in the group of three standing with their backs to the viewer. The play of light and color is heightened by the precious "trimming" of flowers and lights between the animals and the people. For Macke, the zoo was an ideal theme, a source of exotic images in a domesticated setting, dominated by the idea of leisure and offering an opportunity to experience a sense of harmony between man and nature.

August Macke

103 CHILDREN WITH GOAT (Kinder mit Ziege) 1913

Oil on cardboard, 9$\frac{1}{2}$ x 13$\frac{3}{8}$" (24 x 34 cm)
Inscribed "Aug. Macke 1913" (lower right)
Bernhard Koehler Donation, 1965
G 13 331

In October 1913 Macke moved from Bonn to Hilterfingen, a village on the Lake of Thun in Switzerland, where he stayed until June the following year. This was the most productive period of his career: it was in Hilterfingen that the mature, relaxed style of his late pictures evolved. His range of subjects remained limited: the majority of his pictures from this period feature strolling couples, women standing in front of shop-windows, or bathing girls. In her memoirs Macke's wife, Elisabeth, recalls that *Children with Goat* was painted at the beginning of the fall, when the weather was still warm and summery. With her characteristic gift for observation, she gives the following account of her husband's artistic aims: "What most interested August Macke at that time was the sense of dynamic energy conveyed not only by the formal organization of space, but also by the play of colors . . . for him, color had to work, to vibrate, to live. August strove, above all, to balance and reconcile pure colors in a picture, so as to create a sense of harmony and unity, despite the necessary contrasts." In *Children with Goat* the fine nuances of color in the green of the foliage above the children's heads do indeed have a vibrant quality, causing the eye to flicker back and forth. Standing in a pool of light, the children appear protected and sheltered by the surrounding trees, wrapped up in a care-free, innocent world of their own.

The use of color to create a sense of life and movement is one of the most prominent features of Macke's mature work. Although he had already learned a good deal about the depiction of time and movement from Futurism, the most important influence on his style was his encounter with the work of Robert Delaunay, whose cityscapes and pictures of the Eiffel Tower he had seen in the first Blue Rider exhibition. Two years later in 1913, he saw Delaunay's series of "window" pictures in an exhibition at the Gereons-Club in Cologne and was deeply impressed by their prismatic, colored forms. In a note written in 1914 he spoke of his striving "to concentrate life – and space as well – in a single moment. We apprehend light very quickly. We take in the individual parts of the picture very quickly. The difference between sequentiality and simultaneous animation remains." Whereas in Delaunay's work the materiality of the colors themselves – their intervals, contrasts, and formal energy – is the real subject of the picture, Macke uses color to convey the essential unity, the "great harmony" of life.

August Macke

104 MILLINER'S SHOP (Hutladen) 1913

Oil on canvas, 21 ½ x 17 ⅜" (54.5 x 44 cm)
Inscribed "Macke 1913" (lower right)
Bernhard Koehler Donation, 1965
G 13 334

Macke first used the motif of the woman standing in front of a shopwindow in his seminal picture of 1912 *Grosses helles Schaufenster* (*Large Light Shopwindow*; Sprengel Museum, Hanover). This painting was influenced by Futurism – in particular, by Umberto Boccioni's *La strada entra la casa* (*The Street Invades the House;* Sprengel Museum, Hanover) – and depicts a woman standing, with her back to the viewer, in front of a shopwindow in which a street scene is mirrored: the reflection is broken up into a myriad of colored facets. A year later, Macke returned to this motif in the pictures of fashion stores and milliner's shops which he painted in Hilterfingen. In the intervening period he had encountered the art of Robert Delaunay, which was to be a major influence on his mature work. Delaunay's "window" pictures, which caused a considerable stir in the German art world – Paul Klee was also influenced by them – greatly appealed to Macke's sense of form and sensual harmony. In these works, whose subject is the image of the Eiffel Tower as reflected in a window, Macke saw the expression of "a quite heavenly reveling in the sun and in life." He wrote an enthusiastic letter to his wife's uncle, Bernhard Koehler, advising him to buy *Les Fenêtres 2*: "I have just received a reply from Delaunay. I have been thinking about it [his work] a great deal recently. Windows like mirrors, in which, on a sunny day, one sees the city and the Eiffel Tower, the deep violet reflections, on the left the wonderful orange, at the bottom the pale blue houses, from which again and again the green tower rises steeply up into the azure sky, offset by the sharp glint of the windowpane. . . . Above all, you must see for yourself how the colors take on a wonderful depth when one looks at the painting from a distance. It is all so superbly balanced."

In *Milliner's Shop* the motif has a quality of almost magical concentration. The slender figure of the woman, with her royal-blue dress, stands as if mesmerized by the window display. The hats are displayed on golden stands, like some form of precious fetish. Macke dispenses with illusionistic effects in the depiction of the windowpane, which is at once present and absent: there is no division between the two levels of reality. The richly colored, expensive hats offer themselves as objects of consumption and take on a life of their own, casting a spell on the woman. The only direct allusion to the work of Delaunay is to be seen in the angular blocks of yellow and pale violet in the center of the picture. Rather than copying the formal experiments of the French artist, Macke uses intensity of color to evoke a particular vision in an exceptionally precise manner. As Ilse Erdmann wrote to the poet Rainer Maria Rilke, "it is as if the experience of life's essential transience had revealed itself to him [Macke] in the image of a woman standing still and then walking on."

August Macke

105 **PROMENADE** 1913

Oil on cardboard, 20⅛ x 22½" (51 x 57 cm)
Inscribed "August Macke 1913" (lower left)
Bernhard Koehler Donation, 1965
G 13 328

The pictures that Macke painted in Hilterfingen of people strolling by the lake are among the finest in his entire œuvre. These park scenes have an almost dreamlike quality and a quite exceptional charm. After Macke's death, his widow described the pictures as follows: "They are characterized by a loose, relaxed use of glowing color, especially in the greens of the trees, the blue of the sky, and the patches of sunlight on the ground, which darken from the brightest yellow to the deepest reddish brown. In this atmosphere the outlines of the figures are soft, but not without contrast; there are no longer sharp contours, everything is in a state of flux, the color is dematerialized, like melted enamel. In these small pictures, which shine like jewels, one sees an intense concentration. . . . They are truly poetic visions of everyday life painted with unabashed joy and with a deep, fervent commitment."

Macke frequently uses the motif of the bridge or the wall along the promenade, with figures leaning over the parapet and staring at the water below. In *Promenade* two identically dressed men and a schematically outlined woman with a red skirt and white blouse are depicted in this pose, seemingly lost in thought. In the foreground, etched against the curving colored forms of the trees and the path, an elegantly dressed young couple stands in intimate but silent communion. The network of relationships between the outlines of the two figures includes an element of distance: they are together yet at the same time apart. Magdalena Moeller describes *Promenade* thus: "As in many of Macke's park scenes, time appears to stand still. The picture, which shows people at leisure, is a record of a fleeting moment. . . . If one looks at the work more closely, the scene takes on an air of unreality; one notices a strange sense of stillness. Despite the dynamic element in the colors and the composition, everything seems frozen and static." Conveying a sense of the transience of the experience which it depicts, the work has a faint undertone of melancholy.

August Macke

106   TURKISH CAFE (Türkisches Café) 1914

Oil on wood, 23⅝ x 13¾" (60 x 35 cm)
Inscribed "Aug. Macke 1914" (lower right)
Bernhard Koehler Donation, 1965
G 13 325

In April 1914 Macke, Klee, and Louis Moilliet went on the journey to Tunis which was later to acquire legendary status as a milestone in the history of modern art. The Mediterranean light and colors fired Macke's imagination afresh, and he returned home with a bulging portfolio of watercolors and sketches. When he arrived back in Bonn, he painted two versions of *Turkish Café*, one of which – the present work – he presented to Bernhard Koehler, who had helped to finance the trip. According to Moilliet, the subject of the picture is the covered entrance at the foot of the steps leading up to the famous Café des Nattes in Sidi-Bou-Said. Whereas the drawings in Macke's sketchbook are highly detailed, the painting is simple and direct, relying entirely on the power of its strong, pure colors, which have an almost abstract quality. The seated figure of the Arab, dressed in a green robe, seems to have been cut out of the blue wall, whose color is set off by the red of the Arab's fez. This in turn contrasts with the orange and red of the doorway in the center of the picture, while the yellow of the chair and the striped awning is complemented by the blue of the wall. In a manner different from that of Kandinsky or Marc, Macke imbues his pictures with a sense of "inner necessity," using a restricted range of colors and forms.

August Macke

107 GARDEN GATE (Gartentor) 1914

Watercolor on paper, 12¼ x 8⅞" (31 x 22.5 cm)
On permanent loan from the Gabriele Münter and Johannes Eichner Foundation
FH 185

On his trip to Tunis Macke devoted all his artistic energies to
drawing and watercolor painting. The most productive period
of his two-week stay was the four days from April 10 to 13,
which the three friends, Macke, Klee, and Moilliet, spent at
the country house of Dr. Jaeggi in St. Germain near Tunis.
Klee and Macke painted several watercolors of the house and
its surroundings. On April 10 Macke wrote to his wife: "I must
have done a good fifty sketches today; yesterday it was twenty-
five. I am working like the devil and enjoying it more than
ever before." The garden gate of the country house is painted
in partly running colors over a delicate pencil drawing. Despite
the atmospheric quality of the medium, the colors are evenly
handled and succeed in conferring a lyrical form on the motif.

August Macke

108 **ST. GERMAIN NEAR TUNIS**
(St. Germain bei Tunis) 1914

Watercolor on paper, 10¼ x 8¼" (26 x 21 cm)
Bernhard Koehler Donation, 1965
G 14 666

St. Germain near Tunis would appear to be a picture of the view from the house of Macke's host, Dr. Jaeggi: the same motif occurs in Klee's watercolors. Here, as in *Garden Gate* (plate 107), the color is laid over a pencil sketch but liberates itself from the drawing and forms a separate, autonomous structure. Macke seldom used forms as free as those of the squares of blue in the sky, and yet he still succeeds in conveying sensitively the essence of his subject. It was with Macke's supreme confidence in the handling of color that Marc chose to conclude the deeply moving obituary which he wrote following his friend's death in action shortly after the outbreak of World War I: "We painters are well aware that, with the passing of his harmonies, color in German art will pale by several tones and will take on a duller, dryer sound. He gave color the lightest and purest sound, as clear and light as his own personality."

Robert Delaunay

b. 1885 in Paris – d. 1941 in Montpellier

In 1902, having quit school, Robert Delaunay began a two-year apprenticeship as a stage set designer. He first exhibited at the Salon des Indépendants in 1904, showing paintings in a late Impressionist style. At his mother's house he made the acquaintance of the 'naive' painter Henri Rousseau and the writer Guillaume Apollinaire. In 1907, at the Parisian salon of the German art historian Wilhelm Uhde, he met the young Russian painter Sonia Terk. They married a few years later after her divorce from Uhde. In 1907 he began painting his first large original series, *Saint-Séverin*, *La Ville*, and *La Tour*. The Cubisticly fragmented *Tour Eiffel* pictures, of which one was shown at the first exhibition of the Blue Rider, made a strong impression on the German artists. From the spring of 1912 on, Delaunay painted his large series of *Fenêtres* (window paintings), which again influenced German artists such as Paul Klee, Franz Marc and August Macke, who visited Delaunay in his Paris studio.

During World War I, Robert and Sonia Delaunay lived in Portugal, returning to Paris in 1921. In 1931 Delaunay became a member of the Abstraction-Création group, the leading society of abstract artists in France. He quit in 1934, along with Naum Gabo, Hans Arp, Sophie Taeuber-Arp and Otto Freundlich. In 1937, he and his wife were in charge of decorating two pavilions for the Paris World Fair. He painted his last series, *Rythmes sans fin* (Rhythms without End), during these years.

Robert Delaunay

109   WINDOW ON THE CITY (Fenêtre sur la ville) 1914

Encaustic on cardboard, 11⅜ x 7⅞" (28,8 x 20 cm)
Inscribed "r. delaunay" (lower left)
On permanent loan from the Gabriele Münter and Johannes Eichner Foundation
FH 172

Having prepared himself by painting his *La Ville* series, which
showed a view of the Eiffel Tower across the rooftops of Paris
framed by an ornamental curtain – in a fragmented Cubist style
under a Pointillist color grid – Delaunay rapidly completed the
series of *Windows* he started in April 1912. After the 'deconstruc-
tion' of the previous series, he now began constructing a picture solely from autonomous color grids. They no longer serve
an external figurative function but develop two-dimensionally
according to their own laws of motion. Thus the space, volume
and motif, on which a picture is traditionally based, literally
become insubstantial. Despite the fact that a green or bluish silhouette of the Eiffel Tower can still be surmised in all of them,
the *Window* paintings stand for much more than the depiction
of a view of the tower through windowpanes that refract the
light in colorful prisms. It is the material of the colors themselves, their constructive energies, intervals and contrasts, that
here become the subject matter of painting. Delaunay makes
use of the "simultaneous contrasts" discovered by the chemist
M.E. Chevreul in a new way. Unlike complementary contrasts,
these do not attain equilibrium. Rather, each color is attracted to
its complementary color in the neighboring field, thus keeping
the eye in constant motion.

The significance of this far-reaching process of replacing the
painting's subject with vibrating fields of color and of restruc-
turing the painting's message, was clearly understood by the
German artists. The *Window* paintings were received with ap-
plause in Germany, as opposed to France. The first to see and
comment on the new series was Paul Klee in July 1912, at the
exhibition of the *Moderne Bund* (Modern Union) in Zurich.
Similarly enthusiastic were the reactions of Marc and Macke
when they visited Delaunay's studio in Paris in October 1912.
While still on his trip home, Marc wrote to Kandinsky: "He is
working his way through to truly constructive paintings without any representational aspect whatsoever; purely tonal fugues,
as it were."

It was on the occasion of Delaunay's large one-man show in
Berlin and Cologne, which included numerous *Window* paintings, that Guillaume Apollinaire coined the term "Orphism,"
meaning a colorful version of Cubism, in order to characterize
Delaunay's transparent prismatic style of painting. This colorful,
refractive Orphism became fundamental for the work of Franz
Marc and August Macke during their mature period up to 1914.
The small *Window* in the Lenbachhaus collection is not dated,
but according to a list Delaunay made, it was not painted until
1914. The use of wax crayons and white highlights in this work
has caused the transparency of the pictures to make way for a
somewhat greater density. The centrifugal 'propeller forms' in the
upper half of the picture suggest his contemporary series of
Circular Forms. They also embodied what Delaunay considered
pure color energy and a correspondingly turbulent, modern
way of seeing.

Heinrich Campendonk

b. 1889 in Krefeld – d. 1957 in Amsterdam

Heinrich Campendonk, at fifteen, began an apprenticeship at the trade school for textiles in Krefeld. In 1905, however, he switched to the school of arts and crafts there, where the Netherlander Johannes Thorn Prikker became his important teacher and mentor. He soon made the acquaintance of Helmuth Macke, a fellow student who was a cousin of August Macke. From 1909, Campendonk worked on his own in unstable financial conditions. Through Helmuth and August Macke he came into contact with the *Neue Künstlervereinigung München* (New Artists' Association of Munich) in 1910. In the fall of 1911 Campendonk moved from the Rhineland to Sindelsdorf in the immediate vicinity of Franz Marc. For the next few years, his work was strongly influenced by his artist friends working in the area, primarily by Franz Marc but also Kandinsky. After Marc was killed in the war, Campendonk and his young family moved to Seeshaupt on Lake Starnberg in May 1916.

In 1921 Campendonk returned to Krefeld, where the industrialist and patron Paul Multhaupt provided him with a house. After completing a series of public commissions, he was appointed in October 1926 upon the recommendation of Walter Kaesbach to teach the master class in mural painting, stained glass, mosaics and tapestry weaving at the Düsseldorf Academy of Art. In 1933 Campendonck was 'relieved' of this position by the National Socialists. He was appointed to the Royal Academy of Art in Amsterdam in 1935 as Professor of Monumental and Decorative Art. After World War II, despite numerous offers of employment in Germany, Campendonk never returned to his native land.

Heinrich Campendonk

110   **FOREST, GIRL, GOAT**
(Wald, Mädchen, Ziege) 1917

Oil on canvas, 37 x 25¼" (94 x 64 cm)
Inscribed "C./17" (below center)
G 15 388

In his early years as the "youngest of the Blue Riders"
Campendonk was first very much under the spell of Kandinsky's
semi-abstract forms and colors, and later increasingly under that
of Franz Marc. From 1913, Campendonk's artistic individuality
takes on a more distinct form, further developing the earlier
influences in a unique way into the early 20s. In *Forest, Girl, Goat*
dating from 1917, Campendonk's own typical interpretation of
Franz Marc's artistic visions of an original state when people and
animals were one, a 'yearning for a lost paradise,' is mysteriously fairy tale-like. In a darkly glowing, sylvan solitude in predominantly brown and blue-green shades, sits a girl dressed in
rustic clothing with a goat lying behind her. Both are in profile
parallel to the picture plane, side by side in peace and quiet. Her
plain round shapes make the goatherd look like a primitively
carved wooden figure, thus further underscoring the impression
of simplicity and immobility. Overlapping the animal's head is
one of those plant verticals common in Franz Marc's paintings,
where plant forms, such as trees or surrounding bushes, inter-
weave intricately with the animals shown resting among them.
In Campendonk's work, however, the convincing logic of
Franz Marc's transparent structures does not prevail. Rather, an
additive coexistence of forms of various objects often includes
human figures that are thus given a strange floating quality.

The speed and intensity with which Campendonk's decisive
personal and artistic contacts to his Blue Rider friends came
about the moment he moved to Sindelsdorf, are indicated in a
note he wrote to his partner Adda Deichmann on 7 October
1911 shortly after his arrival: "I reached Munich at seven in the
morning, met [Helmuth] Macke an hour later. In the afternoon we went to von Kandinsky's [sic], where we saw grand
things and met, among other gentlemen, Mr Kuno Amiet. On
Monday we went to the Thannhauser Salon and the Pinakothek,
and also met Erbslöh. In the evening we traveled with Macke's
cousin [August] to Penzberg, where Mr. Marc collected us
with a carriage and off we trotted to Sindelsdorf." *Forest, Girl,
Goat* was already painted in Seeshaupt, where Campendonk
moved from Sindelsdorf after Franz Marc had died in the war
in the spring of 1916.

Alfred Kubin
b. 1877 in Litoměřice – d. 1959 in Zwickledt

Alfred Kubin was born in Litoměřice in 1877 in northern Bohemia in the present day Czech Republic. His father was a land surveyor for the imperial Austro-Hungarian government. The family moved to the Austrian heartland shortly afterwards. After dropping out of school, Kubin began a photography apprenticeship in Klagenfurt, Austria. In 1898, Kubin went to study art in Munich. His decisive experience came in 1899 when he saw Max Klinger's cycle of etchings, *Paraphrase über den Fund eines Handschuhs* (*Paraphrase on Finding a Glove*). As Kubin put it, he was overwhelmed by a crisis that caused him to see a "torrent of visions of black-and-white pictures" and led him to discover an expressive world of his own for his nightmarish and fantastic early work.

From then until 1904, hundreds of drawings comprising Alfred Kubin's early works were produced in a special pen and ink technique with wash and spray. In 1903, when the future Munich publisher Hans von Weber issued these sensational drawings in a portfolio of facsimile prints, the so-called the *Weber-Mappe*, Kubin's then rather disreputable fame was established. In 1906 Alfred and Hedwig Kubin moved from Munich to Zwickledt, a small country estate in upper Austria above the river Inn. In a sudden rush of inspiration Kubin wrote his novel, *Die andere Seite* (*The Other Side*) in the fall of 1908, complete with illustrations. They show the fluid, black-and-white pen and ink style of drawing that is characteristic for Kubin's entire late period up to the end of his life. In 1909 Kubin joined the *Neue Künstler-Vereinigung München* and in 1911, he joined the Blue Rider group. Kubin's second major portfolio, *Sansara – Ein Zyklus ohne Ende* (*A Cycle without End*), appeared in 1911. It was followed by a number of other print portfolios in the decades to come, and many illustrations for books. From Zwickledt, Kubin kept in touch with a great deal of people in the second half of his life, mostly through correspondence. Writers such as Hans Carossa, Thomas Mann and Ernst Jünger numbered among them.

Alfred Kubin

111 **WONDERBIRD (Wundervogel)** 1905

Paste and paint, 10 x 14¼" (25.5 x 36.1 cm)
Inscribed "A Kubin" (lower right)
Kub. No. 287

The early period of Kubin's pen and ink drawings, with their sensational and often shocking themes of violence and sexuality from the 'torture chambers of the unconscious,' was followed in 1904 by a reorientation phase, lasting until 1908. In the spring of 1905 he traveled to Vienna in search of new artistic ideas. There he met members of the Vienna *Secession*, including Koloman Moser. Moser introduced him to his paste and paint technique, with which he had achieved ornamental effects and created unusual hues. Kubin produced large numbers of such paste paintings, and as early as June of that year he exhibited many of them at a Munich art salon. The *Wonderbird* belongs to this first series. The bird, an imaginary combination of turkey and peacock, appears all the more exotic against the fairy-tale atmosphere of the diffuse ochre-grey background, which looks like a rubbing. Not all critics approved of Alfred Kubin's new paste and paint technique; some found it too decorative and that its manufacture left too much to chance. Hence the art historian Franz Düllberg, who knew Kubin from the Schwabing circle revolving around Karl Wolfskehl and Countess von Reventlow, wrote: "Unusual and promising, however, is a new technique that Kubin now makes use of a lot: a wet paste is spread on a surface of soft scumbled paints – partly, *horribile dictu*, with a finger – and shaped into an arabesque resembling floral, animal or human forms and then detailed, for instance by means of pen drawing. (…) Seriously, however, the artist could easily find his way from work of this kind to delicately florid and toned col-ored endpapers for bookbinding, and particularly to lovely pottery in the style (not the sense) of English Doulton ware."

Inspired by a trip to the south of France in the autumn of 1905, Kubin worked with paste and paints once again, painting a series of jungle and tropical pictures. He dropped the tech-nique soon afterwards.

Alfred Kubin

112 SMOKING NEGRESSES
(Rauchende Negerinnen) 1905

Tempera on the verso of a cadastral map,
12½ x 15½" (31.8 x 39.2 cm)
Inscribed "A Kubin" (lower left)
Kub. No. 290

Looking back on the end of his experiments with the paste and paint technique during his creative reorientation between 1904 and 1908, Kubin wrote: "After extensive effort, and once the first creative frenzy had dissipated, I realized that my technique made me too dependent on chance, so I turned to pure tempera." At first, after a short stay in Paris in early 1906, Kubin was inspired by Odilon Redon as well as the Barbizon School and painted a series of muddy brown landscapes. That autumn he moved from Munich to Zwickledt, where his better-known "submarine landscapes" and microscopic scenes were painted. However, these did not satisfy Kubin either.

Through Father Willibrod Verkade, who was working in Alexei Jawlensky's studio at the time, Kubin became influenced by the two-dimensional style of Paul Gauguin and the Nabis school in early 1907, falling completely under the spell of models from abroad.

Kubin's *Smoking Negresses* shows his attempt to conform closely to the style of the Nabis by refusing "any originality whatsoever." Even in theme, the broad brown figures of the women, sitting relaxed and facing each other in a two-dimensionally outlined coastal landscape, are borrowed from Gauguin's example. Despite the color highlights of the red fruits and the matte, glowing, yellow landscape and the soft modeling of the figures, the picture remains oddly dull and lifeless. The pair of women is a conception that refers back via Gauguin to 19th century models and Delacroix's orientalism. The latter was surely what secretly fascinated Kubin more than Gauguin's world of forms. The aura of an older tradition in an unconvincing modern adaptation may also contribute to the inconsistent impression made by this painting.

Alfred Kubin

113 **ENCOUNTER (Begegnung)** *c.* 1911

Pen and ink and pencil on the verso of a cadastral map,
7¾ x 5¼" (11⅛ x 7¼") 19.6 x 13.5 cm (28.3 x 18.3 cm)
Inscribed "meinem lieben Kandinsky und dem verehrten Fräulein Münter
Alfred. Kubin" (below the drawing on the right in lead)
GMS3 700

After having written and illustrated his novel *Die andere Seite*
(*The Other Side*) in the winter of 1908, Kubin found the fluid
style of drawing he was to use for the rest of his life. His new,
mobile, black-and-white pen and ink style attained its first
peak with the publication of his *Sansara* portfolio in 1911.
Kubin exhibited some of the original drawings of the *Sansara*
series, including *Der Orgelmann* (*The Organ-Player*), *Zigeunerlager*
(*Gypsy Camp*) and *Schlangen in der Stadt* (*City Snakes*), at the
second Blue Rider exhibition in the spring of 1912. He was
working concurrently on another series of drawings that he
called "direct dream-pieces" in his autobiography of 1917. The
two series exhibit common stylistic features, such as the distorted forms of the "scraps of memory" (Kubin) and their flex-
ible contours. The pen drawing of the *Encounter*, rather plain in
its motif compared to the mysterious swarms of figures in
many works of this period, shows the drawn-out lines of dream
images recorded from memory. This depiction of an encounter
– between a deer or llama and a barely distinguishable snow-
covered tree bending towards it – makes use of the principles
of concealment and disguise applied by Kandinsky in order to
mystify and finally dissolve the pictorial form. "To speak about
secret things in secret terms," as formulated by Kandinsky in
the preface to the catalogue of the second exhibition of the
Neue Künstlervereinigung München (New Artists' Association of
Munich) in 1910, is poetically reflected in this small *Encounter*.
A variant entitled *Lama* (*Llama*), in the Albertina in Vienna,
shows a more clearly recognizable vulture-like bird in the tree-
top which the hoofed animal is looking up at. Kubin gave this
drawing to Wassily Kandinsky and Gabriele Münter with a
dedication.

Alfred Kubin

114　**THE SPIRIT OF AIR (Der Luftgeist)**　*c.* 1912

Pen and ink, watercolor and opaque white on the verso of a cadastral map,
5⅕ x 8⅕" (7⅞ x 12⅜") 14.1 x 21.7 cm (20 x 31.5 cm)
Inscribed "Juli 1912 Kubin für Frl. Münter"
(below the drawing on the right in lead)
GMS 701

The influence of Paul Klee, his artist colleague in the circle around the Blue Rider, who was also working exclusively on drawings at the time, is clearly recognizable for several years in Kubin's drawings from about 1912 on. Some sources indicate that Kubin had known Klee as early as in 1905; it is certainly documented that he first wrote to Klee in November 1910 asking to purchase one of his drawings. This developed into a lively relationship and the mutual exchange of drawings. Kubin was particularly impressed by Paul Klee's illustrations for Voltaire's *Candide*, which Klee had been working on since 1911. He brought the completed series to Kubin in Zwickledt in June 1912. Jürgen Glaesemer, who analyzed these lasting influences in exemplary fashion, sums up: "The impression of the *Candide* illustrations on Kubin's drawing style is striking. Klee's drawings inspired him to similarly dematerialize the figures to

marionette-like schemata in what is superficially a closely related style." While many of these drawings in a calligraphic hand quiver in "the utmost dilution" as a "vision. . . . in the air, like half an idea" (Wilhelm Hausenstein), the drawing of the *Spirit of Air* shows an additional new influence. Kubin had been corresponding and exchanging work regularly with Lyonel Feininger in Berlin since the end of 1911. Their acquaintance had come about through the draughtsman Rudolf Grossmann. In many works by Kubin dated 1912–1915 influences from both Klee and Feininger are superimposed upon each other. Their often typical, angular contour is based on Feininger's almost caricature-like drawing style at the time. The angular, exaggerated gesture of the strange male half-figure in the foreground is repeated in the position of the arm of the 'spirit of the air,' appearing between other phantoms in the sky. While Kubin's forms may be influenced in part by his artist friends, the figures fully belong to the repertoire of 'Kubinesque' chimeras.

According to the dedication, *The Spirit of Air* was given to Gabriele Münter as a gift in July 1912. Like the *Encounter* (plate 113), it did not join the Lenbachhaus collection through the purchase of the Kubin Archive, but was part of Gabriele Münter's gift to the museum.

Paul Klee

b. 1879 in Münchenbuchsee near Bern – d. 1940 in Muralto
near Locarno

Klee was born into a musical family and grew up in Bern;
in 1898 he decided to go to Munich to study painting. From
1900–01 he attended Franz von Stuck's master class at the
Munich Academy, where he briefly encountered Kandinsky.
After traveling to Italy and France, he finally settled in Munich
in 1906. For several years he devoted the major part of his energies to the production of drawings, etchings, and paintings
with a graphic structure. With their sense of rational control
and wealth of intellectual and emotional connotations, these
early works already testify to the originality of Klee's artistic
approach. In 1911 Klee met Macke and Marc and renewed his
acquaintance with Kandinsky; his sense of affinity with these
three artists led him to take part in the second Blue Rider
exhibition in 1912. In the same year he traveled to Paris and
visited Robert Delaunay, whose brilliantly colored "window"
pictures particularly impressed him. Klee's own breakthrough in
the use of color followed two years later, in the course of a stay
in Tunis with Macke and Louis Moilliet in the spring of 1914.

After World War I Klee, together with Kandinsky, Lyonel
Feininger, and Oskar Schlemmer, taught at the Bauhaus in
Weimar, where he remained until 1931. He subsequently held
a further teaching post for a short time at the Academy in
Düsseldorf, but was dismissed by the Nazis in 1933, whereupon
he left Germany and returned to Switzerland.

Straßen Zweigung 1913 27

Paul Klee

115 ROAD JUNCTION (Strassen Zweigung) 1913, 27

Charcoal, pen and ink, and watercolor on paper mounted on cardboard,
5¼ x 10¼" (13.4 x 26 cm)
Inscribed "Klee 1913" (lower right), "Straßen Zweigung 1913 27"
(lower left, on the mount)
G 13 119

Before he created *Road Junction* Klee had experimented for a time with painting on glass and black watercolors; in this drawing, however, he returned to that "original area of psychic improvisation" which corresponded most closely to his artistic nature. After his return from Paris in the spring of 1912 he had written to Alfred Kubin: "From Paris I have brought back all sorts of vivid impressions. Although I have a high opinion of the latest activities there, I have come to realize that I should devote less time to research and work more on my personal style. At present, my *Candide* illustrations seem to offer a suitable basis for this." In these illustrations, on which Klee had begun work in 1911, the physical appearance of the figures is dissolved into a subjective language of graphic signs which exposes the burlesque, farcical dimension of human folly.

Road Junction was done at the same time as the *Candide* illustrations. At the top edge of the narrow, oblong picture, the tiny, antlike human figures are drawn with nervous lines; the yellow of the watercolor is overlaid with violet, green, and red clouds of color which reinforce the impression of flickering haste. The same sense of weightlessness, of stumbling helplessly through space, can be seen in the figures in a number of Klee's other drawings from this period; the depiction of the figures in *Road Junction* reminds one of the great Expressionist street scenes by the Brücke artists and Lyonel Feininger. However, in the fragmentary space of Klee's pictures there is always a narrative thread, a story line relating to some form of adventure: Klee spoke of pictures as experiences, as "journeys into a land of greater possibilities."

The first version of *Road Junction* was a similar pen-and-ink drawing of two intersecting roads, to which Klee applied watercolor wash and added the passersby. This picture was the "construction of the pure graphic expression" of yet another drawing, done in 1912, in which the image was broken up into a series of Cubist surfaces. The decisive motif, the receding lines that appear to suck the tiny figures into a kind of vortex, was only added in the final version of the picture.

Paul Klee

116 **FLOWER STAND WATERING CAN AND BUCKET**
(Blumensteg, Giesskanne und Eimer) 1910, 47

Watercolor on paper mounted on cardboard, 5½ x 5¼" (13.9 x 13.3 cm)
Inscribed "Klee" (lower left), "1910 47" (lower right, on the mount)
G 13 116

In 1910, four years before his journey to Tunis, Klee made a series of small-format watercolors in which he experimented with color, dispensing with line and traditional chiaroscuro. The technique which he used is described in his diary: "Summer in Bern . . . watercolors wet in wet on paper sprinkled with water. Quick, nervous work with a certain sound whose parts are dispersed over the whole." Despite the spontaneously inter-mingling colors, one is struck by the caution with which Klee balances the light and dark sections: he had previously con-ducted numerous experiments on the distribution of light and dark in his black watercolors. The color changes in subtle gra-dations between the flower stand, the watering can, and the bucket. In the quiet economy of the painting one also detects the influence of Cézanne and his dematerialized colored sur-faces. In the spring of 1909 Klee had seen an exhibition which included a number of pictures by Cézanne and which he de-scribed in his diary as "the greatest event in painting so far! For me, he is the teacher *par excellence,* far more so than Van Gogh." These remarks appear in the context of a general discussion of the role of discipline and the will in art, and of that stylistic economy which often creates a seemingly "primitive" effect.

Paul Klee

117 FÖHN IN MARC'S GARDEN
(Föhn im Marc'schen Garten) 1915, 102

Watercolor on paper mounted on cardboard, 7⅞ x 5⅞" (20 x 15 cm)
Inscribed "Klee" (center right), "1915 102" (lower left, on the mount),
"Föhn im Marc'schen Garten" (reverse)
G 13 266

The watercolor *Föhn in Marc's Garden* bears eloquent testimony
to the "conquest of color" which occurred during Klee's famous
trip to Tunis with Macke and Louis Moilliet in April 1914. Until
then, Klee had devoted the major part of his artistic energies to
drawing and etching, advancing in slow, painful stages toward
the use of color, which he saw as a highly problematical means
of expressing reality. Like Macke and Marc, he was deeply
impressed by the simultaneous contrasts of color in Robert
Delaunay's "window" pictures, but it was the Mediterranean
light of Tunis that brought about Klee's final breakthrough in
the use of color. On April 16, 1914, he noted in his diary:
"Color has got me. I no longer need to chase after it. It has got
me for ever, I know it. That is the meaning of this happy hour:
color and I are one. I am a painter."

Föhn in Marc's Garden, which was painted during a visit to
Marc's house in Ried, near Kochel, while Marc was back home
on leave from the front, exhibits a relaxed, confident grasp of
pictorial architecture. The soft colors of the squares, triangles,
and diamond shapes, which in places are almost transparent
and overlap at the edges, convey a vivid impression of the
Föhn, a warm, dry wind which frequently blows from the
Bavarian Alps. The reflections of the sky and the countryside
are evoked by corresponding honeycombs of color which
appear to demonstrate some kind of optical principle: the
rudiments of natural forms are overlaid by geometrical shapes
and reduced to flat surfaces, as in the even triangle of the violet
mountain or the narrow, dark triangles of the fir trees. Here,
Klee follows a system first developed in his Tunis watercolors,
which, however, still contained representational forms, unlike
the present work, in which the motif of the landscape is dissolved into a tissue of pure colors.

1915 102

Paul Klee

118 LEGEND OF THE SWAMP
(Sumpflegende) 1919 / 163 split I (gespalten I)

Oil and pen and ink on reused, painted cardboard, originally together with
Untitled, 1919, 163 18½ x 16" (47 x 40.8 cm)
Inscribed "Klee 1919.163" (lower right), "1919.163 Sumpflegende Klee verkauft
Besitzer Dr. Küppers" (reverse, in the artist's hand on a slip of paper glued
to the cardboard)
G 16 399

For many years Klee confined himself to drawing, etching, and watercolor painting; it was only after World War I that he turned his attention to easel painting. *Legend of the Swamp* is one of his first works in oils. A common feature of the early oil paintings is the combination of organic and inorganic forms, which was to become one of the central metaphors in Klee's œuvre. In *Legend of the Swamp* the geometrical forms of windows and roofs, etched in white, stand out against the damp brown and green vegetation of the swamp. Here and there, one sees small white fir trees and fan-shaped plants; at the very bottom of the picture, there is a tiny, almost transparent matchstick figure. These pictorial elements are enmeshed in an almost invisible network of fine black lines which binds the forms together and assimilates them into the colored space. The dialectic of organized and amorphous form is particularly apparent in the building on the left, which is evidently a church; it is distinguished from the surrounding swamp by its structure alone, rather than by its color. Above the church, to the right, the head of a phantasmagorical human figure, half man and half child, stares with dead eyes into the picture.

Christian Geelhaar, Marcel Franciscono, and Jim M. Jordan have shown that Klee's pictures from 1919–20 are based on a modified version of Cubism. Klee was particularly fascinated by the Cubists' dissolution of form and the possibilities which it offered for creating new and complex relationships between the different elements of a picture, giving equal weight to each part. In 1912 he described the transition from Realism to the new conception of painting which Cubism had made possible: "Houses which are to be fitted into an interesting pictorial structure become crooked. . . . Trees are violated, people become unfit for life, there is a compulsion to render objects unrecognizable, up to the point where the picture becomes a puzzle. For here it is not the law of the world which applies, but the law of art. In the picture, crooked houses do not fall down, trees no longer need to blossom, people do not need to breathe. Pictures are not living images." Klee's interest in the art of children and the mentally ill is apparent in the strange, primitive forms of *Legend of the Swamp*. This interest is illustrated by an entry in his diary, in which he spoke of a particularly happy moment when he felt himself to be "a spectator above this world and, in the world as a whole, a child."

Paul Klee

119   **TOWN R (Stadt R)**   1919/205

Watercolor on plaster-coated gauze mounted on cardboard,
6½ x 8⅝" (16.5 x 22 cm)
Inscribed "Klee/1919 205" (lower right)
On permanent loan from the Gabriele Münter and Johannes Eichner Foundation
FH 188/2

Architecture is one of the main themes of Klee's pictures from the period around 1920. He evidently saw the artificial, "constructed" character of architecture as having special relevance to the laws of art. At the very beginning of his career, during his travels in Italy in 1901–02, he had become aware not only of the fundamentally epigonal nature of art, but also of the close relationship between architectural and pictorial order. The significance of this relationship for his development as a painter is indicated by one of the entries in his diary during his stay in Tunis: "Went to work straight away and painted watercolor in the Arab quarter. Art/Nature/Self. Tackled the synthesis of urban architecture and the architecture of the picture."

In *Town R* a variety of architectural features – walls, chimneys, and roofs – are bound together by a complex geometrical pattern. Some of the elements in this pattern, such as the brick red of the walls and the blue triangle of sky, refer to reality, while others, such as the "walled" moon on the right, have an intermediate status. In the center there is a large black letter "R" and a black comma with a period; it is from the "R" that the picture, like *Villa R* (Kunstmuseum, Basel), painted in the same year, derives its title. Marcel Franciscono describes the Cubist formal principle underlying the picture: "From 1911 onward, and especially after the Cubists began to use collage in 1912, their approach to painting was no longer based simply on the fragmentation of visual perception, but on the arrangement of abbreviated, two-dimensional graphic signs and diagrams which permitted forms and ideas to interpenetrate and mingle in a variety of interesting ways. The foundation of a picture – its structure, space, and motifs – were linked to a common visual and conceptual core, so that even letters or words could be included without disturbing the balance of the whole." The introduction of letters was a particularly important source of inspiration to Klee. However, whereas the letters used by the Cubists refer to reality – for example, to newspapers or advertising placards – the letters in Klee's work take on a symbolic significance akin to that of other geometrical or emblematic signs, such as the arrow, the heart, or the sun. The meaning of the "R" ultimately remains a mystery, as does the overall architecture of the picture. Meaning, in Klee's work, can only be inferred from the picture as a whole, since the artist himself, according to Klee, is "a creature within the whole." In his essay "Wege des Naturstudiums" ("Ways of Studying Nature"), published in 1923, Klee described how this conception of the artist emerges in the gradual process by which "a totalization occurs in the image of the natural object – be it vegetable, animal, or human, in a domestic space or in the space of landscape or the world – a totalization which begins with a more spatial image of the object."

Paul Klee

120 DESTROYED PLACE (Zerstörter Ort) 1920, 215

Oil on paper mounted on cardboard, 8¾ x 7⅝" (22.3 x 19.5 cm)
Inscribed "Klee" (lower left), "1920/215" (lower left, on the mount),
"Zerstörter Ort" (lower right, on the mount)
G 15 638

Like *Town R* (plate 119), *Destroyed Place* is based on an architectural motif, but its style is quite different. Together with *Zerstörtes Dorf* (*Destroyed Village;* private collection), it is one of the very few pictures in which Klee directly referred to the horrors of World War I. Klee's attitude to the war was one of detachment, as the following, oft-quoted words indicate: "I already had this war within myself. Hence it no longer concerns me." In this picture the ghostly gray and violet ruins of a village stand out against the blue-black sky, which is lit up by the reflection of a fire. The windows, which in many of Klee's pictures symbolize the dialectic of interior and exterior and connote a sense of comfort and security, are here like yawning black chasms. In the foreground, one sees the remains of a ruined church; the pale clumps of vegetation next to it may be interpreted as metaphors of rebirth and renewal. However, the associations which the small picture evokes are dominated by the absence of living things and the emptiness of the anonymous place. Here, Klee has succeeded in the "visualization of nonvisual impressions and ideas," to which he referred in his essay "Wege des Naturstudiums" ("Ways of Studying Nature") as an essential feature of modern art. In a private obituary of his friend Marc, Klee spoke of the particular quality of "dispassionate fervor" in pictures such as *Destroyed Place,* whose effect on the viewer is quite different from that induced by the work of Kandinsky or the Brücke artists. Comparing his own art with that of Marc, he wrote: "My fervor is more like that of the dead or the as yet unborn. . . . I adopt a distant, original standpoint, where I presuppose formulas for man, animals, plants, rocks, and the elements, for all the circulating forces at once. A thousand questions fall silent before they are answered." However, the "silent," dispassionate quality of Klee's pictures owes more to their carefully calculated gestural vocabulary and their seismographic recording of a given state of mind than to the artist's adoption of a superior creative standpoint.

1920 / 215   zerstörter Ort

Paul Klee

121 **ROSE GARDEN** (Rosengarten) 1920, 44

Oil and pen and ink on paper mounted on cardboard,
19¼ x 16¾" (49 x 42.5 cm)
Inscribed "Klee 1920/44" (center right)
Gabriele Münter and Johannes Eichner Foundation/Städtische Galerie im
Lenbachhaus
G 16 102

In the period around 1920 Klee painted a series of pictures in which organic and inorganic structures are fused into a rhythmical whole. There can be no doubt that *Rose Garden* is the most significant of these works. The idea of the garden, which has a central place in Klee's thinking, encompasses both the principle of artificial order and that of natural, organic growth. In *Rose Garden* irregular narrow triangles and trapezoid forms, with fine black borders, give rise to a structure that resembles a wall made up of a variety of vivid red, orange, and pink bricks. The same reds are used for the buildings with pointed triangular roofs, whose vertical lines contrast with the horizontal structuring of the garden. With their long stems and round, spiral-shaped blooms, the roses rhythmically distributed throughout the picture are reminiscent of musical notes.

Klee did indeed see an analogy between painting and music. In his notes on "Bildnerisches Denken" ("Pictorial Thinking"), written while he was teaching at the Bauhaus, he spoke of "cultural rhythms" and referred to "the structure of the beat as an ordering rhythm in landscape." This link between music and painting is fundamental to Klee's ideas concerning the principles of pure artistic construction, an issue in which Kandinsky was also keenly interested. Yet whereas Kandinsky contented himself with discussing the general "inner sound" of pictures, Klee sought to discover precise formal laws, calling for "exact research" of the kind which had long since been undertaken in music – although in some respects, for example in the use of polyphony, he thought that art had already overtaken music. In a diary entry, written in 1917, he cited the simultaneous contrasts in Robert Delaunay's "window" pictures, which had so impressed Marc and Macke, as an example of "polyphonous painting" which he saw as superior to music, since "the temporal has a more spatial quality. The idea of simultaneity emerges in an even more complex form. . . . By his choice of a particularly long format, Delaunay endeavored to accentuate the temporal dimension of the picture, in the manner of a fugue." The melodic structure of *Rose Garden* also expands rhythmically from the center outward. It is known that Klee trimmed the edges of the finished picture, as he frequently did with his early paintings and watercolors, in order to achieve precisely the desired structural effect.

Paul Klee

122   WILD BERRY (Waldbeere) 1921, 92

Watercolor and pencil on paper, cut and rearranged, with gouache and pen
and ink, mounted on cardboard, approx ½" strip added to bottom by the artist,
sheet 14 x 10⅝" (35.7 x 27 cm)
Inscribed "Klee" (lower right), "1921/92 Waldbeere" (lower center, on the
mount)
G 15 694

The world of the stage held a continuing fascination for Klee:
the theater, the circus, variety artistes, and magicians form the
subject of many of his pictures, in which bizarre imaginary
figures are seen performing some sort of act which is far
removed from reality. In *Wild Berry* a strange puppet-like
creature with an enormous head stands on a kind of stage in
the middle of a dark wood. Armin Zweite describes the picture
as follows: "The scene reminds one of a stage set. The diminutive figure stands out against the dark violet background; at
its feet, there is a row of stylized plants. It seems as though the
figure is straining to lift its huge balloonlike head. Together
with the leaf forms and diamond shapes of its costume, the
semitransparent head lends the bizarre, hermaphroditic creature an air of mystery: it is seemingly part human and part
vegetable. This symbiosis confers a puzzling, quietly uncanny
quality on the picture."

The year 1920 saw the publication of several books on Klee's
art, and a major exhibition of his work was held at the Goltz
gallery in Munich. He had at last begun to secure the recognition for which he had longed. In the same year he was appointed to a teaching post at the Bauhaus in Weimar, where
he gave his first classes in January 1921; in the fall of that
year he finally moved to Weimar with his family. With its
geometrical forms, *Wild Berry* bears a certain resemblance
to the puppets of Oskar Schlemmer, who also taught at the
Bauhaus. However, the intentions which inform Klee's bizarre
poetic creature are quite different from those underlying the
work of Schlemmer, whose aim was to demonstrate the mechanical, functional character of the human body. Although *Wild
Berry* adumbrates the theme of the relationship between natural
and artificial, mathematical forms which preoccupied Klee
while he was working at the Bauhaus, it is emphatically a
product of the artist's own imagination, rather than of a purely
rational, mechanical approach to painting. It originates from
an anthropocentric view of the world, through which the artist
takes possession of nature. Klee describes this process in his
essay "Wege des Naturstudiums" ("Ways of Studying Nature"),
where he speaks of a "humanization of the object . . . which
establishes a relationship of resonance between the self and the
object which goes beyond the visual basis."

1921/92   Waldbeere

Paul Klee

123 THE WILD MAN (Der wilde Mann) 1922, 43

Pencil, oil tracing, watercolor and gouache on plaster-coated gauze,
mounted on paper,
23 x 15¼" (58.6 x 38.8 cm)
Inscribed "Klee" (lower right), "S. Cl." "1922/43 Der wilde Mann" (lower left
and center, on the mount)
FH 207

In *The Wild Man* a schematic male figure in harlequin costume
is shown as the helpless victim of conflicting drives, symbolized
by the arrows pointing in opposite directions. Against the
chalk ground, which was deliberately prepared to absorb the
paint, the figure is seen as a kind of marionette, torn this way
and that by the variety of human urges. The large brown
arrows emerging from his head, which is covered by a transparent veil, would appear to signify intellectual or psychological obsession; the smaller arrows shooting out of his staring
eyes symbolize the incompatibility of conflicting desires. In
the center of the picture, the figure's drooping chin, covered
with curly hair, resembles a pair of testicles, a sexual connotation that is echoed by the red and brown arrows emerging
from his groin. As in the early *Held mit Flügeln* (*Hero with
Wings*), an etching dating from 1905, where the central figure
is trapped by his carnal "weakness," Klee depicts the eternal
conflict between the promptings of the flesh and the striving
for higher things, between id and superego.

The arrow also appears as a symbol of sexual desire and
aggression in such pictures as *Der Pfeil* (*The Arrow,* 1920; Kunstmuseum, Bern) and *Analyse verschiedener Perversitäten* (*Analysis
of Diverse Perversities;* Centre Georges Pompidou, Paris), where
Klee dissects human sexuality in the manner of Max Ernst.
At the same time, Klee endows the arrow with a rich variety
of other connotations: it indicates a particular direction, an increase of energy, a tendency to exceed the given. He discusses
the significance of this symbol, which is central to his work, in
his *Pädagogisches Skizzenbuch* (*Pedagogical Sketchbook*): "The father
of the arrow is the question: how do I extend my range to get
there? . . . Man's ability in the sphere of ideas to traverse the
earthly and the celestial worlds conflicts with his physical im-
potence, and this is the origin of human tragedy. Man is half
free and half prisoner." However, the arrow also has a certain
Utopian dimension: "The longer the journey, the greater the
tragedy of not already being there. . . . The recognition that
where there is a beginning, there can never be infinity.
Consolation: a little further than usual, than possible?" In view
of Klee's use of the principle of montage, combining figures
with abstract signs, it is hardly surprising that the Surrealists
invited him to take part in their first group exhibition in Paris
in 1925.

1922 / 43   Der wilde Mann

Paul Klee

124 BOTANICAL THEATER
(Botanisches Theater) 1934, 219 (U19)

Oil, watercolor, brush and pen and ink on paper mounted on cardboard,
19¾ x 26⅜" (50 x 67 cm)
Inscribed "Klee/1924/=1934" (top left), "1924/198" (lower right)
Gabriele Münter and Johannes Eichner Foundation
G 15 632

Klee painted *Botanical Theater* in 1924, reworked it in 1934, and exhibited it the following year at his major one-man show in Bern. With its dramatic *mise-en-scène* of the processes of creation and growth, it offers a key to one of the main ideas informing Klee's art. In pictures such as *Fruits on Red* (plate 117) Klee frequently addressed the theme of hidden life-forces, of creation and metamorphosis. However, the specific repertoire of forms seen in *Botanical Theater* appears to have held a special interest for him. Similar forms are to be seen in many of his pictures from the 1920s: *Bühnenlandschaft* (*Stage Landscape,* 1922; private collection) and the watercolor *Kosmische Flora* (*Cosmic Flora,* 1923; Kunstmuseum, Bern) exhibit a form of order which directly anticipates Klee's first work on *Botanical Theater.*

Despite the mysterious, pulsating energy of the work and the bizarreness of the individual forms, order is the basic principle of the picture. The framework of twiglike forms, leaves, seeds, and flowers resembles the proscenium arch of a stage, in the center of which one sees a plantlike structure with a red teardrop-shaped heart, surrounded by a profusion of strange offshoots. Armin Zweite writes of this structure: "It is, so to speak, the *Urpflanze,* the original plant, from which the various species appear to evolve. The picture speaks at one and the same time of natural laws and the mystery of organic growth." One has the impression of looking into an alchemist's laboratory in which the materials and the instruments are identical: the small, neatly ordered elements at the top and bottom of the picture are arranged like tools for the creation of larger forms of plant life. Using Klee's own vocabulary, Christian Geelhaar has interpreted *Botanical Theater* as an evocation of the workings of the *Urgesetz,* the primal law which governs all creation. This sense of organic growth is conveyed not only by the objects themselves, but also by the way in which they are painted, with fur-like structures of fine lines and cross-hatching which cover the forms. The idea of creation as a continuing process is also emphasized by the materiality of the picture, by the layering of the colors, the slight cracks in the center, and the variety of media: oil, watercolor, and ink. Addressing his pupils at the Bauhaus, Klee remarked on one occasion that the task of the artist was to present "not form, but the process of shaping." This analogy between natural and artistic creation is central to Klee's aesthetic theory. With its theme of imaginary growth, initiated by the artist, *Botanical Theater* is without a doubt one of the finest examples of Klee's mature work.

Paul Klee

125 **FRUITS ON RED (Fruechte auf rot)** 1930, 263 (AE 3)

Watercolor, brush, pen and ink on silk, 24 x 18⅛" (61.2 x 46.2 cm)
"S. Cl.1930 AE 2", "Fruechte auf rot" (left and right, on the mount)
FH 222

Like *Botanical Theater* (plate 24), *Fruits on Red* deals with the theme of natural growth, of the development from flower to fruit. The watercolor is painted on a piece of fine copper-colored silk which is mounted on cardboard painted blue. The forms of the fruits and leaves are also cut from silk and glued to the surface; the branches, on the other hand, are painted with a fine brush or pen. Christian Geelhaar describes the picture thus: "The dominant image is one of growth: flowers and fruits shoot up from the ground and grow inward from the edges. The central structure is a tall plant or tree which resembles a candelabrum, with branches running off in several directions. In the bottom right-hand corner a number of small plants with berries and bell-shaped flowers rise up from the base. All the plants are straining upward, toward the light." Geelhaar mentions a further significant detail: the elongated triangular shape in the top left-hand corner, which suggests a theater curtain. "This motif frequently crops up in Klee's pictures from 1918 onward. Here, the curtain not only serves to round off the composition, it also conveys an idea of visionary revelation in the depiction of natural growth. Hence *Fruits on Red* is thematically aligned with the group of works which includes the painting *Botanical Theater.*"

Fruits on Red was painted after the Bauhaus had moved from Weimar to Dessau. While working at the Bauhaus, Klee experimented with a number of new artistic techniques. In 1930 he began to paint on primed surfaces; in his late, expressive work he often used such coarse materials as jute and sackcloth. The delicate silk collage of *Fruits on Red* uses highly artificial means to observe and analyze natural processes: the organic forms appear to be seen in crosssection, with their inner structure exposed. In his essay "Wege des Naturstudiums" ("Ways of Studying Nature") Klee wrote: "Man takes the object apart and exposes its innards on cut surfaces: the nature of the object determines the number and character of the cuts. It is this visible penetration into hidden regions – sometimes with a simple sharp knife and sometimes with the help of delicate instruments – which clearly opens up the material structure or the material function. The sum of the experiences gained in this way enables us to judge the inner nature of the the object intuitively, looking only at its outer surface." The delicate architecture of *Fruits in Red* perfectly exemplifies this precision in the anatomy of objects.

The silk cloth on which the picture is painted was originally used by Klee while playing the violin, in order to avoid damage to the instrument from perspiration.

Paul Klee

126 **RHYTHMICAL MORE RIGOROUS AND FREER**
(rhythmisches strenger und freier) 1930, 59 (O 9)

Gouache on paper mounted on cardboard, 18½ x 24¼" (47 x 61.5 cm)
Inscribed "Klee" (lower right), "1930 0.9", "rhythmisches strenger und
freier" (lower left and right, on the mount)
G 16 155

In 1923 Klee began producing pictures based on the form of a
chessboard, and repeatedly returned to this motif throughout
the rest of his career. Although he subjected what Will
Grohmann has called his "magic squares" to intensive theoretical
scrutiny during his time at the Bauhaus, their essential character as images of balance and harmony remained unchanged.
Around 1930 he painted several pictures of this kind, including
rhythmical more rigorous and freer. The entry for it in his personal
catalogue of his works reads: "Large watercolor, i.e., thick, water-
based paste applied with a palette knife, German Ingres" (the
name of the paper used for the picture). Combining squares
and irregular oblongs of black, reddish brown, blue, and gray
into a large square which is set against a pink background,
Klee experiments with the alternating rhythms of form and
color, subtly varying and distorting the shapes to produce a
pattern quite unlike that of an ordinary chessboard, whose
even, symmetrical structure he found lacking in "the stimulus
of increase or decrease.... Despite the variety, the formal result
is unproductive." In his notes on "Bildnerisches Denken"
("Pictorial Thinking") he wrote: "Whereas in the ordinary chessboard the division follows the eye, in the *Überschach* [superchess]
it is to be viewed as a measure and a functional basis" – in other
words, a system which may or may not be visible and whose
absolute laws enable the movement of the parts to unfold in a
"more rigorous and freer" manner.

Paul Klee

127 CLIFFS BY THE SEA
(Klippen am Meer) 1931, 154 (R 14)

Oil on white ground on canvas on stretcher, 17⅜ x 24⅜" (44 x 62 cm)
Inscribed "Klee" (lower right), "R.14 Klippen am Meer" (on the stretcher)
On permanent loan from the Gabriele Münter and Johannes Eichner Foundation
FH 211

In April 1931 Klee left the Bauhaus and went to teach at the
Academy in Düsseldorf. It was at this point that he became
particularly interested in the use of a technique which he
himself termed "so-called Pointillism," in reference to the
work of Georges Seurat and the Neo-Impressionists, who had
dissolved the surface appearance of reality into minute dots of
color. Klee's approach is somewhat different. In his "Division-
ist" paintings he first seals off the surface of the picture with
thick white paint, which is often applied in successive layers,
and then covers this with a dense mosaic of colors. Often
painted over several times, the individual particles of color
create a surface relief, as in *Cliffs by the Sea*. The dots of color
in this picture form an animated pattern in which one vaguely
recognizes the outlines of a seaside landscape, with cliffs, the
sea, and the sky. As in his famous pictures *Ad Parnassum* (Kunstmuseum, Bern) and *Das Licht und Etliches* (*Light and Various
Things;* private collection), both painted in 1931, Klee experiments with the representation of light; here, he takes the
experiment to its ultimate conclusion, beyond which lies total
abstraction. The mosaic of colors is a logical extension of the
chessboard patterns in pictures such as *rhythmical more rigorous
and freer* (plate 126), whose rectangles of color have dwindled
here into isolated dots. In order to recreate a visual connection
between the dots of color, the viewer has to concentrate far
harder on the picture than in the case of Neo-Impressionist
painting, where the technique of Pointillism serves to convey
an immediate sensual experience of reality.

Paul Klee

128 **ARCHANGEL (Erzengel)** 1938, 82 (G 2)

Oil and distemper on cotton on jute on a stetcher, $39\frac{3}{8}$ x $25\frac{5}{8}$" (100 x 65 cm)
Inscribed "Klee" (lower right), "1938 Y Erzengel" (on the stretcher)
On permanent loan from the Gabriele Münter and Johannes Eichner Foundation
FH 182

Klee returned to Switzerland in 1933, after being dismissed by the Nazis from his teaching post at the Düsseldorf Academy. Two years later he contracted sclerodermia, a fatal skin disease from which he eventually died in 1940. In 1936 he painted very little, but, beginning in the following year, a new burst of creativity resulted in over two thousand pictures, an astonishing figure in view of the illness that was gradually destroying the artist. One of the main themes of these late pictures is the figure of an angel. The motif occasionally occurs in his earlier work, but in pictures from the late 1930s, such as *Archangel,* the figure takes on an entirely new dimension: it is used to convey a sense of the thin line separating life from death, of the transience of earthly existence, beyond which lies immortality.

The heavy black lines in *Archangel* stand out boldly against the translucent background, whose variegated colors have been absorbed by the coarse jute and whose pale glow lends the picture a semireligious aura. Despite the disparate character of the formulaic signs, there is an overriding sense of hierarchical order which welds them into an intelligible whole. The image of the angel's face embodies an awareness of imminent death and a longing for transcendence, and simultaneously evokes the pessimistic mood of the time, when the world faced the threat of Fascism and war.

Paul Klee

129 **INTOXICATION (Rausch)** 1939, 341 (Y 1)

Oil and watercolor on jute, 25⅝ x 31½" (65 x 80 cm)
Inscribed "Klee" (top right), "1939 Y 1 Rausch Klee" (reverse, top left
on the stretcher)
Purchased with the help of the Gabriele Münter and Johannes Eichner
Foundation
G 15 953

Toward the end of Klee's life, his painting takes a pronounced
"primitive" turn and reaches a final creative climax. The fragmentary figures in *Intoxication* are like hieroglyphs which, as
Rosel Gollek has pointed out, allude to "the intoxication of
eternal processes of change within nature" and which also
indicate the isolation of human, animal, and vegetable existence. The cosmos of the general concept of art formulated by
Klee in his "Schöpferische Konfession" ("Creative Confession")
of 1920 has clearly fallen apart. There appears to be no way out of
the closed world of *Intoxication,* which, like *Archangel* (plate 128),
is painted on coarse jute. The depiction of growth as a coherent
process has given way to the presentation of individual forms
which lack any sense of inner connection.

Selected Bibliography

GENERAL

Der Blaue Reiter. Exhibition catalogue. Ed. Hans Christoph von Tavel, with contributions by Andreas Meier, Hans Christoph von Tavel, Felix Thürlemann, Klaus Lankheit, Jessica Boissel, Günter Krüger, and Wolfgang Kersten. Kunstmuseum, Bern, 1986.

Der Blaue Reiter. Exhibition catalogue. Ed. by Christine Hopfengart, with contributions by Christine Hopfengart, Andreas Hüneke, Magdalena Bushart, et al. Kunsthalle Bremen, 2000

Der Blaue Reiter: Dokumente einer geistigen Bewegung. Ed., and with an afterword by, Andreas Hüneke. Leipzig, 1986.

Der Blaue Reiter im Lenbachhaus München. Edited and with an introduction by Armin Zweite, plate commentaries by Annegret Hoberg. Munich, 1989

Der Blaue Reiter und das Neue Bild. Von der 'Neuen Künstlervereinigung München' zum 'Blauen Reiter'. Exhibition catalogue. Ed. by Annegret Hoberg and Helmut Friedel, with contributions by Sabine Fehlemann, Michael Koch, Mario-Andreas von Lüttichau, et al. Städtische Galerie im Lenbachhaus, Munich, 1999

Expressionistische Bilder. Ahlers Collection. Exhibition catalogue. Käthe-Kollwitz-Museum Berlin, Städtische Galerie im Lenbachhaus, Munich, Wilhelm-Lehmbruck-Museum, Duisburg, 1993/94

Gollek, Rosel. *Der Blaue Reiter im Lenbachhaus München: Katalog der Sammlung in der Städtischen Galerie.* Munich, 1974. 2nd rev. and enl. ed., Munich, 1982. 3rd rev. ed., Munich, 1985.

Moeller, Magdalena M. *Der Blaue Reiter.* Cologne, 1987.

Stationen der Moderne. Exhibition catalogue. Berlinische Galerie, Berlin, 1988/89

The Blaue Reiter Almanac. Ed. Wassily Kandinsky and Franz Marc. Documentary ed. by Klaus Lankheit. London and New York, 1974.

Vogt, Paul. *Der blaue Reiter: Sammelband, Ausstellungen, Künstler.* Cologne, 1977.

HEINRICH CAMPENDONK

Heinrich Campendonk – Ein Maler des Blauen Reiter. Exhibition catalogue. Kaiser-Wilhelm-Museum Krefeld and Städtische Galerie im Lenbachhaus, Munich, 1989

Firmenich, Andrea. *Heinrich Campendonck (1889–1957) – Leben und expressionistisches Werk.* With a catalogue of works. Recklinghausen, 1989

Wember, Paul, *Heinrich Campendonck, Krefeld 1889–1957 Amsterdam.* Krefeld, 1961

ROBERT DELAUNAY

Albrecht, H.J. *Farbe als Sprache: Robert Delaunay, Josef Albers, Richard Paul Lohse.* Cologne, 1974

Robert Delaunay (1885–1941). Exhibition catalogue. Orangerie des Tuileries, Paris, Staatliche Kunsthalle Baden-Baden, 1976

Robert et Sonia Delaunay. Exhibition catalogue. Musée d'Art Moderne de la Ville de Paris, 1985

Delaunay und Deutschland. Ed. by Peter-Klaus Schuster. Exhibition catalogue. Staatsgalerie moderner Kunst im Haus der Kunst, Munich, 1985/86

Sonia und Robert Delaunay. Exhibition catalogue. Kunstmuseum Bern, 1991

Robert Delaunay, Retrospektive. Exhibition catalogue. Grand Palais Paris, Kunsthalle Hamburg, 1999

Robert Delaunay, Werke von 1909–1914. Exhibition catalogue. Deutsche Guggenheim Berlin, 1997

Robert Delaunay. Zur Malerei der Reinen Farbe. Schriften 1912 bis 1940. Ed. by Hajo Düchting. Munich, 1983

Dorival, Bernard. *Robert Delaunay 1885–1941.* Paris/Brussels, 1975

Düchting, Hajo. *Robert und Sonia Delaunay. Triumph der Farbe.* Cologne, 1993

Vriesen, Gustav. *Robert Delaunay – Licht und Farbe.* Cologne, 1967/1992

ALEXEI JAWLENSKY

Alexej Jawlensky 1864–1941. Exhibition catalogue. Ed. Armin Zweite, with contributions by Jelena Hahl-Koch, Armin Zweite, Bernd Fäthke, Jürgen Schultze, and Katharina Schmidt. Städtische Galerie im Lenbachhaus, Munich, and Staatliche Kunsthalle, Baden-Baden, 1983.

Alexej Jawlensky. Exhibition catalogue. Serge Sabarsky Gallery, New York, 1982.

Alexej Jawlensky: Vom Abbild zum Urbild. Exhibition catalogue. Comp. Gottlieb Leinz. Galerie im Ganserhaus, Wasserburg, in cooperation with the Bayerische Staatsgemäldesammlungen, Munich, 1979.

Demetrion, James T. "Alexei Jawlensky: Variation and Meditation." In *Alexei Jawlensky: A Centennial Exhibition.* Exhibition catalogue. The Pasadena Museum, Pasadena, California, 1964.

Jawlensky, Alexei. *Meditationen.* Ed. W. A. Nagel, intro. Ewald Rathke. Hanau, 1983.

Jawlensky, Maria, Lucia Pironi-Jawlensky, and Angelica Jawlensky. *Alexej von Jawlensky. Catalogue Raisonné: Oil Paintings.* 3 vols., Munich, 1991/1992/1993

Jawlensky and the Serial Image. Exhibition catalogue. Text by Shirley Hopps and John Coplans. Art Gallery, University of California at Irvine and University of California at Riverside, 1966.

Schultze, Jürgen. *Alexej Jawlensky.* Cologne, 1970.

Weiler, Clemens. *Alexej Jawlensky.* Cologne, 1959.

Weiler, Clemens. *Alexej Jawlensky: Köpfe, Gesichte, Meditationen.* Hanau, 1970.

WASSILY KANDINSKY

Barnett, Vivian Endicott. *Kandinsky at the Guggenheim.* New York, 1983.

Bowlt, John E., and Rose-Carol Washton-Long, eds. *The Life of Vasilii Kandinsky in Russian Art: A Study of "On the Spiritual in Art."* Newtonville, Massachusetts, 1980.

Brucher, Günter. *Kandinsky – Wege zur Abstraktion.* Munich, 1999

Das bunte Leben. Wassily Kandinsky im Lenbachhaus. Ed. by Helmut Friedel, with Vivian Endicott Barnett. Städtische Galerie im Lenbachhaus. Munich, 1995/96

Der frühe Kandinsky 1900–1910. Exhibition catalogue. Ed. by Magdalena M. Moeller. Brücke-Museum Berlin/Kunsthalle Tübingen, 1994/95

Eichner, Johannes. *Kandinsky and Gabriele Münter: Von Ursprüngen der modernen Kunst.* Munich, 1957.

Emmert, Claudia. *Bühnenkompositionen und Gedichte von Wassily Kandinsky.* Frankfurt am Main, 1998

Fineberg, Jonathan David. *Kandinsky in Paris 1906–1907.* Ann Arbor, 1984.

Gollek, Rosel, intro. *Wassily Kandinsky: Frühe Landschaften.* Munich and Zurich, 1978.

Grohmann, Will. *Wassily Kandinsky: Life and Work.* New York, 1958.

Hahl-Koch, Jelena, ed. *Arnold Schönberg, Wassily Kandinsky: Briefe, Bilder und Dokumente einer aussergewöhnlichen Begegnung.* With an essay by Hartmut Zelinsky. Salzburg and Vienna, 1980.

Hanfstaengl, Erika. *Wassily Kandinsky: Zeichnungen und Aquarelle – Katalog der Sammlung in der Städtischen Galerie im Lenbachhaus München.* Munich, 1974. 2nd ed., Munich, 1981.

Hoberg, Annegret. *Wassily Kandinsky und Gabriele Münter in Murnau und Kochel 1902–1914. Briefe und Erinnerungen.* Munich, 1994

Kandinsky, Vassily. *Complete Writings on Art.* Ed. Kenneth C. Lindsay and Peter Vergo. 2 vols. Boston, 1982.

Kandinsky: The Munich Years 1900–1914. Exhibition catalogue. The Scottish Arts Council Gallery, Edinburgh, and The Museum of Modern Art, Oxford, 1979.

Kandinsky: The Road to Abstraction. Exhibition catalogue. Marlborough Fine Art Limited, London, 1961.

Kandinsky and his Friends: Centenary Exhibition. Exhibition catalogue. Marlborough Fine Art Limited, London, 1966.

Kandinsky: Das druckgraphische Werk – Zum 100. Geburtstag. Exhibition catalogue. Städtische Galerie im Lenbachhaus, Munich, 1966.

Kandinsky in Munich 1896–1914. Exhibition catalogue. Text by Peg Weiss. The Solomon R. Guggenheim Museum, New York, 1982.

Kandinsky: The Russian and Bauhaus Years. Exhibition catalogue. The Solomon R. Guggenheim Museum, New York, 1983/84.

Kandinsky in Paris: 1934–1944. Exhibition catalogue. The Solomon R. Guggenheim Museum, New York, 1985.

Kandinsky: Œuvres de Vassily Kandinsky (1866–1944). Exhibition catalogue. Comp. Christian Derouet and Jessica Boissel. Musée National d'Art Moderne, Centre Pompidou, Paris, 1984.

Kandinsky und München. Begegnungen und Wandlungen 1896–1914. Exhibition catalogue. Ed. by Armin Zweite. Städtische Galerie im Lenbachhaus, Munich. 1982

Lindsay, Kenneth C. "The Genesis and Meaning of the Cover Design for the First Blaue Reiter Exhibition Catalogue." *The Art Bulletin,* 35, no. 1 (1953), pp. 47–52.

Ringbom, Sixten. *The Sounding Cosmos: A Study in the Spiritualism of Kandinsky and the Genesis of Abstract Painting.* Abo, 1970.

Robbins, Daniel. "Vasily Kandinsky: Abstraction and Image." *Art Journal,* 12 (Spring 1963), pp. 145–47.

Roethel, Hans K. *Kandinsky: Das graphische Werk.* Cologne, 1970.

Roethel, Hans K. *Kandinsky.* Munich and Zurich, 1982.

Roethel, Hans K., with Jean K. Benjamin. *Kandinsky.* New York, 1979.

Roethel, Hans K., and Jean K. Benjamin. *Kandinsky: Catalogue Raisonné of the Oil Paintings.* Vol. 1: *1900–1915,* vol. 2: *1916–1944.* London and New York, 1982, 1984.

Thürlemann, Felix. *Kandinsky über Kandinsky: Der Künstler als Interpret eigener Werke.* Bern, 1986.

Vasily Kandinsky: Painting on Glass (Hinterglasmalerei) – Anniversary Exhibition. Exhibition catalogue. Text by Hans K. Roethel. The Solomon R. Guggenheim Museum, New York, 1966.

Washton-Long, Rose-Carol. "Kandinsky and Abstraction: The Role of the Hidden Image." *Artforum,* 10 (June 1972), pp. 42–49.

Washton-Long, Rose-Carol. "Kandinsky's Abstract Style: The Veiling of Apocalyptic Folk Imagery." *Art Journal,* 34, no. 3 (1975), pp. 217–28.

Washton-Long, Rose-Carol. *Kandinsky: The Development of an Abstract Style.* Oxford, 1980.

Wassily Kandinsky à Munich: Collection Städtische Galerie im Lenbachhaus. Exhibition catalogue. With contributions by Armin Zweite, Rosel Gollek, Hans K. Roethel, Jelena Hahl-Koch, and Michael Hoog. Galerie des Beaux-Arts, Bordeaux, 1976.

Weiss, Peg. *Kandinsky in Munich: The Formative Jugendstil Years.* Princeton, New Jersey, 1979.

Whitford, Frank. *Kandinsky.* The Colour Library of Art. London, 1967.

Zander Rudenstine, Angelica. In *The Guggenheim Museum Collection: Paintings 1880–1945.* Vol. 1, pp. 204–391. New York, 1976.

PAUL KLEE

Boulez, Pierre. *Le pays fertile. Paul Klee.* Paris, 1989

Catalogue raisonné Paul Klee. Vol. 1. Ed. by the Paul-Klee-Stiftung. Kunstmuseum Bern, 1998

Düchting, Hajo. *Paul Klee. Malerei und Musik.* Munich, 1997

Geelhaar, Christian. *Paul Klee and the Bauhaus.* Greenwich, Connecticut, New York, and Bath, England, 1973.

Geelhaar, Christian. *Paul Klee: Life and Work.* New York, 1982.

Geelhaar, Christian, ed. *Paul Klee: Schriften, Rezensionen und Aufsätze.* Cologne, 1976.

Glaesemer, Jürgen. *Paul Klee: Handzeichnungen.* Vol. 1: *Kindheit bis 1920,* vol. 2: *1921–1936,* vol. 3: *1937–1940.* Bern, 1973, 1984, 1979.

Glaesemer, Jürgen. *Paul Klee: The Coloured Works in the Kunstmuseum Bern.* Bern, 1979.

Grohmann, Will. *Paul Klee.* New York, 1954.

Grohmann, Will. *Der Maler Paul Klee.* Cologne, 1966.

Haftmann, Werner. *The Mind and Work of Paul Klee.* New York, 1954.

Haxthausen, Charles Werner. *Paul Klee: The Formative Years.* New York, 1981.

Franciscono, Marcel. "Paul Klee's Italian Journey and the Classical Tradition." *Pantheon,* 32 (1974), pp. 54–64.

Kagan, Andrew. *Paul Klee. Art and Music.* London, 1983

Jordan, Jim M. *Paul Klee and Cubism.* Princeton, New Jersey, 1984.

Klee and Kandinsky: Erinnerung an eine Künstlerfreundschaft anlässlich Klees 100. Geburtstag. Exhibition catalogue. Staatsgalerie, Stuttgart, 1979.

Klee, Felix, ed. *Paul Klee: His Life and Work in Documents.* New York, 1962.

Klee, Felix, ed. *Paul Klee: Briefe an die Familie.* Vol. I: *1893–1906,* vol. 2: *1907–1940.* Cologne, 1979.

Klee, Paul. *Tagebücher, 1898–1918: Texte und Perspektiven.* Ed. and intro. Felix Klee. Cologne, 1957. 2nd ed., Cologne, 1968; repr. 1979.

Klee, Paul. *The Notebooks of Paul Klee.* Ed. Jürg Spiller. Vol. 1: *The Thinking Eye,* vol. 2: *The Nature of Nature.* London and New York, 1961, 1973.

Klee, Paul. *Beiträge zur bildnerischen Formenlehre.* Facsimile edition of the manuscript of Klee's first series of lectures at the Bauhaus in Weimar, 1921/22. Ed. Jürgen Glaesemer. Basel and Stuttgart, 1979.

Klee, Paul. *Tagebücher 1898–1918: Textkritische Neuedition.* Ed. Wolfgang Kersten. Stuttgart and Teuffen, 1988.

Kornfeld, Eberhard W. *Verzeichnis des graphischen Werkes von Paul Klee.* Bern, 1963.

Kornfeld, Eberhard W. *Paul Klee in Bern: Aquarelle und Zeichnungen von 1897 bis 1915.* Bern, 1973.

Paul Klee: Aquarelle, Handzeichnungen. Exhibition catalogue. Kunsthalle, Bremen, 1967.

Paul Klee: Das Werk der Jahre 1919–1933 – Gemälde, Handzeichnungen, Druckgraphik. Exhibition catalogue. With contributions by Marcel Franciscono, Christian Geelhaar, Eva-Maria Triska, Siegfried Gohr, Placido Cherchi, and Per Kirkeby. Kunsthalle, Cologne, 1979.

Paul Klee: Das graphische und plastische Werk – Mit Vorzeichnungen, Aquarellen und Gemälden. Exhibition catalogue. With contributions by Marcel Franciscono, Christian Geelhaar, Jürgen Glaesemer, and Mark Rosenthal. Wilhelm-Lehmbruck-Museum, Duisburg, 1975.

Paul Klee (1879–1940): Innere Wege. Exhibition catalogue. Wilhelm-Hack-Museum, Ludwigshafen, 1981/82.

Paul Klee: Das Frühwerk 1883–1922. Exhibition catalogue. Ed. Armin Zweite, with contributions by Rosel Gollek, Christian Geelhaar, Marcel Franciscono, Jürgen Glaesemer, Charles Werner Haxthausen, Otto K. Werckmeister, Jim M. Jordan, Magdalena Droste, and others. Städtische Galerie im Lenbachhaus, Munich, 1979/80.

Paul Klee. Exhibition catalogue. Ed. Carolyn Lanchner. The Museum of Modern Art, New York, The Cleveland Museum of Art, and Kunstmuseum, Bern, 1987/88.

Paul Klee in der Pinakothek der Moderne. Collections cat., vol. 2. Ed. by the Pinakothek der Moderne/Bayerische Staatsgemäldesammlungen, with Cathrin Klingsöhr-Leroy. Munich, 1999

Paul Klee – Im Zeichen der Teilung. Die Geschichte zerschnittener Kunst Paul Klees 1883–1940. Ed. by Wolfgang Kersten and Osamu Okuda. Kunstsammlung Nordrhein-Westfalen, Düsseldorf, and Staatsgalerie Stuttgart, 1995

Paul Klee – Wachstum regt sich. Klees Zwiesprache mit der Natur. Ed. by Ernst-Gerhard Güse, with contributions by Lorenz Dittmann, Meinrad Maria Grewenig, Ernst-Gerhard Güse, and Richard Verdi. Saarland Museum Saarbrücken and Prinz-Max-Palais, Karlsruhe. Munich, 1990

Paul Klee. In der Maske des Mythos. Ed. by Pamela Kort, with texts by Stefan Frey, Pamela Kort, Gregor Wedekind, and Otto Karl Werckmeister, Haus der Kunst, Munich, and Museum Boijmans Van Beuningen, Rotterdam, Munich, 1999/2000

Paul Klee. Die Kunst des Sichtbarmachens. Materialien zu Klees Unterricht am Bauhaus. Ed. by the Kunstmuseum Bern/Paul-Klee-Stiftung and Seedamm Kulturzentrum Pfäffikon. Bern, 2000

Plant, Margaret. *Paul Klee: Figures and Faces.* London, 1978

Prange, Regine. *Das Kristalline als Kunstsymbol. Bruno Taut und Paul Klee. Zur Reflexion der Abstraktion in Kunst und Kunsttheorie der Moderne.* Hildesheim, 1991

Rewald, Sabine. *Paul Klee: The Berggruen Collection in The Metropolitan Museum of Art.* New York, 1988.

Schmalenbach, Werner. *Paul Klee: The Düsseldorf Collection.* Munich, 1986.

Smith Pierce, James. *Paul Klee and Primitive Art.* New York and London, 1976.

Tower, Beeke Sell. *Klee and Kandinsky in Munich and at the Bauhaus.* Ann Arbor, 1981.

Verdi, Richard. *Klee and Nature.* London, 1984.

Werckmeister, Otto K. *Versuche über Paul Klee.* Frankfurt, 1981.

ALFRED KUBIN

Alfred Kubin zum 100. Geburtstag. Exhibition catalogue. Kunsthalle Bielefeld, 1977

Alfred Kubin. Das zeichnerische Frühwerk bis 1904. Exhibition catalogue. Staatliche Kunsthalle Baden-Baden/Bayerische Akademie der Schönen Künste/Graphische Sammlung Albertina, Vienna, 1977

Alfred Kubin. Exhibition catalogue. Städtische Galerie im Lenbachhaus, Munich, Kunsthalle Hamburg, 1990/91

Hoberg, Annegret. *Alfred Kubin. Das lithographische Werk.* Munich, 1999

Raabe, Paul. *Alfred Kubin Leben – Werk – Wirkung.* Hamburg, 1957

AUGUST MACKE

August Macke: Handzeichnungen und Aquarelle. Exhibition catalogue. Kunsthalle, Bremen, 1965.

August Macke: Die Tunisreise – Aquarelle und Zeichnungen von August Macke. 2nd ed., Cologne, 1978.

August Macke: Gemälde, Aquarelle, Zeichnungen. Exhibition catalogue. Kunstverein, Hamburg, 1969.

August Macke und die Rheinischen Expressionisten aus dem Städtischen Kunstmuseum Bonn. Exhibition catalogue. Kestner-Gesellschaft, Hanover, 1978/79.

August Macke: Aquarelle und Zeichnungen. Exhibition catalogue. Westfälisches Landesmuseum für Kunst und Kulturgeschichte, Münster, Städtisches Kunstmuseum, Bonn, and Kaiser Wilhelm Museum, Krefeld, 1976/77.

August Macke: Gemälde, Aquarelle, Zeichnungen. Exhibition catalogue. Ed. Ernst-Gerhard Güse, with contributions by Ernst-Gerhard Güse, Rosel Gollek, Katharina Schmidt, Johannes Langner, Ursula Heiderich, Klaus Lankheit, and others. Westfälisches Landesmuseum für Kunst und Kulturgeschichte, Münster, Städtisches Kunstmuseum, Bonn, and Städtische Galerie im Lenbachhaus, Munich, 1987.

August Macke. "Gesang von der Schönheit der Dinge." Aquarelle und Zeichnungen. Exhibition catalogue. Kunsthalle Emden, Ulmer Museum, Kunstmuseum Bonn, 1992/93

Die Rheinischen Expressionisten: August Macke und seine Malerfreunde. Exhibition catalogue. Städtisches Kunstmuseum, Bonn, Kaiser Wilhelm Museum, Krefeld, Von der Heydt-Museum, Wuppertal, 1979.

Güse, Ernst-Gerhard, ed. *Die Gemälde von Franz Marc und August Macke im Westfälischen Landesmuseum Münster.* Münster, 1982.

Heiderich, Ursula. *August Macke. Aquarelle. Werkverzeichnis.* Stuttgart, 1997

McCullagh, Janice Mary. "August Macke and the Vision of Paradise: An Iconographic Analysis." Diss., University of Texas at Austin, 1980.

Macke, August. *Briefe an Elisabeth und die Freunde.* Ed. Werner Frese and Ernst-Gerhard Güse. Munich, 1987.

Macke, Wolfgang, ed. *August Macke, Franz Marc: Briefwechsel.* Cologne, 1964.

Moeller, Magdalena M. *August Macke.* Cologne, 1988.

Vriesen, Gustav. *August Macke.* Stuttgart, 1953. 2nd, enl. ed., Stuttgart, 1957.

FRANZ MARC

Franz Marc. Exhibition catalogue. Foreword by Hans K. Roethel, intro. Rudolf Probst. Städtische Galerie im Lenbachhaus, Munich, 1963.

Franz Marc. Exhibition catalogue. Text by Mark Rosenthal. University Art Museum, Berkeley, 1979.

Franz Marc – Else Lasker-Schüler, "Der Blaue Reiter präsentiert Eurer Hoheit sein Blaues Pferd," Karten und Briefe. Edited and with a commentary by Peter-Klaus Schuster. Munich, 1987

Franz Marc: Gemälde, Gouachen, Zeichnungen, Skulpturen. Exhibition catalogue. Intro. Hans Platte. Kunstverein, Hamburg, 1963/64.

Franz Marc. Kräfte der Natur, Werke 1912–1915. Exhibition catalogue. Ed. by Erich Franz, with contributions by Andrea Firmenich, Andreas Hüneke, Armin Zweite, Peter-Klaus Schuster, Annegret Hoberg, et al. Staatsgalerie moderner Kunst, Munich/Westfälisches Landesmuseum Münster, 1993/94

Franz Marc. Pferde. Exhibition catalogue. Ed. by Christian von Holst, with contributions by Karin von Maur, Andreas Schalhorn, Andreas K. Vetter, Klaus Zeeb. Staatsgalerie Stuttgart, 2000

Franz Marc 1880–1916. Exhibition catalogue. Ed. Rosel Gollek, with contributions by Rosel Gollek, Johannes Langner, Frederick S. Levine, and Carla Schulz-Hoffmann. Städtische Galerie im Lenbachhaus, Munich, 1980.

Lankheit, Klaus. *Franz Marc im Urteil seiner Zeit: Texte und Perspektiven.* Cologne, 1960.

Lankheit, Klaus. *Franz Marc: Katalog der Werke.* Cologne, 1976.

Lankheit, Klaus. *Franz Marc: Sein Leben und seine Kunst.* Cologne, 1976.

Lankheit, Klaus. *Franz Marc: Schriften.* Cologne, 1978.

Levine, Frederick S. *The Apocalyptic Vision: The Art of Franz Marc as German Expressionism.* New York, San Francisco, and London, 1979.

Marc, Franz. *Skizzenbuch aus dem Felde.* Facsimile ed. with text vol. by Klaus Lankheit. Berlin, 1956.

Maria Marc, Leben und Werk 1876–1955. Exhibition catalogue. Ed. by Annegret Hoberg. Städtische Galerie im Lenbachhaus, Munich 1995/96

März, Roland. *Franz Marc.* Berlin, 1984.

Wassily Kandinsky, Franz Marc: Briefwechsel – Mit Briefen von und an Gabriele Münter und Maria Marc. Ed. and intro. Klaus Lankheit. Munich and Zurich, 1983.

GABRIELE MÜNTER

An Exhibition of Unknown Work by Gabriele Münter 1877–1962: "Hinterglasmalerei" (Painting on Glass), Woodcuts in Color, Etchings, Collages. Exhibition catalogue. Intro. Alfred Werner. Leonard Hutton Galleries, New York, 1966/67.

Cole, Brigitte M. "Gabriele Muenter and the Development of her Early Murnau Style." Diss., University of Texas at Arlington, 1980.

Eichner, Johannes. *Kandinsky und Gabriele Münter: Von Ursprüngen der modernen Kunst.* Munich, 1957.

Gabriele Münter. Exhibition catalogue. Ed. Karl-Egon Vester. Kunstverein, Hamburg, Hessisches Landesmuseum, Darmstadt, and Sammlung Eisenmann, Aichtal-Aich, 1988.

Gabriele Münter 1877–1962. Exhibition catalogue. Intro. Hans K. Roethel. Städtische Galerie im Lenbachhaus, Munich, 1962.

Gabriele Münter: Das druckgraphische Werk. Städtische Galerie im Lenbachhaus München: Sammlungskatalog 2. Comp. Sabine Helms, foreword by Hans K. Roethel. Munich, 1967.

Gabriele Münter 1877–1962: Gemälde, Zeichnungen, Hinterglasbilder und Volkskunst aus ihrem Besitz. Exhibition catalogue. Comp. Rosel Gollek. Städtische Galerie im Lenbachhaus, Munich, 1977.

Gabriele Münter 1877–1962. Retrospektive. Exhibition catalogue. Ed. by Annegret Hoberg and Helmut Friedel. Städtische Galerie im Lenbachhaus, Munich/Schirn Kunsthalle Frankfurt am Main, 1992/93

Gollek, Rosel, intro. *Gabriele Münter: Hinterglasbilder.* Munich and Zurich, 1981.

Gollek, Rosel. *Das Münter-Haus in Murnau.* N. p., 1984.

Kleine, Gisela. *Gabriele Münter und Wassily Kandinsky. Biographie eines Paares.* Frankfurt am Main, 1990

Lahnstein, Peter. *Gabriele Münter.* Ettal, 1971.

Mochon, Anne. *Gabriele Münter: Between Munich and Murnau.* Cambridge, Massachusetts, 1980.

Pfeiffer-Belli, Erich. *Gabriele Münter: Zeichnungen und Aquarelle.* With a catalogue by Sabine Helms. Berlin, 1979.

Roethel, Hans K., intro. *Gabriele Münter.* Munich, 1957.

MARIANNE VON WEREFKIN

Marianne Werefkin 1860–1938. Ed. by Franz Stöckli. Exhibition catalogue. Kunsthaus Zürich, 1938

Marianne Werefkin 1860–1938. Exhibition catalogue. With a text by Clemens Weiler. Museum Wiesbaden, 1958

Marianne Werefkin. Brief an einen Unbekannten. 1901–1905. Ed. by Clemens Weiler. Cologne, 1960

Marianne Werefkin. Exhibition catalogue. Städtische Galerie im Lenbachhaus, Munich, 1959

Marianne Werefkin, Gemälde und Skizzen. Exhibition catalogue. Museum Wiesbaden, 1980

Marianne Werefkin. Leben und Werk. Exhibition catalogue. Ed. By Bernd Fäthke. Monte Verità, Museo Comunale d'Arte Moderna, Ascona. Munich, 1988

Weiler, Clemens. *Marianne Werefkin.* Cologne, 1960

DATE DUE

MAY 18 2006			
GAYLORD			PRINTED IN U.S.A.